SELF-ESTEEM

THE PUZZLE OF
LOW SELF-REGARD

THE PLENUM SERIES IN SOCIAL / CLINICAL PSYCHOLOGY

Series Editor: C. R. Snyder

University of Kansas
Lawrence Kansas

DESIRE FOR CONTROL
Personality, Social, and Clinical Perspectives
Jerry M. Burger

HOW PEOPLE CHANGE
Inside and Outside Therapy
Edited by Rebecca C. Curtis and George Stricker

SELF-DEFEATING BEHAVIORS
Experimental Research, Clinical Impressions, and Practical Implications
Edited by Rebecca C. Curtis

SELF-ESTEEM
The Puzzle of Low Self-Regard
Edited by Roy F. Baumeister

SELF-HANDICAPPING
The Paradox That Isn't
Raymond L. Higgins, C. R. Snyder, and Steven Berglas

THE SELF-KNOWER
A Hero under Control
Robert A. Wicklund and Martina Eckert

SELF-ESTEEM

THE PUZZLE OF
LOW SELF-REGARD

EDITED BY

Roy F. Baumeister

Case Western Reserve University
Cleveland, Ohio

PLENUM PRESS • NEW YORK AND LONDON

Library of Congress Cataloging-in-Publication Data

Self-esteem : the puzzle of low self-regard / edited by Roy F.
  Baumeister.
       p.   cm. -- (The Plenum series in social/clinical psychology)
    Includes bibliographical references and index.
    ISBN 0-306-44373-2
    1. Self-esteem.   I. Baumeister, Roy F.   II. Series.
    [DNLM: 1. Self Concept. 2. Behavior.   BF 697 S4654 1993]
  RC455.4.S42S443   1993
  155.2'32--dc20
  DNLM/DLC
  for Library of Congress   93-7043
                                                                CIP

ISBN 0-306-44373-2

© 1993 Plenum Press, New York
A Division of Plenum Publishing Corporation
233 Spring Street, New York, N.Y. 10013

Printed in the United States of America

CONTRIBUTORS

GLENN AFFLECK, Department of Psychiatry, University of Connecticut Health Center, Farmington, Connecticut 06030

NALINI AMBADY, Department of Psychology, Harvard University, 33 Kirkland Street, Cambridge, Massachusetts 02138

ROY F. BAUMEISTER, Department of Psychology, Case Western Reserve University, Cleveland, Ohio 44106-7123

BRUCE BLAINE, Department of Psychology, State University of New York at Buffalo, Amherst, New York 14260

JOEL BROCKNER, Columbia University Graduate School of Business, 715 Uris Hall, New York, New York 10027

JONATHON D. BROWN, Department of Psychology, NI-25, University of Washington, Seattle, Washington 98195

JENNIFER D. CAMPBELL, Department of Psychology, University of British Columbia, Vancouver, B.C., Canada V6T 1Z4

JENNIFER CROCKER, Department of Psychology, State University of New York at Buffalo, Amherst, New York 14260

CHRIS DE LA RONDE, Department of Psychology, University of Texas at Austin, Austin, Texas 78712

SUSAN HARTER, Department of Psychology, University of Denver, 2155 South Race Street, Denver, Colorado 80208

TODD F. HEATHERTON, Department of Psychology, Harvard University, 33 Kirkland Street, Cambridge, Massachusetts 02138

ROBERT A. JOSEPHS, Department of Psychology, University of Texas at Austin, Austin, Texas 78712

MICHAEL H. KERNIS, Department of Psychology, University of Georgia, Athens, Georgia 30602

LORAINE F. LAVALLEE, Department of Psychology, University of British Columbua, Vancouver, B.C., Canada V6T 1Z4

BRETT W. PELHAM, Department of Psychology, University of California at Los Angeles, 1285 Franz Hall, 405 Hilgard Avenue, Los Angeles, California 90024-1563

DAPHNA F. RASKAS, Columbia University Graduate School of Business, 715 Uris Hall, New York, New York 10027

STEVEN J. SPENCER, Department of Psychology, University of Michigan, Ann Arbor, Michigan 48106

CLAUDE M. STEELE, Department of Psychology, Stanford University, Stanford, California 94305

WILLIAM B. SWANN, JR., Department of Psychology, University of Texas at Austin, Austin, Texas 78712

HOWARD TENNEN, Department of Psychiatry, University of Connecticut Health Center, Farmington, Connecticut 06030

DIANNE M. TICE, Department of Psychology, Case Western Reserve University, Cleveland, Ohio 44106-7123

BATIA M. WIESENFELD, Columbia University Graduate School of Business, 715 Uris Hall, New York, New York 10027

PREFACE

Researchers have been studying self-esteem for decades. It is quite clear that there are important individual differences in self-esteem, and that these can be measured in reliable, valid ways. It is also clear that self-esteem is one of the central, most important aspects of the self-concept (Greenwald, Bellezza, & Banaji, 1988).

But once one begins to look more closely at the large mass of published data about self-esteem, it becomes clear that many things are *not* clear. Do people with low self-esteem hate and disrespect themselves? Do they seek failure and humiliation? Or are they similar in many respects to people with high self-esteem? Are they willing to gamble recklessly in order to gain some esteem, or are they supremely cautious? Is their low self-esteem well-founded in a widespread incompetence and unattractiveness, or is it merely a self-critical attitude? These and similar questions have confused and misled theorists over the years.

It should be emphasized that interest in self-esteem is not confined to academic research laboratories. Beginning, perhaps, with Nathaniel Branden (1974), a flood of popular psychologists have exploited the general public's large and growing interest in self-esteem as a promising key to health and happiness. Perhaps the epitome of the general public's interest in the benefits of self-esteem was embodied in the California Task Force to Promote Self-Esteem and Personal and Social Responsibility. The high hopes of this task force are reflected in the assertion that self-esteem "is the likeliest candidate for a *social vaccine*" which, it was hoped, would inoculate individuals and society "against the lures of crime, violence, substance abuse, teen pregnancy, child abuse, chronic welfare dependency, and educational failure." The task force's final report went on to assert that "the lack of self-esteem is central to most personal and social ills plaguing our state and nation" (1990, p. 4).

Indeed, California State Assemblyman John Vasconcellos, the driving force behind the self-esteem initiative, was initially stimulated by concern over California's multibillion-dollar budget deficit. He eventually reached the conclusion that raising self-esteem would solve California's economic problems and produce a balanced budget. "People with self-esteem produce income and pay taxes," he said. "Those without [self-esteem] tend to be users of taxes" (Winegar, 1990).

Although research typically focuses on differences between people with high versus low self-esteem, the truly puzzling questions and issues are nearly all linked with low levels of self-esteem. People with high self-esteem are no mystery. They generally want and expect to succeed, and they generally want and expect other people to like them, even to admire them. They approach new situations with a confident optimism that helps them to thrive.

Rather, it is people with low self-esteem who are the puzzle. Low self-esteem is usually established on the basis of a questionnaire measure, on which these individuals describe themselves less favorably than people with high self-esteem. But why do these people say bad things about themselves on a questionnaire? Do they really believe themselves to be inferior and inadequate? Are they trying to manipulate the reader into feeling sorry for them, or into something else? If so, what could they hope to gain in their social and work lives? After all, it is unclear what one can hope to accomplish once one portrays oneself to others as inept and unattractive. At one conference I attended, an eminent researcher considered this aspect of low self-esteem and concluded, "Well, these people are just stupid." In his view, it simply made no sense for people to start off by presenting themselves in unfavorable terms.

About seven years ago, I began to think that what the field needed was a volume, like this one, that would bring together the leading researchers on self-esteem and ask them to summarize their views and findings. If the contributions by the various personality and social psychologists could be juxtaposed, some clear insights and conclusions might emerge about the nature of self-esteem. When I examined the current literature in 1986, however, I concluded that although there were interesting ideas available, research had not yet progressed to a point where the findings were conclusive. And so I decided to postpone the project.

Finally, after years of waiting and watching the research literature, I concluded that the time was ripe. The series of important, influential research articles on self-esteem that were published in the late 1980s and early 1990s confirmed the wisdom of my initial decision to wait. Those articles provided enough pieces of the jigsaw puzzle that it seemed appropriate to try, at last, to put them together. The result is this book.

To put this volume together, I contacted the leading researchers in self-esteem. Naturally, people may disagree as to who exactly the leading researchers are, but my goal was to include those who were actively conducting and publishing empirical work on self-esteem. It is therefore not surprising that the majority of contributors to this book are relatively young researchers. This relative youth is also a reassuring sign of the enduring appeal of the topic of self-esteem. Although empirical work on self-esteem was already moving into high gear in the 1950s, the topic continues to attract the ideas and energies of bright young scholars just entering the field now.

I asked these researchers to provide brief overviews of their research programs. Some readers may be surprised that certain chapters fail to integrate large amounts of other work in developing their arguments, but this is because I encouraged authors to focus on their own contributions. This strategy enabled us to produce short chapters with minimal overlap; each researcher summarizes what he or she has contributed. To pull things together, the book ends with three commentaries from different perspectives. Howard Tennen, a clinical psychologist and editor of the *Journal of Personality*, provides a perspective on the implications of this work for clinical theory and practice. Joel Brockner, who first bridged social, personality, and organizational psychology in his book *Self-Esteem at Work* (1988), here offers a management/organizational perspective on how these contributions fit together. Finally, my own commentary is rooted in social and personality theory.

I began reading the literature on self-esteem in 1973, and my very first empirical research project was on self-esteem. I have remained active in the area, publishing a series of studies in the 1980s and an ambitious literature review in 1989 (Baumeister, Tice, & Hutton, 1989). Because of that long involvement, I thought I knew the self-esteem literature very well. It was, however, a pleasant surprise to discover that there was plenty I did not know; I learned something from each and every chapter in this book. The other two contributors of commentaries had similar reactions. They also had cause to think that they knew the literature very well, and yet each of them also remarked on how much they learned from reading these chapters. It is my hope and expectation that readers of this work will have the same experience.

REFERENCES

Baumeister, R. F., Tice, D. M., & Hutton, D. G. (1989). Self-presentational motivations and personality differences in self-esteem. *Journal of Personality, 57,* 547–579.

Branden, N. (1974). *The psychology of self-esteem: A new concept of man's nature.* New York: Bantam.

Brockner, J. (1988). *Self-esteem at work: Research, theory, and practice.* Lexington, MA: Lexington Books.

California Task Force to Promote Self-Esteem and Personal and Social Responsibility. (1990). *Toward a state of self-esteem.* Sacramento: California State Department of Education.

Greenwald, A. G., Bellezza, F. S., & Banaji, M. R. (1988). Is self-esteem a central ingredient of the self-concept? *Personality and Social Psychology Bulletin, 14,* 34–45.

Winegar, K. (1990, November 27). Self-esteem is healthy for society. *Minnesota Star Tribune,* pp. 1E–2E.

CONTENTS

Chapter 3

Dianne M. Tice

Chapter 4

Bruce Blaine and Jennifer Crocker

Chapter 5

Causes and Consequences of Low Self-Esteem
    in Children and Adolescents 87

Susan Harter

PART II. ADVANCES

Chapter 6

Motivational Conflict and the Self: The Double-Bind
    of Low Self-Esteem 117

Jonathon D. Brown

Chapter 7

Self-Esteem, Self-Prediction, and Living Up to Commitments 131

Todd F. Heatherton and Nalini Ambady

Chapter 8

Caught in the Crossfire: Positivity and Self-Verification Strivings
Among People With Low Self-Esteem 147

Chris La Ronde and William B. Swann, Jr.

Chapter 9

The Roles of Stability and Level of Self-Esteem in Psychological
Functioning 167

Michael H. Kernis

Chapter 10

Brett W. Pelham

PART III. INTEGRATION AND COMMENTARY

Chapter 11

Roy F. Baumeister

Chapter 12

Self-Esteem and Expectancy-Value Discrepancy: The Effects
    of Believing That You Can (or Can't) Get What You Want 219

Joel Brockner, Batia M. Wiesenfeld, and Daphna F. Raskas

Chapter 13

The Puzzles of Self-Esteem: A Clinical Perspective 241

Howard Tennen and Glenn Affleck

PART I

FOUNDATIONS

CHAPTER 1

WHO AM I?
THE ROLE OF SELF-CONCEPT CONFUSION IN UNDERSTANDING THE BEHAVIOR OF PEOPLE WITH LOW SELF-ESTEEM

JENNIFER D. CAMPBELL AND LORAINE F. LAVALLEE

Research on self-esteem has had a long, prolific history in psychology. Although several reasons could be cited for the topic's popularity, the most important, in our view, is that self-esteem has been shown to have a pervasive and powerful impact on human cognition, motivation, emotion, and behavior. Research has demonstrated, for example, self-esteem effects in such diverse areas as competition, conformity, attraction, causal attribution, achievement, helping, and coping with stressful life events (DeLongis, Folkman, & Lazarus, 1988; Wells & Marwell, 1976; Wylie, 1974, 1979). Despite decades of empirical and theoretical activity, however, little consensus has been achieved with regard to the locus of these effects. In particular, as reflected in the title of this volume, there is still considerable debate surrounding the specific characteristics of people low in trait self-esteem that somehow cause them to respond in ways that are often detrimental to their psychological well-being (Taylor & Brown, 1988).

JENNIFER D. CAMPBELL AND LORAINE F. LAVALLEE • Department of Psychology, University of British Columbia, Vancouver, British Columbia, Canada V5A 1S6.

Self-Esteem: The Puzzle of Low Self-Regard, edited by Roy F. Baumeister. Plenum Press, New York, 1993.

3

In this chapter, we will argue that an important concomitant of self-esteem is the clarity of the self-concept. Whereas people with high self-esteem have positive, well-articulated views of the self, the prototypical person low in self-esteem does not, in contrast, have a well-defined negative view of the self. The self-views of low self-esteem individuals are in fact evaluatively neutral and, more importantly, are characterized by high levels of uncertainty, instability, and inconsistency. We will further argue that these differences in clarity of the self-knowledge structure are particularly useful in understanding the pervasive effects of self-esteem on social functioning. To accomplish this, we first distinguish evaluative and knowledge components of the self and define our use of the terms *self-esteem* and *self-concept* clarity. Then we briefly review empirical evidence for the suggestion that people low in self-esteem have more poorly defined self-concepts. Next, we outline two broad differences in the social behavior of low and high self-esteem people in order to highlight the utility of self-concept confusion in enhancing our understanding of self-esteem differences in behavior. Finally, we discuss the possible causal mechanisms underlying our portrait of low self-esteem people and then address some limitations of the portrait.

EVALUATIVE AND KNOWLEDGE COMPONENTS
OF THE SELF

The self-concept is broadly defined as an organized schema that contains episodic and semantic memories about the self and controls the processing of self-relevant information (Kihlstrom & Cantor, 1983; Kihlstrom et al. 1988; Markus, 1977). In order to make a theoretically useful distinction between self-knowledge ("Who am I?") and self-evaluation ("How do I feel about who I am?"), we use the term *self-concept* here to refer only to the knowledge aspects of the self-schema—that is, the beliefs that an individual holds about his or her attributes. The evaluative component of the self-schema is conceptualized here as self-esteem; a self-reflexive attitude that is the product of viewing the self as an object of evaluation.

Both components of the self, evaluative and knowledge, can be treated as states or traits. That is, feelings of self-regard can certainly fluctuate over situations, roles, and events (Burke, 1980; Campbell & Tesser, 1985; Wells & Marwell, 1976), but it is also true that trait self-esteem or global judgments of self-worth remain remarkably stable over time (Epstein, 1983; Mortimer, Finch, & Kumka, 1982; O'Malley & Bachman, 1983). Similarly, self-knowledge can refer to the configuration of self-beliefs that are currently accessible or salient to the individual (the dynamic or working self-concept, Markus & Wurf, 1987; or identity images, Schlenker, 1985), or to a set of relatively stable beliefs about one's global attributes.

Are the knowledge and evaluative components of the self related to one another? With respect to state views of the components, there is now a large literature demonstrating the systemic interplay between affective or evaluative states and the accessibility or salience of compatible self-beliefs (Greenwald & Pratkanis, 1984; Kihlstrom & Cantor, 1983). Our focus is on describing the relations between trait conceptualizations of self-esteem and the self-concept. Later, however, we will discuss how the global self-concept of low self-esteem people interacts with the social environment to affect the working self-concept and temporary feelings of self-regard.

The self-concept or knowledge component of the self can be described in terms of both its contents and its structure. The traditional self-esteem literature assumes that self-esteem is related to the self-concept only via the positivity of its contents; that is, people low and high in self-esteem differ only in the positivity of their self-beliefs. That people high in self-esteem describe themselves with more positive attributes is well-known; indeed, it is such a well-established phenomenon that positivity of self-descriptions has sometimes been used to define self-esteem operationally (e.g., Sherwood, 1962; reprinted in Robinson & Shaver, 1973). There is increasing evidence, however, that self-esteem may also be associated with the *structure* of the self-concept. For example, self-esteem appears to be positively related to the number of self-beliefs (Greenwald, Bellezza, & Banaji, 1988) and to the complexity of the knowledge structure (Campbell, Chew, & Scratchley, 1991).

Our concern here is with the clarity of the knowledge structure—the extent to which the contents or self-beliefs are clearly and confidently defined, temporally stable, and internally consistent. Although self-concept clarity has some obvious overlap with the more traditional construct of identity, identity is typically accorded a much richer (but less empirically tractable) set of elements than those conveyed by self-concept clarity. Nonetheless, given the overlap, it is important to acknowledge that the suggestion that people low in self-esteem have more poorly articulated self-concepts is not a particularly new one. Classic and contemporary personality theorists (Adler, 1959; Allport, 1961; Erikson, 1959; Marcia, 1980) have typically assumed that higher levels of identity (achievement, integration, status) are associated with higher levels of self-esteem. Tests of this assumption, however, have been mostly limited to correlating two self-report measures of the constructs (e.g., correlating a self-esteem scale with an identity diffusion scale).

EVIDENCE FOR THE SELF-ESTEEM–SELF-CONCEPT CLARITY RELATION

To provide some evidence for a relation between self-esteem and self-concept clarity, we briefly review studies that have examined the relations between self-report scales of self-esteem and indirect or unobtrusive indicants of self-concept clarity. Specifically, the studies examined the relations between self-esteem and the extremity, confidence, temporal stability, and internal consistency of self-descriptions. In all of the studies, subjects were pretested on self-esteem—either the Rosenberg (1965) scale, the Revised Janis-Field scale (Eagly, 1967), or the Texas Social Behavior Inventory (Helmreich, Stapp, & Ervin, 1974)—at least 1 month prior to the study and were unaware that self-esteem was a focus of investigation.

ARTICULATION OR EXTREMITY OF SELF-BELIEFS

Campbell (1990, Study 1) reasoned that if people low in self-esteem have more poorly defined self-concepts, they should exhibit less extremity in their self-descriptions. That is, to the extent that people are uncertain of their standing along some descriptive dimension, they should tend to give more intermediate ratings on the dimension. Subjects rated themselves on 15 bipolar trait scales such as predictable-unpredictable, tactful-candid, cautious-risky, and unconventional-conventional. The bipolar pairs were specifically chosen to have anchors that were roughly equal in terms of social desirability, a feature that is important in order to avoid confounding any differences in extremity with the well-established self-esteem differences in positivity that we noted above. Three different measures of extremity showed that people lower in self-esteem gave ratings that were, on average, nearer the midpoint of the scales. That is, low-self-esteem subjects tended to describe themselves in noncommittal, middle-of-the-road terms.

CONFIDENCE OF SELF-BELIEFS

More poorly articulated self-knowledge structures should also be associated with self-descriptions that are accompanied by lower levels of subjective confidence. Subjects in Study 1 were also asked to rate how confident they were of each bipolar rating. Self-esteem was positively correlated with average self-reported confidence. A subsequent study (Study 4, described below in the section on internal consistency) examined self-esteem differences in reaction times on a self-descriptive task, an unobtrusive measure of subjective confidence. Subjects lower in self-esteem exhibited longer response latencies.

Baumgardner (1990) reported conceptually similar results. Her subjects were asked to rate themselves and their friends on a set of traits and then to bracket each rating with a subjective confidence interval. Low self-esteem subjects exhibited significantly broader confidence intervals (Studies 1 and 2) and longer reaction times (Study 3) than high self-esteem subjects when rating their own traits, but not when rating the traits of their friends. Taken together, these results indicate that, compared to people high in self-esteem, people low in self-esteem are vague and uncertain, particularly when asked to describe their own attributes.

TEMPORAL STABILITY OF SELF-BELIEFS

If, at any given point in time, the self-schemas of low self-esteem people are more equivocal and uncertain, their self-schemas should also exhibit less stability across time than those of high self-esteem people. That is, to the extent that one is uncertain about the "correct" answer on one occasion, he or she should be more likely to give a different answer on another occasion. Campbell (1990, Study 2) asked low and high self-esteem subjects to provide trait descriptions (how they generally behave in social situations) on a set of 20 unipolar adjectives (e.g., considerate, confident, friendly, assertive, defensive, shy, rude, awkward). Three months later, they were asked to make the same ratings again. The temporal stability of these two sets of self-descriptions was operationalized in four different ways, and self-esteem was reliably associated with each of the four measures. Low self-esteem people's beliefs about their general behavioral tendencies or traits exhibited less absolute stability and less relative stability than did those of people with high self-esteem.

A subsequent study (Campbell, 1990, Study 3) tested two variations of the temporal stability hypothesis. First, rather than measuring the congruence (stability) between trait perceptions at Time 1 and Time 2, it measured the congruence between perceived traits at Time 1 and beliefs about behaviors in a specific social situation at Time 2. It was anticipated that the self-concept (trait beliefs) measured at Time 1 would be less predictive of subjects' beliefs about their subsequent situation-specific behavior for subjects low in self-esteem than for subjects high in self-esteem. Subjects rated their social traits on the same 20 adjectives used in the previous study (the self-concept measure). Three months later, they participated in a 15-minute getting-acquainted interaction with another naive same-sex subject. Following the interaction, subjects rated how they believed they and their partner had behaved "during the interaction" on the same 20 adjectives. High self-esteem subjects exhibited more congruence between their self-concept ratings and their subsequent ratings of situation-specific behavior than did low self-esteem subjects.

This higher congruence on the part of subjects with high self-esteem could derive from one of two mechanisms, both of which are consistent with the overall argument that high self-esteem people have more clearly defined self-concepts. First, high self-esteem subjects may have given more biased interpretations of their current behavior. That is, holding well-articulated schemas about how they generally behave, high self-esteem people may simply ignore or be insensitive to their actual behavior in a particular situation. It is also possible, however, that the better-defined self-schemas of high self-esteem people either reflect or direct situational behavior that is in fact more consistent with their self-schemas. Although the issue of "accuracy" could not be rigorously examined with our data, a comparison of subjects' interaction ratings with those given by their interaction partners suggested that high self-esteem subjects were not less accurate in their descriptions of their interactional behavior. Indeed, high self-esteem subjects' ratings were marginally more congruent with their partners' ratings of their behavior than were those of low self-esteem subjects. Therefore, the higher congruence between the self-concept ratings and ratings of situation-specific behavior exhibited by subjects with high self-esteem was not achieved at the expense of reduced agreement with their partners' views of their situational behavior (see Campbell & Fehr, 1990, for additional research on self-esteem differences in the accuracy of self-perceptions).

The second variation of the temporal stability hypothesis focused on self-esteem differences in the extent to which the self-schema would bias self-relevant memory. Cognitive research has consistently shown that schemas are used as default mechanisms to "fill in" forgotten information, and that well-articulated schemas are more likely to serve that function than poorly articulated schemas (Millar & Tesser, 1986; Taylor & Crocker, 1981). To examine the impact of subjects' self-schemas on memory errors, Study 3 subjects were recontacted 2 weeks after their interaction and asked to recall, as accurately as possible, the self-ratings they had given during the interaction. Generally, all subjects remembered their previous ratings quite accurately, and there were no self-esteem differences in the overall accuracy of recalled ratings.

There were, however, reliable self-esteem differences in the *direction* of the recall errors that were made. The recall errors of high self-esteem subjects were systemtically biased or pulled in the direction of their self-schemas (i.e., initial self-concept ratings), whereas the recall errors of low self-esteem subjects were more or less random with respect to their initial self-concept ratings. Stated differently, the recalled ratings of high self-esteem subjects were significantly more congruent with their self-schemas than were their interaction ratings. Low self-esteem subjects' recalled ratings and interaction ratings both exhibited lower congruence with their self-schemas than did those of high self-esteem subjects, and their recalled and interaction ratings did not differ in the extent to which they were congruent with the self-concept ratings.

INTERNAL CONSISTENCY OF SELF-BELIEFS

Finally, we examine evidence for the hypothesis that the self-beliefs of people with high self-esteem are more internally consistent than those of people with low self-esteem. Campbell (1990, Study 4) asked subjects to make me/not-me decisions for a set of adjectives. The adjectives were presented by a microcomputer in a randomized order, but embedded within the adjective set were 25 pairs that anchored opposite ends of a descriptive dimension (e.g., nervous-calm, proud-humble, impatient-patient, disorganized-organized). Internal consistency was measured by the number of consistent response patterns, where an internally consistent response pattern was defined as responding "me" to one adjective and "not me" to its descriptive opposite. Low self-esteem subjects gave fewer consistent response patterns than did high self-esteem subjects, indicating that people lower in self-esteem are more confused or ambivalent with respect to their standing along descriptive dimensions.

There is also evidence that low self-esteem people are less evaluatively consistent in their self-descriptions. When Campbell and Fehr (1990) examined how subjects rated themselves on sets of adjectives that were either uniformly positive or uniformly negative, subjects with low self-esteem not only gave ratings that were (on average) less positive or more negative, but their ratings within each set exhibited more individual scatter or greater variance. High self-esteem subjects strongly and consistently endorsed the positive adjectives and rejected the negative adjectives. Low self-esteem subjects did not, in contrast, strongly and consistently endorse the negative adjectives and reject the positive adjectives. Rather, they gave more intermediate ratings and more variable ratings to both types of adjectives. Therefore, it appears that low and high self-esteem individuals differ not only in the average positivity of their self-views, but also in the extent to which their self-views are evaluatively and descriptively consistent with one another.

SELF-CONCEPT CONFUSION AND LOW SELF-ESTEEM BEHAVIOR

Having presented evidence that people low in self-esteem have more poorly defined self-concepts, we now examine the utility of self-concept confusion for increasing our understanding of the behavior of low self-esteem people. To accomplish this, we outline some evidence for two very broad differences in the social functioning of people who are low and high in self-esteem. Specifically, we attempt to show that people low in self-esteem are (a) generally more reactive to external self-relevant cues in the social environment, and (b) more conservative or cautious in their orientation to this environment. We highlight these particular differences because they are ones that we believe cannot be readily understood in terms of self-esteem differences in the positivity of self-beliefs, but are quite directly implied by self-esteem differences in the clarity of self-beliefs.

Low Self-Esteem Reactivity to the Social Environment

Space limitations preclude a detailed review here (see Campbell, 1990; Campbell, Chew, Scratchley, 1991), but the existing self-esteem literature supports the proposition that people low in self-esteem are generally more dependent on and more susceptible to external cues that carry self-relevant implications. Of particular relevance is the research that has examined self-esteem differences in reactions to self-relevant feedback or information (see Jones, 1973; Shrauger, 1975; Swann, Pelham, & Krull, 1989, for reviews). The current interpretation of this literature, predicated on self-esteem differences in the positivity of self-beliefs, is that affective reactions to feedback adhere to a self-enhancement formulation and that cognitive reactions to feedback adhere to a self-consistency formulation.

The self-enhancement formulation of affective reactions (pleasure/displeasure, moods, preferences) to feedback has two versions, a weak version and a strong version. The weak version states that everyone prefers or responds with more pleasure to positive feedback than to negative feedback. The strong version further suggests that because low self-esteem people have more negative self-views, they have greater needs for self-enhancement and therefore show more pronounced differences in their affective responses to positive and negative feedback. Studies show that people generally exhibit pain in response to negative feedback and pleasure in response to positive feedback, and that when self-esteem differences are found, the differences indicate that subjects low in self-esteem show more pronounced affective reactions. The fact that low self-esteem people tend to be more threatened by negative feedback and more gratified by positive feedback is, of course, also congruent with our claim that such individuals are more reactive to their social environment.

Cognitive reactions to feedback (acceptance measures such as perceived accuracy, attributions, or diagnosticity) have been interpreted as conforming to a consistency formulation that states that people are more cognitively accepting of external information that is consistent with their self-schemas. The consistency formulation predicts that people with low self-esteem, having more negative self-views, will exhibit greater acceptance of or susceptibility to negative or threatening feedback than will high self-esteem people. This difference is reliably and consistently supported by the research evidence. The consistency formulation, however, also predicts that low self-esteem people should be less accepting of or susceptible to positive feedback than high self-esteem people. This latter prediction is not well supported; self-esteem differences in the acceptance of positive feedback are generally weak or unreliable (Zuckerman, 1979). More importantly, studies that have included the critical no-feedback or control condition indicate that low self-esteem people accept and are affected by both positive and negative information, in contrast to high self-esteem people, who accept and are affected by only positive (i.e., consistent) feedback (e.g., Campbell & Fairey, 1985).

In Brockner's review (1984) of the self-esteem literature, he noted that people with low self-esteem are also more susceptible to influence attempts, anxiety-provoking stimuli, and evaluatively neutral stimuli such as suggestibility, expectancy, and self-focus manipulations. Combining this evidence with the reactions-to-feedback results, he concluded that the empirical self-esteem literature was best characterized as revealing a pattern of "low self-esteem plasticity," that is, people low in self-esteem are generally more susceptible to self-relevant social cues than high self-esteem people.

Although the research reviewed above is consistent with our description of low self-esteem reactivity to environmental cues, it consists mostly of laboratory experiments. This method has been criticized on the grounds that experimenter-manipulated (i.e., false) feedback may elicit different responses from high and low self-esteem subjects because the feedback is differentially discrepant from the cues that people low and high in self-esteem normally encounter in their daily lives. Campbell, Chew, and Scratchley (1991) recently tested the low self-esteem reactivity hypothesis in the natural ecology by examining naturally occurring events, appraisals of these events, and moods. Subjects kept a daily dairy for 14 consecutive days in which they rated the overall pleasantness of their mood five times each day and, at the end of each day, provided objective descriptions of what they perceived to be the most positive and negative events of the day. These events were rated on six scales assessing subjects' appraisals of the events (attributions, perceived impact on mood, personal importance).

We reasoned that if low self-esteem people are generally more reactive to the self-relevant implications of daily events, they should exhibit more fluctuations in their daily moods (i.e., their moods should tend to be pushed around more by the winds of changing circumstances). The results showed that the moods of subjects low in self-esteem were less pleasant on average than those of subjects high in self-esteem. More importantly, the moods of subjects low in self-esteem also exhibited more variability; that is, they changed more frequently than did the moods of subjects high in self-esteem.

Furthermore, subjects' appraisals of their daily events replicated the low self-esteem plasticity effects obtained in experimental designs. Whereas high self-esteem subjects cognitively accepted the self-relevant implications of their positive events and rejected the self-relevant implications of their negative events, subjects low in self-esteem were equally accepting of both types of events. For example, high self-esteem subjects made more characterological (internal, stable, and global) attributions for their positive daily events than for their negative daily events, whereas low self-esteem subjects made characterological attributions for *both* types of daily events. In short, the results were consistent with the view that people low in self-esteem are more reactive to their social environments.

Parenthetically, it is interesting to note that when we asked a new sample of subjects to read the event descriptions provided by low and high self-esteem diary subjects and rate them on the same six appraisal measures, these subjects were generally unable to distinguish between the daily events that had occurred to low and high self-esteem diary subjects. This latter result suggests that although people low and high in self-esteem differ substantially in their cognitive and affective reactions to daily events, the daily events that they experience may not be objectively different.

The low self-esteem plasticity pattern described above is not easily or parsimoniously accounted for by reference to self-esteem differences in the positivity of the contents of the self-concept. For example, positivity differences cannot account for the fact that low self-esteem people are more susceptible to evaluatively neutral cues such as self-focus, or for the fact that the moods of low self-esteem people fluctuate more frequently than do those of high self-esteem people. On the other hand, low self-esteem plasticity is quite directly implied by self-concepts that are poorly articulated, confused, and uncertain. Low levels of perceived expertise, competence, or confidence in any domain substantially increase people's susceptibility to external influence in that domain. For example, the conformity literature demonstrates that people conform more to the judgments of others when they lack confidence or perceived competence in the judgment domain (e.g., Campbell, Tesser, & Fairey, 1986). Similarly, when people lack clear and confidently held internal standards of self-definition, they must be more dependent on, and hence more susceptible to, external cues that convey self-relevant information.

Low Self-Esteem Conservatism and Caution

A second pervasive difference between people low and high in self-esteem is that low self-esteem people are more conservative or cautious in their responses to the social environment. Again, we cannot undertake a detailed review here, but we will attempt to show that whereas the cognitive and behavioral responses of high self-esteem people are overtly (and probably overly) positive and motivated by self-enhancement, the responses of low self-esteem people are *not* overtly negative and motivated by self-derogation. Rather, the responses of people low in self-esteem are more appropriately characterized as conservative or cautious, and as motivated by self-protection.

First, it is important to note that within normal populations, people classified as low in self-esteem are low only in a relative sense. Self-esteem is typically assessed via subjects' endorsements of structured evaluative questions about the self. Subjects are then classified as low or high in self-esteem based on a median split of self-esteem scores. With this procedure, it can be shown that people classified as high self-esteem are those who strongly endorse the positive and strongly reject the negative items in self-esteem scales. In contrast, however, people classified as low self-esteem do not strongly endorse the negative and strongly reject the positive scale items. Indeed, the modal response of those identified as low in self-esteem is in fact near the theoretical or conceptual midpoint of the scale (Bachman & O'Malley, 1984; Baumeister, Tice, & Hutton, 1989). Also, as noted earlier, low self-esteem people tend to give ratings near the scale midpoint when asked to rate themselves on valanced trait adjectives (Campbell & Fehr, 1990). Therefore, the prototypical self-evaluations of low self-esteem people are best characterized as being neutral or intermediate, not overtly negative.

A second type of evidence that low self-esteem people exhibit a cautious orientation comes from the literature on biases and illusions. The evidence clearly indicates that people high in self-esteem exhibit robust positive illusions or biases about themselves and the world (Taylor & Brown, 1988). There is little evidence, however, that low self-esteem people exhibit robust or reliable negative biases. The perceptions of people low in self-esteem are better described as evenhanded, less exaggerated or optimistic, or perhaps even more realistic (Taylor & Brown, 1988). For example, Campbell (1986) found that in general, individuals overestimate the percentage of people who share their opinions and underestimate the percentage of people who share their abilities, a self-enhancing pattern that exaggerates the consensual validation for one's opinions and the uniqueness of one's abilities. This self-serving pattern was very pronounced and highly significant among subjects high in self-esteem. Low self-esteem subjects did not, however, exhibit a reliable self-deprecating pattern. In fact, they exhibited the same pattern as high self-esteem subjects, but in their case, the pattern was attenuated and unreliable. In other words, the consensus estimates of subjects low in self-esteem were conservative, cautious, and relatively evenhanded.

Finally, Baumeister et al. (1989) recently summarized evidence that people low and high in self-esteem tend to adopt different self-presentational styles. The evidence suggests that people high in self-esteem employ self-enhancing styles, characterized by a willingness to take risks, focusing on their outstanding qualities, engaging in strategic ploys, and calling attention to themselves. In contrast, low self-esteem people utilize self-protective strategies, characterized by unwillingness to take risks, focusing on avoiding their bad qualities, avoidance of strategic ploys, and reluctance to call attention to the self. In other words, the self-presentational styles of people with low self-esteem are not self-derogatory but self-protective, cautious, and conservative.

The phenomena we have described are again not well understood when self-esteem is viewed as simply reflecting differences in the positivity of people's self-beliefs. Differences in positivity anticipate a pattern of behaviors, thoughts, and feelings that reflect average differences in the *direction* of people's orientation but do not anticipate the pervasive differences that exist in the confidence or certainty of the orientations displayed by people low and high in self esteem. A cognitive-behavioral orientation to the social environment that is cautious, conservative, and self-protective is, however, directly implicated by a self-concept characterized by confusion and uncertainty.

CONCLUDING COMMENTS

We have drawn a portrait of the prototypical low self-esteem person as an individual whose global self-evaluation is neutral, whose self-concept is uncertain and confused, who is highly susceptible to and dependent on external self-relevant cues, and whose social perceptions and behaviors reflect a cautious or conservative orientation. In this last section, we first discuss the causal relations among these characteristics and then address some potential limitations of this portrait.

CAUSAL RELATIONS

The research we presented suggests that self-esteem is correlated with self-concept clarity, but it is mute with respect to the causal direction of the association. One could argue that low self-concept clarity could cause low self-esteem; indeed, classic personality theorists have usually assumed that higher levels of identity somehow cause higher levels of self-esteem (Erikson, 1959; Marcia, 1980). In support of this causal direction, Baumgardner (1990, Study 4) reported that manipulated self-certainty increased temporary feelings of positive affect and self-regard.

It also seems plausible, however, that low self-esteem or temporary negative affect could cause people to experience self-uncertainty and confusion. We recently tested this possibility in a study that examined the joint effects of trait self-esteem and manipulated mood on the internal consistency and the temporal stability of self-descriptions. Subjects pretested on self-esteem participated in a two-session laboratory experiment. In the first session, they underwent a mood manipulation (Eich & Metcalfe, 1989) designed to place them in either a happy or sad mood, and then made me/not-me judgments regarding 25 pairs of opposite traits presented in a randomized order. Two days later, half of the subjects were placed in the same mood state (happy/happy and sad/sad subjects) and the remainder in the opposite mood state (happy/sad or sad/happy subjects), followed by the identical judgment task.

The internal consistency of subjects' self-descriptions in the first session was examined as a function of mood (happy vs. sad) and self-esteem (low vs. high). The only reliable effect was a main effect for mood; subjects in the happy-mood condition gave more consistent responses than did subjects in the sad-mood condition. The temporal stability of subjects' self-descriptions (across the two sessions) was affected by both self-esteem and the mood manipulations. High self-esteem subjects exhibited higher temporal stability than did low self-esteem subjects. In addition, subjects in the same-mood conditions showed higher temporal stability than did subjects in the changed-mood conditions. These results suggest that negative mood states and fluctuating mood states, both of which are more characteristic of people low in self-esteem (see Campbell, Chew, and Scratchley, 1991, described earlier), can cause increases in self-concept confusion and uncertainty.

Having presented some evidence that both causal directions of the relation between self-esteem and self-concept clarity are plausible, we argue more broadly that the causal relations among self-evaluation, self-concept clarity, susceptibility to the social environment, and a cautious orientation are probably all reciprocal and systemic. For example, if one assumes that all daily lives in fact contain a mixture of positive and negative self-relevant cues, people who tend to accept these environmental cues indiscriminately are more likely to acquire a self-schema characterized by lower levels of positivity and clarity. It also seems reasonable to postulate that although the adoption of cautious self-presentational strategies may serve to protect the self from embarrassing or humiliating experiences, they also limit the possibility of attaining outcomes, such as gaining visible prestige or acquiring diagnostic feedback, that might increase the positivity or clarity of self-beliefs.

The notion of affective-cognitive crossfire advanced by Swann (Swann, Griffin, Predmore, & Gaines, 1987) describes the process that we believe underlies these systemic relations. This process assumes that (a) everyone desires or is motivated to hold positive beliefs about the self, but that (b) people will tend cognitively to accept information that is more consistent with their current self-view. When the current self-view is a confidently held positive one (e.g., for people high in self-esteem), there is no problem; people cognitively accept only those environmental cues that convey the affectively preferred positive information. But when the current self-view is less positive or uncertain, people are caught in an emotional-cognitive crossfire between what they *want* to believe is true of them and what they *think* just might be true of them. These conflicting cognitive and emotional reactions to social cues can lead, in turn, to increased self-concept uncertainty. For example, studies have shown that when people are led to believe that they might possess some negative attribute, they seem to prefer or seek uncertainty in that they actively avoid acquiring certain or diagnostic information about the attribute (Berglas & Jones, 1978; Campbell, Fairey, & Fehr, 1986; Flett, Vredenburg, Pliner, & Krames, 1987). Therefore cognitive-affective crossfire is not only elicited by a self-concept that is evaluatively neutral and uncertain, but also may serve to maintain a self-concept that is characterized by intermediate levels of evaluation and a lack of clarity.

LIMITATIONS OF THE PORTRAIT

Because our research program has not studied clinical or dysfunctional samples, there is a possibility that the relation between self-esteem and self-concept clarity is in fact curvilinear; that is, perhaps people with very low self-esteem hold negative beliefs about the self with high certainty. Our own data (based on college samples) have provided no reliable evidence for a curvilinear relation, despite the fact that we have studied some subjects whose self-esteem scores were well below the theoretical midpoint on the self-esteem scale. Nonetheless, this possibility raises the issue of whether or not the dysfunctional effects of increased negativity might somehow be offset by the "improvement" in self-concept clarity. There is little empirical evidence regarding this issue, but the existing evidence and theory suggest that holding negative beliefs with certainty can be highly detrimental to psychological health. For example, Andersen and Lyon (1987) provided experimental evidence for the suggestion by Garber, Miller, and Abramson (1980) that the absolute certainty of expectancies about being unable to avoid negative outcomes (or obtain positive outcomes) may be a potent component of depression.

Even if the positive relation between self-esteem and self-concept clarity is limited to "normal" populations, we believe that the theoretical benefits of highlighting the self-concept confusion and uncertainty of people low in self-esteem are substantial. Self-esteem has been shown to have robust and pervasive effects on thoughts, feelings, and behavior, and most of these effects have been demonstrated in normal samples (Wells & Marwell, 1976; Wylie, 1979). We attempted to demonstrate here that our ability to understand these effects is greatly enhanced by knowing that the self-concepts of people low in self-esteem are relatively confused and uncertain.

Despite our claim that self-concept uncertainty provides a more coherent explanation for some self-esteem phenomena than negativity, however, we do not believe that it would be a useful enterprise to attempt to compare or weigh the relative impact of negativity and uncertainty in accounting for self-esteem effects. Recent studies aimed at developing and validating a self-report measure of self-concept clarity (Campbell, Katz, Lavallee and Trapnell, 1991; Campbell, Trapnell, Katz and Lavallee, 1992) indicate that clarity scores are substantially correlated with self-esteem, as well as related scales, including negative and positive affectivity, anxiety, and neuroticism. Furthermore, when the scales are used to predict subsequent behavior, self-esteem and clarity scales often exhibit very comparable effects, a result that probably derives from the fact that the causal relations between self-esteem and self-concept clarity are reciprocal and systemic. Therefore, rather than asking whether the evaluative component or the knowledge component of the self is the better piece of the low self-esteem puzzle, it seems more reasonable to view them as one interlocking piece that we hope will be joined with other pieces in this volume to bring the portrait of low self-esteem people into sharper focus.

REFERENCES

Adler, A. (1959). *The practice and theory of individual psychology.* Totowa, NJ: Littlefield, Adams.

Allport, G. (1961). *Pattern and growth in personality.* New York: Holt, Rinehart and Winston.

Andersen, S. M., & Lyon, J. E. (1987). Anticipating undesired outcomes: The role of outcome certainty in the onset of depressive affect. *Journal of Experimental Social Psychology, 23,* 428–443.

Bachman, J. G., & O'Malley, P. M. (1984). Black-white differences in self-esteem: Are they affected by response styles? *American Journal of Sociology, 90,* 624–639.

Baumeister, R. F., Tice, D. M., & Hutton, D. G. (1989). Self-presentational motivation and personality differences in self-esteem. *Journal of Personality, 57,* 547–579.

Baumgardner, A. H. (1990). To know oneself is to like oneself: Self-certainty and self-affect. *Journal of Personality and Social Psychology, 58,* 1062–1072.

Berglas, S., & Jones, E. E. (1978). Drug choice as a self-handicapping strategy in response to noncontingent success. *Journal of Personality and Social Psychology, 36,* 405–417.

Brockner, J. (1984). Low self-esteem and behavioral plasticity: Some implications for personality and social psychology. In L. Wheeler (Ed.), *Review of personality and social psychology* (Vol. 4, pp. 237–271). Beverly Hills, CA: Sage.

Burke, P. J. (1980). The self: Measurement requirements from an interactionist perspective. *Social Psychology Quarterly, 43,* 18–29.

Campbell, J. D. (1986). Similarity and uniqueness: The effects of attribute type, relevance, and individual differences in self-esteem and depression. *Journal of Personality and Social Psychology, 50,* 281–294.

Campbell, J. D. (1990). Self-esteem and clarity of the self-concept. *Journal of Personality and Social Psychology, 59,* 538–549.

Campbell, J. D., Chew, B., & Scratchley, L. S. (1991). Cognitive and emotional reactions to daily events: The effects of self-esteem and self-complexity. *Journal of Personality, 59,* 473–505.

Campbell, J. D., & Fairey, P. J. (1985). Effects of self-esteem, hypothetical explanations, and verbalization of expectancies on future performance. *Journal of Personality and Social Psychology, 48,* 1097–1111.

Campbell, J. D., Fairey, P. J., & Fehr, B. (1986). Better than me or better than thee? Reactions to intrapersonal and interpersonal performance feedback. *Journal of Personality, 564,* 479–493.

Campbell, J. D., & Fehr, B. (1990). Self-esteem and perceptions of conveyed impressions: Is negative affectivity associated with greater realism? *Journal of Personality and Social Psychology, 58,* 122–133.

Campbell, J. D., Katz, I. M., Lavallee, L. F., & Trapnell, P. D. (1991, June). *Development and validation of a self-report scale of self-concept clarity.* Paper presented at the meeting of the American Psychological Society, Washington, D.C.

Campbell, J. D., & Tesser, A. (1985). Self-evaluation maintenance processes in relationships. In S. Duck & D. Perlman (Eds.), *Understanding personal relationships: An interdisciplinary approach,* (Vol. 1, pp. 107–135). London: Sage.

Campbell, J. D., Tesser, A., & Fairey, P. J. (1986). Conformity and attention to the stimulus: Some temporal and contextual dynamics. *Journal of Personality and Social Psychology, 51,* 315–324.

Campbell, J. D., Trapnell, P. D., Katz, I. M., & Lavallee, L. F. (1992). *Personality and self-knowledge: Development of the self-concept confusion scale and examination of its personality correlates.* Unpublished manuscript, University of British Columbia, Canada.

DeLongis, A., Folkman, S., & Lazarus, R. S. (1988). The impact of daily stress on health and mood: Psychological and social resources as mediators. *Journal of Personality and Social Psychology, 54,* 486–495.

Eagly, A. H. (1967). Involvement as a determinant of response to favorable and unfavorable information. *Journal of Personality and Social Psychology, 7,* 1–15 (Monograph, whole no. 643).

Eich, E., & Metcalfe, J. (1989). Mood dependent memory for interval versus external events. *Journal of Experimental Psychology: Learning, Memory and Cognition, 15,* 443–455.

Epstein, S. (1983). The unconscious, the preconscious, and the self-concept. In J. Suls & A. Greenwald (Eds.), *Psychological perspectives on the self* (Vol. 2, pp. 219–247). Hillsdale, NJ: Lawrence Erlbaum.

Erikson, E. (1959). Identity and the life cycle. In G. S. Klein (Ed.), *Psychological issues* (pp. 1–171). New York: International Universities Press.

Flett, G. L., Vredenburg, K., Pliner, P., & Krames, L. (1987). Depression and social comparison information-seeking. *Journal of Social Behavior and Personality, 2,* 473–484.

Garber, J., Miller, S. M., & Abramson, L. Y. (1980). On the distinction between anxiety and depression: Perceived control, certainty, and probability of goal attainment. In J. Garber & M. E. P. Seligman (Eds.), *Human helplessness: Theory and applications* (pp. 131–169). New York: Academic Press.

Greenwald, A. G., Bellezza, F. S., & Banaji, M. R. (1988). Is self-esteem a central ingredient of the self-concept? *Personality and Social Psychology Bulletin, 14,* 34–45.

Greenwald, A. G., & Pratkanis, A. R. (1984). The self. In R. S. Wyer & T. K. Srull (Eds.), *Handbook of social cognition* (Vol. 3, pp. 129–178). Hillsdale, NJ: Lawrence Erlbaum.

Helmreich, R., Stapp, J., & Ervin, C. (1974). The Texas Social Behavior Inventory (TSBI): An objective measure of self-esteem or social competence. *JASA Catalog of Selected Documents in Social Psychology, 4,* 79 (Ms. No. 681).

Jones, S. C. (1973). Self and interpersonal evaluations: Esteem theories versus consistency theories. *Psychological Bulletin, 79*, 185–199.

Kihlstrom, J. F., & Cantor, N. (1983). Mental representations of the self. In L. Berkowitz (Ed.), *Advances in experimental social psychology* (Vol. 17, pp. 1–47). New York: Academic Press.

Kihlstrom, J. F., Cantor, N., Albright, J. S., Chew, B. R., Klein, S. B., & Neidenthal, P. M. (1988). Information processing and the study of the self. In L. Berkowitz (Ed.), *Advances in experimental social psychology* (Vol. 21, pp. 159–187). New York: Academic Press.

Marcia, J. E. (1980). Identity in adolescence. In J. Adelson (Ed.), *Handbook of adolescent psychology* (pp. 159–187). Toronto: John Wiley.

Markus, H. (1977). Self-schemata and processing information about the self. *Journal of Personality and Social Psychology, 35*, 63–78.

Markus, H., & Wurf, E. (1987). The dynamic self-concept: A social psychological perspective. *Annual Review of Psychology, 38*, 299–337.

Millar, M. B., & Tesser, A. (1986). Thought-induced attitude change: The effects of schema structure and commitment. *Journal of Personality and Social Psychology, 52*, 156–176.

Mortimer, J. T., Finch, M. D., & Kumka, D. (1982). Persistence and change in development: The multidimensional self-concept. In P. B. Baltes & O. G. Brim, Jr. (Eds.), *Life-span development and behavior* (Vol. 4, pp. 263–313). New York: Academic Press.

O'Malley, P. M., & Bachman, J. G. (1983). Self-esteem: Change and stability between ages 13 and 23. *Developmental Psychology, 19*, 257–268.

Robinson, J. P., & Shaver, P. R. (1973). *Measures of social psychological attitudes.* Ann Arbor, MI: Institute for Social Research.

Rosenberg, M. (1965). *Society and the adolescent self-image.* Princeton, NJ: Princeton University Press.

Schlenker, B. R. (1985). Identity and self-identification. In B. R. Schlenker (Ed.), *The self and social life* (pp. 65–100). New York: McGraw-Hill.

Sherwood, J. J. (1962). *Self-identity and self-actualization: A theory and research.* Unpublished doctoral dissertation, University of Michigan.

Shrauger, J. S. (1975). Responses to evaluation as a function of initial self-perceptions. *Psychological Bulletin, 82*, 581–596.

Swann, W. B., Jr., Griffin, J. J., Jr., Predmore, S. C., & Gaines, B. (1987). The cognitive-affective crossfire: When self-consistency confronts self-enhancement. *Journal of Personality and Social Psychology, 52*, 881–889.

Swann, W. B., Jr., Pelham, B. W., & Krull, D. S. (1989). Agreeable fancy or disagreeable truth? Reconciling self-enhancement and self-verification. *Journal of Personality and Social Psychology, 57*, 782–791.

Taylor, S. E., & Brown, J. D. (1988). Illusion and well-being: A social psychological perspective on mental health. *Psychological Bulletin, 103*, 193–210.

Taylor, S. E., & Crocker, J. (1981). Schematic bases of social information processing. In E. T. Higgins, C. P. Herman, & M. P. Zanna (Eds.), *Social cognition: The Ontario symposium* (pp. 89–134). Hillsdale, NJ: Lawrence Erlbaum.

Wells, L. E., & Marwell, G. (1976). *Self-esteem.* Beverly Hills, CA: Sage.

Wylie, R. (1974). *The self-concept, vol. 1.* Lincoln: University of Nebraska Press.

Wylie, R. (1979). *The self-concept, vol. 2.* Lincoln: University of Nebraska Press.

Zuckerman, M. (1979). Attribution of success and failure revisited, or the motivational bias is alive and well in attribution theory. *Journal of Personality, 47*, 245–287.

CHAPTER 2

LOW SELF-ESTEEM
THE UPHILL STRUGGLE FOR SELF-INTEGRITY

STEVEN J. SPENCER, ROBERT A. JOSEPHS, AND
CLAUDE M. STEELE

SELF-ESTEEM AND RESILIENCY TO SELF-IMAGE THREATS

> I have wondered why it is that some people are less affected and torn by the
> verities of life and death than others. Una's death cut the earth from under
> Samuels's feet and opened his defended keep and let in old age. On the other
> hand Liza, who surely loved her family as deeply as did her husband, was
> not destroyed or warped. Her life continued evenly. She felt sorrow but she
> survived it. (Steinbeck, 1952, p. 258)

Like Steinbeck, we have wondered why some people are more resilient
to the vicissitudes of life than others, that is, why their sense of worth
and the psychological states that vary with it (e.g., defensiveness, efficacy, positive affect) are less affected by particular threats to their self-
image. They have "thicker skins." Clearly all of us fluctuate in this

STEVEN J. SPENCER • Department of Psychology, University of Michigan, Ann Arbor, MI
48106.   ROBERT A. JOSEPHS • Department of Psychology, University of Texas, Austin,
TX 78712.   CLAUDE M. STEELE • Department of Psychology, Stanford University, Stanford, CA 94305.

Self-Esteem: The Puzzle of Low Self-Regard, edited by Roy F. Baumeister. Plenum Press,
New York, 1993.

respect; sometimes and in some settings, we are more resilient than at other times or in other settings. But personal experience suggests there are reliable individual differences in this capacity. For example, one of the authors was presented with an option to buy a particularly risky stock by his brother. Like most such stocks, there was a good chance of a high payoff, coupled with a good chance of a big loss. The author's brother, thick of skin, was eager to buy. If the stock failed, he may have calculated, he had lots of esteem cushioning, a happy family, a good career as a lawyer, and so on. But the author, who had a thinner skin (perhaps because he was a poor graduate student at the time), was wary of the gamble. He focused on the possibility that the stock might lose value, and how foolish he would feel if he gambled away his tenuous financial security.

We would like to set forth a theory of individual differences in resiliency to self-image threat based on the idea that such resiliency may be related to self-esteem. We reason that high self-esteem people have more resources (i.e., positive aspects of their self-concepts) with which to affirm their overall sense of self-integrity, and therefore, like Steinbeck's Liza and the author's brother, are less disturbed when a particular threat arises. Conversely, low self-esteem people with fewer such resources are, like Samuel and the author, more distraught by and wary of each threat.

This theory is derived from theories of self-esteem maintenance (e.g., Greenberg, Pyszczynski, Solomon, & Rosenblatt, 1990; Rosenblatt, Greenberg, Solomon and Pyszczynski, 1989; Tesser, 1988) and particularly from self-affirmation theory (Liu & Steele, 1986; Steele, 1988; Steele & Liu, 1983), which assumes a self-system for maintaining an image of self-integrity, that is, overall moral and adaptive adequacy. This theory assumes that the process of self-affirmation is begun by a threat to this image. Such threats can arise form negative life events, negative judgments of others, or even one's own behavior (e.g., a contradiction of one's values or a failure). In response, this system interprets and reinterprets one's experience and the world so as to restore this image. Importantly, the goal of the system is a global sense of self-integrity, not necessarily refutation of each specific threat. A particular threatening event, even an important one, might be left unrationalized if one could affirm a valued aspect of the self that reinforces one's overall image of self-adequacy, even when that self-aspect is unrelated to the threat. The individual thus has substantial flexibility in responding to specific self-image threats. For example, the college student who fails a test may deal with the inherent self-image threat by arguing herself into a higher grade or derogating the test. Or she might do something that does nothing to deflect the specific threat but affirms her overall self-integrity, such as working harder for a good cause.

Maintaining a sense of self-integrity may be especially difficult for low self-esteem people. These individuals have fewer and less distinct positive aspects of their self-image (Baumeister, Tice, & Hutton, 1989; Brown, 1986; Campbell, 1990), and therefore fewer specific self-aspects with which to affirm a sense of global self-integrity. Thus, when they are threatened, it may be more difficult for them to restore feelings of adequacy by recruiting valued self-aspects. Compared to high-esteem people, they may be forced to restore a sense of integrity more by rationalizing the threatening event or by dismissing its self-image implications.

This is our working hypothesis of how the level of self-esteem moderates resilience to self-image threat. In the remainder of this chapter, we present research testing this formulation in paradigms selected to show, as a first step in this program of research, the importance of this functioning in basic social psychological processes and everyday life.

Dissonance and Self-Esteem Functioning

We begin with an examination of the implications of this model for basic dissonance processes. To put our reasoning in terms of an example, consider the student in a classic dissonance experiment whose self-image is threatened by freely writing a public essay favoring a tuition hike at his university, something he deeply opposes. He can rationalize his action by changing his attitude about the tuition hike, as has been shown in many such experiments (Cooper & Fazio, 1984), or he can access some other centrally important aspect of his self-image that restores a sense of self-integrity, as has been shown in a number of self-affirmation experiments (Steele, 1988). If the student has high self-esteem, he should have numerous self-aspects capable of affirming a sense of global self-integrity and thus may recruit them to counter the threat. But if the student has low self-esteem, he will likely have few such self-aspects, and therefore will be more pressured to cope with his actions by changing his attitude about the tuition hike.

But the relationship between self-esteem and self-affirmational processes may not be quite so simple. A central proposition of self-affirmation theory is that after a self-image threat, people will affirm their self-adequacy through whatever means is most available or salient (Steele, 1988). It may be that after a self-image threat, one's attention is focused on the threat, and all people (regardless of their level of self-esteem) will try to affirm themselves by deflecting or diminishing the threat. That is, the threat itself may draw their attention and make them less mindful of their affirmational resources, thus preempting any effect of individual differences in these resources.

If this reasoning is correct, self-affirmational resources may have to be salient, or "on line," in what Markus and Wurf (1987) have called the "working self-concept" in order for there to be reliable individual differences in the use of these resources. In real life, a variety of factors may conspire to make one's characterological resources more salient and thus part of the affirmation process. Anything that diverts attention toward the self—a question from a friend, or the mere passage of time without having dismissed the threat—may focus attention on one's characterological resources, bringing them on line and thus into the affirmation process. For a person with many esteem resources (i.e., a high self-esteem person), this awareness is likely to help restore a favorable self-image, making it less important to resolve the provoking threat. For a person with fewer or less secure esteem resources (i.e., a low self-esteem person), this awareness will be less restorative, and in fact may motivate the person to gain affirmation through some dismissal of the provoking threat. Returning to our example, recall the student who was induced to write a counterattitudinal (and thus self-threatening) essay. Were he allowed to leave the laboratory so that other events and conversations could make salient different self-knowledge, he would be likely to rebound rather quickly if this knowledge affirmed his overall adequacy. But if it did not, he might suffer a bit and begin rationalizing the essay, thus changing his attitude, as his most promising means of restoring self-integrity.

Accordingly, we reasoned that if people are not focused on their affirmational resources following a self-image threat, both high- and low-esteem people will attempt to rationalize or dismiss the threat per se; however, when something does focus them on their resources, high-esteem people (being cognizant of a broader set of affirmational resources) will rationalize the threat less than low-esteem people.

We tested this prediction by examining subject's responses to the self-image threat inherent in the classic free-choice dissonance paradigm (Brehm, 1956). In our view, this paradigm is self-threatening because choosing between closely valued alternatives challenges the subject's competence as a decision maker. In the version of this paradigm that we used (Steele, Spencer, & Lynch, in press), subjects rated and ranked 10 compact discs, ostensibly as part of a marketing survey. They were then given a choice between their fifth and sixth-ranked discs. After a 10-minute delay, they were asked to rerate the discs. Self-justifying rationalization is measured as the extent to which subjects raised their rating of the chosen disc and lowered their rating of the nonchosen disc at the time of the second rating, thus "spreading the alternatives," as this measure of rationalization is called in the dissonance literature.

To manipulate self-focus, approximately half of the subjects in each esteem condition completed the Rosenberg Self-Esteem Scale (1965) when they arrived for the experiment, just prior to the free-choice procedure. The items on this scale require subjects to access directly their global self-esteem, as well as many constituent self-concepts, and thus should make their self-evaluative resources more salient.

We expected that when subjects were not self-focused, both high and low self-esteem subjects would show the standard dissonance effect. They would be focused on the threatening possibility that they may have made a bad decision and thus will spread the alternatives in justification and self-affirmation. But when they were focused on their affirmational resources (via the earlier self-esteem scale), we expected little if any rationalizing spread of alternatives among high self-esteem subjects, but significant rationalization among low-esteem subjects.

The results conformed to these predictions. Indeed, when subjects were focused on their self-images, there were reliable self-esteem differences. Low self-esteem people showed marked rationalization of their decisions, whereas high self-esteem people showed none. But when subjects were not so focused, both high and low self-esteem subjects showed moderate rationalization of their decisions.

Self-Esteem and Downward Social Comparison

Up to this point, we have emphasized the difficulty that low self-esteem people may have in recruiting positive self-aspects with which to restore a sense of global self-integrity after it is threatened. For this reasoning we suggested that low self-esteem people may feel more pressured to restore this sense of integrity by rationalizing away the provoking threat. But there is a further alternative: Low self-esteem people might also recover from a threatened sense of self-integrity by engaging in downward social comparisons.

Social comparisons are contacts between people in which performances or opinions are made known. Festinger (1954) has argued that in general, people have a tendency to compare themselves with others who are doing slightly better than themselves—that is, to make upward social comparisons—in order to gain more information about a task. Yet considerable research has shown that people often make comparisons with others who are performing poorly, that is, make downward social comparisons (Brickman & Bullman, 1977; Taylor & Lobel, 1989; Wills, 1981). This research suggests that people make downward social comparisons to bolster their self-image and thus, we speculate, to recover a threatened sense of self-integrity. Focusing on the negative aspects of another's performance puts one's own performance in a relatively positive light. Thus, in social comparison situations, people may sometimes make upward comparisons, presumably to gain more information about a task, or they may make downward comparisons, presumably to bolster their self-image.

From this standpoint of our resource model of psychological resiliency, we reason that people will make upward comparisons in social comparison situations to maximize information gain, unless they are focused on their self-image. Then we expect an esteem difference: Low self-esteem individuals, now mindful of their relatively negative self-concept, may strive to bolster their self-image by engaging in downward social comparisons, whereas high self-esteem people, now mindful of their positive self-image, should be freed from the need for downward social comparisons and compare upward.

We tested this prediction by investigating social comparison in an interview setting (Spencer, Fein, & Steele, 1992). All subjects were told that they would be engaging in an interview in which they should try to make a favorable impression. But, ostensibly to familiarize them with the procedure, subjects were asked to listen to two brief excerpts of previous interviews. After listening to the excerpts, subjects were asked to choose one interview to listen to in its entirety. The two excerpts portrayed very different interviews. In one interview a respondent made a very favorable impression; in the other, a respondent made a negative impression. The dependent variable was which tape the subject chose to listen to in its entirety. Did the subject choose the good interview (making an upward social comparison), which should provide the more useful information, or the bad interview (making a downward social comparison), which presumably would bolster the subject's self-image? As in the previous experiment, approximately half of the subjects in each self-esteem condition completed the Rosenberg Self-Esteem Scale (1965) when they arrived for the experiment, just prior to the social comparison task. This manipulation served to focus subjects on their self-evaluative resources.

We predicted that without the self-focus manipulation, subjects would focus on the social comparison task, and both high and low self-esteem subjects would listen to the good interview, making upward social comparisons; however, when subjects were self-focused, low self-esteem subjects would tend to listen to the bad interview to boost their self-image through downward comparison, whereas high self-esteem subjects would have the resilience to listen to the good interview. As illustrated in Table 1, the result conformed to our predictions.

Taken together, these two studies provide good initial support for our resources model of resiliency to self-image threats. When people are focused on their self-image, high self-esteem people seem to utilize positive self-aspects to cope with the threat by affirming an overall sense of self-integrity. Low self-esteem people seem to have difficulty using this route to affirmation; instead, they appear to utilize affirmational opportunities that do not require self-resources. They are more likely to rationalize and dismiss provoking threats and to engage in downward social comparisons.

Importantly, though, the findings also suggest that people may not immediately access esteem resources in the effort to recover from a self-image threat. Both high and low self-esteem subjects, when not explicitly focused on the self, attempted to resolve the threat presumably without consulting their standing esteem resources. For these resources to affect the affirmation process, they had to be primed. In everyday real life, such factors as the elapse of time or the failure to resolve the provoking threat eventually direct people to use standing esteem resources in affirmation. But the present findings establish that once they become salient, esteem resources can influence the affirmation process, and thus that such resources may be an important source of individual difference in resilience to self-image threat.

On a more speculative note, we assume that resolving the provoking threat and engaging in downward social comparisons are not the only means available for low self-esteem people to restore a sense of self-integrity. Our primary hypothesis has been that low self-esteem people may have particular difficulty recruiting positive aspects of their self-concept that confer a sense of moral and adaptive adequacy. Yet there must be other routes to self-affirmation that do not require access to esteem resources. One strategy that may be of particular importance is engaging in stereotypic and prejudiced behaviors. Like social compari-

TABLE 1. Type of Interview Chosen Most Often

	Self-Focus Condition	No Self-Focus
High self-esteem	GOOD	GOOD
Low self-esteem	BAD	GOOD

NOTE: Interviews provided social comparison information such that choosing the good interview led to upward comparison and choosing the bad interview led to downward comparison.

sons, these negative views of others may serve to bolster one's self-image. If this reasoning is correct, then when low self-esteem people are focused on their self-image, they may be more likely to use stereotypes and to display prejudice.

LOW SELF-ESTEEM AND SELF-CONSISTENCY: AVOIDING SELF-IMAGE THREATS

In uncertainty, I am certain that underneath their topmost layers of frailty men want to be good and want to be loved. (Steinbeck, 1952, p. 367)

Our model suggests that both high and low self-esteem people strive to maintain an overall sense of self-integrity. The only difference is that high self-esteem people have more positive aspects of their self-image than low self-esteem people that they can use to affirm self-integrity. This position seems to be in conflict with a large body of research suggesting that at times, low self-esteem people prefer to act and obtain information that is consistent with their negative self-image (i.e., they seem not to strive to maintain a sense of moral and adaptive adequacy). The 1940s, 1950s, and 1960s saw the birth of several prominent consistency and balance theories (Aronson, 1969; Festinger, 1957; Heider, 1958; Lecky, 1945; Secord & Backman, 1965). An important implication of these theories, as described by Swann, Pelham, and Krull (1989), is that self-verifying information "acts like the rudder of a ship, bolstering people's confidence in their ability to navigate through the sometimes murky seas of everyday social life" (p. 763).

Self-verification theory (Swann, 1983) paints the individual as one who desires a world that is both predictable and controllable, and thus provides stable self-conceptions. To this end, there is evidence that people choose interaction partners who support their self-views (Swann, Hixon, Stein-Seroussi, & Gilbert, 1990), and that they regard self-consistent information as more accurate, credible, and diagnostic (e.g., Crary, 1966; Korman, 1968; Markus, 1977; Shrauger & Lund, 1975; Swann, Griffin, Predmore, & Gaines, 1987).

These results might seem to suggest that people pursue self-consistency, even heroically—as when low self-esteem subjects, given a choice between a roommate who likes them and one who doesn't like them, prefer the one who doesn't like them, or when after an important performance, low-esteem subjects prefer to hear negative rather than positive evaluations of their work. We think that if one looks "underneath their topmost layers of frailty," however, this may not be the case.

Although we admire the quality and replicability of these effects, we argue that such sacrifices for consistency are more apparent than real. These people are simply foregoing self-enhancement for another self-integrity motive that in these situations is more powerful (e.g., avoiding a roommate who may expect them to be someone they don't believe they can be, or getting an evaluation that, though negative, may help them perform better in the future).

A central proposition of self-affirmation theory (Steele, 1988) is that people consider the costs and benefits of different routes to self-affirmation and prefer modes of affirmation that have favorable cost-benefit ratios. We argue that because of individual differences in self-affirmational resources, routes to self-affirmation may differ in their costs to high and low self-esteem people. In particular, modes of affirmation in which the individual's self-image might be further threatened should have greater costs for low than high self-esteem people. If high self-esteem people choose routes to self-affirmation that may impeach the self, they have many positive aspects of their self-image to fall back on and therefore should be more likely, barring any better alternatives, to do so. Conversely, if low self-esteem people choose a route that threatens their self-image, they will have few affirmational resources to counteract this threat; such a mode of affirmation would therefore have a higher potential cost for them than for high-esteem people.

For example, if a person chooses a roommate who likes her, but the roommate eventually decides that this person is a slob and an awful roommate, a high self-esteem person could recruit self-affirmational resources to counteract this threat. She may react by saying, "Oh well, I am a good student, and I have lots of other friends. I will get by this year, and everything will be all right." But a low self-esteem person who may not have these self-evaluative resources must face this threat each day without an easy way to counter it. He may say, "Try as I may I just can't get this person to like me. It really gets me down."

If this reasoning is correct, then manipulating the presence of future self-image threats (i.e., manipulating the cost to low self-esteem people) should affect the strategies that low self-esteem people use to maintain an overall sense of self-integrity. Low self-esteem people will likely avoid a route to self-affirmation that includes the possibility of future self-image threat, as the costs will be relatively high. If the possibility of self-image threat is removed, however, they will use this strategy. High self-esteem subjects, on the other hand, will use routes to self-affirmation without worrying about the self-image threat that may occur. To them, these self-image threats are small costs because they have other aspects of their self-image that can counteract the threat.

SELF-ESTEEM AND ESTIMATES OF PERFORMANCE

We tested this reasoning by investigating high and low self-esteem people's estimates of their performance on a difficult intelligence test (Spencer & Steele, 1992). We manipulated self-image threat by giving subjects different amounts of feedback about their performance. In one condition, subjects were told that they would find out their actual performance immediately after they made their estimates. In a second condition subjects were told that their performance would be anonymous, under the guise that they were being sent to another department. Lastly, some subjects were informed that the machine that scores the intelligence test was broken, but that they could see their score in a couple of days.

We hypothesized that when subjects expected immediate feedback on the intelligence test, the potential humiliation stemming from the possibility that they might overestimate their test score would have different effects on high and low self-esteem people. High self-esteem people, knowing that they had many positive aspects of their self-image to fall back on, would be relatively undaunted by this threat. Conversely, low self-esteem people would be concerned with this threat, as they had few self-evaluative resources to counteract it, and so they would lower their estimates of their performance to protect against the threat. For subjects not receiving immediate feedback, either when the results were anonymous or delayed, the threat that they might embarrass themselves by overestimating their performance was removed; here we expected that low self-esteem subjects would not lower their estimates. The results confirmed these predictions.

These results suggest that even though high self-esteem people report higher estimates of their performance than low self-esteem people when they expect feedback, they are not simply being consistent with their self-image. Both high and low self-esteem people may be trying to maintain a sense of self-integrity, but the costs of pursuing a self-enhancing strategy may be different for these two groups of people. For high self-esteem people, restoring self-integrity is relatively easy; they can affirm themselves without worrying about possible self-image threats. But for low self-esteem people the task is harder; they face the possibility of incurring a self-image threat that they will not be able to overcome. If this threat is removed, these low self-esteem people will also pursue self-enhancement.

SELF-ESTEEM AND RISKY DECISION MAKING

Spencer & Steele (1992) provided a useful first step in showing that routes to self-affirmation may have different costs for high and low self-esteem people if these routes include possible self-image threats. Josephs, Larrick, Steele, and Nisbett (1992) extended these findings to the domain of risky decision making. Low self-esteem people may avoid risk more than high-esteem people because the cost of losing a gamble may be higher for low-esteem people, as they have fewer self-evaluative resources to counter such a threat. This reasoning is consistent with the literature on risk taking and self-esteem, which finds that generally high self-esteem people are more risk seeking, whereas low self-esteem people are risk averse (see Baumeister et al., 1989, for a review).

In these experiments, subjects were asked to choose between pairs of monetary gambles. In each pair, there was one gamble in which there was a certain payoff (100% chance) and one gamble in which there was an uncertain payoff (20% to 80% chance). Thus, subjects were forced to choose between an option where they knew the outcome and an option where the outcome would be determined by chance. Sometimes these pairs were framed in terms of gains, in which subjects were given a choice between a sure win and a chance of winning a greater amount of money; sometimes they were framed as losses, in which subjects were given the choice between a sure loss and a chance of losing a greater amount of money.

We argued that the threat in this gambling task arises from the regret associated with choosing the probabilistic gamble and finding later that the gamble did not pay off. It is in this situation that the subject must contend with the knowledge that a poor decision was made. In essence, the subject can kick himself or herself for passing up a certain, albeit modest, sum for a larger sum that carries with it the risk of not paying off. Presumably, by eschewing the bird-in-the-hand logic, the subject opens himself or herself up to the possibility that he or she will wind up with nothing.

Our resources model suggests that the threat that one's choices will not pay off will have different effects on high and low self-esteem subjects. High-esteem subjects should be able to withstand this threat, because they can counter with many positive aspects of their self-image. Low self-esteem subjects, on the other hand, have fewer self-evaluative resources to dispel such a threat; for these people, the threat will incur greater costs. Therefore, we expected that low self-esteem people would be more likely to choose the certain payoff than high self-esteem people.

This reasoning is true as long as subjects know the outcome of their gambles. We reasoned that if one did not expect to know the outcome of various gambles chosen, the threat that one's gambles might not pay off (and thus result in feelings of regret and foolishness) would be greatly diminished. In this situation, we would expect low self-esteem subjects to behave similarly to high self-esteem subjects. In the experiment, we removed this threat of regret by telling subjects that they would not be informed as to the outcome of any of the gambles they were about to choose. Thus subjects would not be threatened by the possibility that their gambles would not pay off. A subject could choose a risky gamble and imagine a successful outcome, resulting in a profitable payoff, without ever worrying about reality interfering to dispel the fantasy. As a result, we expected subjects high and low in self-esteem not to differ in their choice of gambles. The results confirmed this prediction.

SELF-ESTEEM AND INFORMATION SEEKING

In Spencer and Steele (1992) and Josephs et al. (1992), the costs that strategies of self-affirmation entail were manipulated by varying whether subjects were informed about the outcomes of possible self-image threats. When they learned the outcomes of these threats, high and low self-esteem people incurred different costs. High self-esteem people were faced with a relatively small cost, as they have many positive aspects of their self-concept to counteract the self-image threat. The self-image threat posed a much bigger cost, however, for low self-esteem people, who have fewer self-evaluative resources. But when subjects did not learn of the outcomes of these self-image threats, the cost of using a route to self-affirmation was the same for high and low self-esteem people.

In Steele, Spencer, and Josephs (1992), rather than manipulating whether people learn the outcomes of self-image threats, we manipulated the nature of these threats. In these experiments, using a procedure developed by Swann and Read (1981), subjects completed a questionnaire that ostensibly measured aspects of their personality; it was supposedly evaluated by two graduate students in clinical psychology. The subjects were then presented with preliminary evaluations of their personality, purportedly from each of the graduate students. One of these students ostensibly evaluated the subject favorably, and the other negatively. In addition, subjects were told that the aspects of personality being evaluated were either changeable or stable. Subjects were then asked which complete evaluation they wanted to read, the favorable one or the negative one.

We reasoned that when subjects were told that the aspects of personality being evaluated were changeable, they would face the following self-image threat: In order to choose the self-enhancing positive feedback, they would face the threat that the positive evaluation might be proven wrong, thus passing up the opportunity to get feedback that might help them improve themselves. Further, these threats would have higher costs for low self-esteem people than for high self-esteem people.

Therefore we predicted that in this situation, low self-esteem people would be more likely to pick the negative evaluation, and high self-esteem people the positive one—a finding obtained many times by Swann and his colleagues (Swann, 1983; Swann et al., 1989; Swann, Pelham, Hixon, & De La Ronde, 1990; Swann & Read, 1981; Stein-Seroussi, Giesler, & Swann, 1992). But when the aspects of personality that were being evaluated were purportedly stable, then the self-image threat that a positive evaluation might be proven wrong would seem unlikely, and hope for self-improvement would be prohibited. In this condition, we expected that both high and low self-esteem subjects would choose the positive evaluation. As illustrated in Table 2, these predictions were confirmed.

CONCLUSIONS

Taken together, these results provide strong support for our reasoning that some routes to self-affirmation may entail costs that may not be equal for high and low self-esteem individuals. If these costs are self-image threats, high self-esteem individuals will be able to recruit positive aspects of their self-concept to counteract these threats. Low self-esteem individuals may have more difficulty accessing such positive self-images; therefore, the cost of strategies of self-affirmation that entail self-image threats will be higher for low self-esteem than for high self-esteem people.

Although at times it may appear as if low self-esteem people are acting to maintain self-consistency, we would argue that they are simply striving for self-affirmation through a route that offers them the fewest costs and the largest benefits. It is important to keep in mind that the motive for perceived self-integrity is not just a motive for self-enhancement, as is sometimes implied, but a motive to perceive the self as morally and adaptively adequate. We readily concede that subjects can be induced to forgo self-enhancements (especially the rather trivial

TABLE 2. Type of Feedback Chosen Most Often

	Changeable Trait	Stable Trait
High self-esteem	GOOD	GOOD
Low self-esteem	BAD	GOOD

NOTE: The feedback provided subjects with an evaluation of their performance on a supposed personality test that measured either changeable or stable personality traits.

ones offered in research) to fend off more profound threats to their self-integrity.

These findings and those reviewed earlier suggest that high and low self-esteem people do not differ dramatically in their motivations to affirm themselves: Both strive to maintain a sense of self-integrity. The difference is that high self-esteem people have a relatively larger number of positive self-concepts that they can recruit to counter self-image threats. Low self-esteem people face the difficult challenge of maintaining a sense of moral and adaptive adequacy with few self-evaluative resources that may dismiss such a threat.

To summarize our theoretical position, we argue the following:

1. People strive to maintain a sense of self-integrity, that is, a sense of moral and adaptive adequacy. When this sense of self-integrity is threatened, people are motivated to restore it, either by dismissing the provoking threat or by affirming their overall sense of worth by accessing a valued aspect of the self. The strategy of self-affirmation that people use will depend on what strategies are available and what strategies have the best cost-benefit ratio.

2. Because high self-esteem people have more positive aspects of their self-image (self-evaluative resources) than low self-esteem people, they can respond to self-image threats by accessing self-evaluative resources. This strategy is more difficult for low self-esteem people, however, because they have relatively few resources.

3. In order for self-evaluative resources to be utilized, they may have to be accessible in thought and memory; that is, they may have to be brought "on line" in the working self-concept.

4. Some routes to self-affirmation may have different costs for high and low self-esteem people. In particular, self-affirmational strategies in which people's self-image might be threatened may have relatively small costs for high self-esteem people, as they have many self-evaluative resources to counter such a threat; however, the potential cost is greater to low self-esteem people, who have few such resources.

Acknowledgments

The preparation of this chapter and some of the research reported herein was supported by a National Science Foundation Predoctoral Fellowship and a National Institute for Mental Health Predoctoral Fellowship to the first author; a National Institute for Mental Health Predoctoral Fellowship to the second author; and a grant from the National Institute of Mental Health to the third author. Address correspondence to Steve Spencer, 5237 ISR, Box 1248, University of Michigan, Ann Arbor, MI 48106–1248.

REFERENCES

Aronson, E. (1969). The theory of cognitive dissonance: A current perspective. In L. Berkowitz (Ed.), *Advances in experimental social psychology* (Vol. 4, pp. 1–34). New York: Academic Press.

Baumeister, R. E., Tice, D. M., & Hutton, D. G. (1989). Self-presentational motivations and personality differences in self-esteem. *Journal of Personality, 57,* 547–579.

Brehm, J. (1956). Postdecision changes in the desirability of alternatives. *Journal of Abnormal and Social Psychology, 52,* 384–389.

Brickman, P., & Bullman, R. J. (1977). Pleasure and pain in social comparison. In J. M. Suls & R. L. Miller (Eds.), *Social comparison processes: Theoretical and empirical perspectives.* Washington, DC: Hemisphere.

Brown, J. (1986). Evaluation of self and others: Self-enhancement biases in social judgments. *Social Cognition, 4,* 353–376.

Campbell, J. (1990). Self-esteem and clarity of the self-concept. *Journal of Personality and Social Psychology, 59,* 1–12.

Cooper, J., & Fazio, R. J. (1984). A new look at dissonance theory. In L. Berkowitz (Ed.), *Advances in experimental social psychology* (Vol. 17, pp. 229–266). New York: Academic Press.

Crary, W. G. (1966). Reactions to incongruent self-experiences. *Journal of Consulting Psychology, 30,* 246–252.

Festinger, L. (1954). A theory of social comparison processes. *Human Relations, 7,* 117–140.

Festinger, L. (1957). *A theory of cognitive dissonance.* Evanston, IL: Row, Peterson.

Greenberg, J., Pyszczynski, T., Solomon, S., & Rosenblatt, A. (1990). Evidence for terror management theory: II. The effects of mortality salience on reactions to those who threaten or bolster the cultural worldview. *Journal of Personality and Social Psychology, 58,* 308–318.

Heider, F. (1958). *The psychology of interpersonal relationships.* New York: John Wiley.

Josephs, R., Larrick, R., Steele, C., & Nisbett, R. (1992). Protecting the self from the consequences of risky decisions. *Journal of Personality and Social Psychology, 62,* 26–37.

Korman, A. K. (1968). Task success, task popularity, and self-esteem as influences on task liking. *Journal of Applied Psychology, 52,* 484–490.

Lecky, P. (1945). *Self-consistency: A theory of personality.* New York: Island.

Liu, T. J., & Steele, C. M. (1986). Attribution as self-affirmation. *Journal of Personality and Social Psychology, 51,* 351–360.

Markus, H. R. (1977). Self-schemas and processing information about the self. *Journal of Personality and Social Psychology, 22,* 90–107.

Markus, H. R., & Wurf, E. (1987). The dynamic self concept: A social psychological perspective. *Annual Review of Psychology, 38,* 299–337.

Rosenberg, M. (1965). *Society and the adolescent self-image.* Princeton, NJ: Princeton University Press.

Rosenblatt, A., Greenberg, J., Solomon, S., & Pyszczynski, T. (1989). Evidence for terror management theory: I. The effects of mortality salience on reactions to those who violate or uphold cultural values. *Journal of Personality and Social Psychology, 57,* 681–690.

Secord, P. F., & Backman, C. W. (1965). An interpersonal approach to personality. In B. Maher (Ed.), *Progress in experimental personality research* (Vol. 2, pp. 91–125). New York: Academic Press.

Shrauger, J. S., & Lund, A. (1975). Self-evaluation and reactions to evaluations from others. *Journal of Personality, 43,* 94–108.

Spencer, S., & Steele, C. (1992). *Judging our abilities and the nature of self-esteem functioning.* Unpublished manuscript, University of Michigan.

Spencer, S. J., Fein, S., & Steele, C. M. (1992). *Availability of self-evaluative resources and downward social comparisons.* Unpublished manuscript, University of Michigan.

Steele, C. M. (1988). The psychology of self-affirmation: Sustaining the integrity of the self. In L. Berkowitz (Ed.), *Advances in experimental social psychology* (Vol. 21, pp. 261–302). New York: Academic Press.

Steele, C. M., & Liu, T. J. (1983). Dissonance processes as self-affirmation. *Journal of Personality and Social Psychology, 45,* 5–19.

Steele, C., Spencer, S., & Josephs, R. (1992). *Seeking self-relevant information: The effects of self-esteem and stability of the information.* Unpublished manuscript, University of Michigan.

Steele, C. M., Spencer, S. J., & Lynch, M. (in press), Dissonance and affirmational resources: Resilience against self-image threats. *Journal of Personality and Social Psychology.*

Steinbeck, J. (1952). *East of Eden.* New York: Viking.

Swann, W. B., Jr., Stein-Seroussi, A., & Giesler, R. B. (1992). Why people self-verify. Journal of Personality and Social Psychology, 62, 392–401.

Swann, W. B., Jr. (1983). Self-verification: Bringing social reality into harmony with the self. In J. Suls & A. G. Greenwald (Eds.), *Social psychological perspectives on the self* (Vol. 2, pp. 33–66). Hillsdale, NJ: Lawrence Erlbaum.

Swann, W. B., Jr., & Read, S. J. (1981). Acquiring self-knowledge: The search for feedback that fits. *Journal of Personality and Social Psychology, 41,* 1119–1128.

Swann, W. B., Jr., Griffin, J. J., Predmore, S., & Gaines, B. (1987). The cognitive affective crossfire: When self-consistency confronts self-enhancement. *Journal of Personality and Social Psychology, 52,* 881–889.

Swann, W. B., Jr., Hixon, G. J., Stein-Seroussi, A., & Gilbert, D. T. (1990). The fleeting gleam of praise: Cognitive processes underlying behavioral reactions to self-relevant feedback. *Journal of Personality and Social Psychology, 59,* 17–26.

Swann, W. B., Jr., Pelham, B. W., Hixon, J. G., & De La Ronde, C. (1990). *Getting out when the getting gets good: Choice of relationship partners and the self.* Unpublished manuscript, University of Texas.

Swann, W. B., Jr., Pelham, B. W., & Krull, D. S. (1989). Agreeable fancy or disagreeable truth? How people reconcile their self-enhancement and self-verification needs. *Journal of Personality and Social Psychology, 57,* 782–791.

Taylor, S. E., & Lobel, M. (1989). Social comparison activity under threat: Downward evaluation and upward contacts. *Psychological Review, 96,* 569–575.

Tesser, A. (1988). Toward a self-evaluation maintenance model of social behavior. In L. Berkowitz (Ed.), *Advances in experimental social psychology* (Vol. 21, pp. 181–227). New York: Academic Press.

Wills, T. A. (1981). Downward comparison principles in social psychology. *Psychological Bulletin, 90,* 245–271.

CHAPTER 3

THE SOCIAL MOTIVATIONS OF PEOPLE WITH LOW SELF-ESTEEM

DIANNE M. TICE

Low self-esteem people have always been a puzzle to researchers. For years, many theorists began with the plausible yet probably false assumption that people with low self-esteem were generally the opposite of those with high self-esteem; by this reasoning, if people with high self-esteem want to succeed and be liked, then people with low self-esteem must want to fail and be disliked. More recent theorists (e.g., S. Jones, 1973; Shrauger, 1975) have suggested that the notion that low self-esteem people desire failure and rejection is false. The question remains, however: What do these people want?

The purpose of this chapter is to address the issue of motivation. What do the data tell us about people with low self-esteem? By examining studies on self-handicapping, allocation of free-choice time, task persistence, self-presentation, and responses to feedback, it will be possible to furnish a picture of the motivations and goals of the typical person with low self-esteem. To anticipate my conclusions, the picture is as follows: People with low self-esteem would very much like to succeed, to win love and admiration, to become rich and famous, and so

DIANNE M. TICE • Dept. of Psychology, Case Western Reserve University, 10900 Euclid Ave., Cleveland OH 44106–7123.

Self-Esteem: The Puzzle of Low Self-Regard, edited by Roy F. Baumeister. Plenum Press, New York, 1993.

forth, but such goals seem out of reach to them and are not part of their ongoing concerns. Instead, their first goal in most situations is to avoid failure, humiliation, rejection, and other disasters. Well acquainted with and sensitive to the costs and pains of failure, they focus on protecting themselves against such distressing outcomes. They lean toward neutral, noncommittal self-presentations and in fact find it difficult to present themselves in either a highly negative or a highly positive fashion. They focus on their shortcomings and try to remedy them. They show little interest in strategic ploys (such as self-handicapping) designed to enhance credit for potential success, but they may use similar strategies in order to protect themselves from the implications of failure.

SELF-PROTECTION, SELF-ENHANCEMENT, OR SELF-HATRED?

EARLY THEORIES

Current thinking about the motivational side of self-esteem has evolved through a series of hypotheses. Researchers began with the plausible but ultimately false view that low self-esteem motivations were the opposite of high self-esteem motivations. If people with high self-esteem wanted success and social acceptance, then people with low self-esteem must want failure and social rejection, according to this line of reasoning. The consistency theories of the 1960s provided the most powerful and appealing framework for this view (e.g., Aronson & Carlsmith, 1962; Aronson & Meettee, 1968; Maracek & Mettee, 1972).

This view has been largely discarded. Attempted replications and other studies employing analogous methods were not always able to reproduce the consistency findings (especially the findings that low self-esteem people or people with low expectations preferred failure feedback; e.g., Brock, Edelman, Edwards, & Schuck, 1965; Ward & Sandvold, 1963). In the seventies, S. Jones (1973) published a literature review that concluded that there was little support for consistency theory and suggested that low self-esteem people, like high self-esteem people, usually prefer approval and success over rejection and failure.

In a subsequent review of the literature, Shrauger (1975) proposed an elegant solution to the question of whether low self-esteem individuals prefer success or failure feedback. He observed that when *affective reactions* (e.g., pleasure or disappointment with feedback) are being assessed, low self-esteem people prefer to receive positive, success feedback, as do high self-esteem people. On the other hand, when *cognitive reactions* (e.g., recall, judgments of the accuracy of the feedback) are being assessed, findings favor the consistency model. In other words, low self-esteem people expect to fail and are more likely to believe failure feedback than are high self-esteem people, because failure feedback is consistent with their cognitive structures and expectations. There are no differences between high and low self-esteem people in their affective responses to feedback; everyone prefers success. Differences between high and low self-esteem persons emerge in the cognitive realm: People with high self-esteem expect to excel, whereas those with low self-esteem expect to do more poorly.

Direct empirical support for Shrauger's hypothesis that cognitive reactions to social feedback conform to self-consistency theory and affective reactions conform to self-enhancement theory was provided by McFarlin and Blascovich (1981). They found that low self-esteem people desire success just as much as high self-esteem people, but cognitively they continue to expect failure. Low self-esteem people were less willing to boast in advance that they would achieve success, perhaps because they lacked confidence in their abilities to live up to highly favorable predictions. Cognitive consistency dynamics may influence expectancies and willingness to believe feedback, but they do not dictate desires and motivations. In addition, an important conceptual replication of McFarlin and Blascovich's findings was provided by Swann, Griffin, Predmore, and Gaines (1987), who also concluded that the affective motivations that accompany low self-esteem scores are indistinguishable from those that accompany high self-esteem scores, and only cognitive differences exist between the two groups of people. Thus, although people with low self-esteem may believe criticism more than praise, they would rather have praise.

After consistency theories were largely rejected as an all-encompassing explanation for the motivations of low self-esteem people, another theory of self-esteem emerged that suggested that people with low self-esteem are strongly oriented toward self-enhancement, whereas those with high self-esteem are oriented toward protecting themselves. This view (e.g., Dinner, Lewkowicz, & Cooper, 1972; see also Cohen, 1959) may have been based on an analogy to financial investors. People with low self-esteem presumably have nothing to lose, so they should adopt risky, self-aggrandizing, get-rich-quick schemes to enhance their views of themselves. In contrast, people with high self-esteem were seen as comparable to wealthy individuals, who have much to lose and little to gain and so should be cautious investors who seek to avoid loss.

Like the consistency theories, this view too appears to be false. Risky, self-aggrandizing strategies do not appear to be common among people with low self-esteem, who instead persistently show caution, modesty, restraint, malleability, and so forth (see Crocker & Schwartz, 1985; Roth, Harris, & Snyder, 1988; Roth, Snyder, & Pace, 1986; Wolfe, Lennox, & Cutler, 1986). For example, Baumeister (1982) has shown that compensatory self-enhancement characterizes high, not low, self-esteem.

Who Are These People With Low Self-Esteem?

Some of the confusion in previous motivational hypotheses may derive from a mistaken view of the nature of low self-esteem. Many theorists seem to have begun with a stereotype impression of the person with low self-esteem as someone with a strong dislike, even hatred, of self. People with low self-esteem were assumed to be those who regarded themselves as incompetent, unlovable, and generally worthless individuals. Although there may be a few individuals who fit that description, it does not appear to apply to the majority of people with low self-esteem.

In a review of published studies on self-esteem, my colleagues and I found a consistent pattern in the distributions of self-esteem scores (Baumeister, Tice, & Hutton, 1989). Researchers usually set up their samples by giving subjects a self-esteem measure and dividing the range of scores in half to create roughly equal-sized groups of high and low self-esteem. For study after study, we compared the range of scores actually obtained on whatever self-esteem measure was used with the range of *possible* scores on that scale. Invariably the actual scores clustered in the middle and upper ranges of possible scores. For example, if the range of possible scores on self-esteem ran from 0 to 100, a researcher might expect actual scores to run from approximately 40 to 80. The dividing line between high and low self-esteem therefore might come around 60, rather than at 50. We found this sort of pattern with every different scale used to measure self-esteem.

Thus, although high self-esteem scores were high in an absolute sense, low scores were not truly low but were only low in a relative sense. Apparently, "low" self-esteem scores typically result from endorsing the intermediate, not the low, responses. A median split of self-esteem scores on a variety of different self-esteem scales typically produced two groups: a high self-esteem group, in which the participants endorsed the most favorable statements about themselves, and a "low" self-esteem group, in which the participants endorsed the midpoint response for each question. To put it bluntly, high scores are high, but low scores are medium, in an absolute sense.

This fact needs to be taken into account to understand the nature of trait self-esteem. People with high self-esteem are those who really endorse very positive statements about themselves—basically, people who claim to be terrific in many ways. Low self-esteem, however, is not the opposite. People with low self-esteem do not depict themselves as worthless, incompetent losers. Rather, they are people who are essentially neutral in their self-descriptions, attributing neither strongly positive nor strongly negative traits to themselves. They are low in self-esteem only in a relative sense, that is, in comparison to the very flattering way that people with high self-esteem portray themselves. Low self-esteem, then, is not self-hatred, but rather it is typically a matter of regarding and presenting oneself in a neutral, noncommittal fashion.

The analogy to financial investors thus may need revision in light of this finding. People with low self-esteem are not those who have nothing to lose, like the totally poor and destitute. Rather, they are people with modest means and limited resources. High-stakes speculators are rarely found among such people; instead, such people are among the most cautious investors. Most high-stakes speculators, in fact, are found among the very wealthy, which is comparable to people with high self-esteem who are rating themselves in extremely positive terms. Thus, the link between self-esteem and self-enhancement versus self-protection should be formulated opposite to the traditional view. Instead of linking low self-esteem with self-enhancement and high self-esteem with self-protection, it is low self-esteem people who are motivated to protect their sense of self-esteem and will therefore behave in a cautious, noncommittal fashion. High self-esteem people, on the other hand, are motivated to enhance their sense of self-esteem and will therefore behave in a self-aggrandizing, risk-taking fashion.

PROTECTION, ENHANCEMENT, AND SELF-ESTEEM

A number of studies by a variety of researchers have provided support for the assertion that high self-esteem people are more concerned with self-enhancement, and low self-esteem people are more concerned with self-protection. For example, Wolfe et al. (1986) and Arkin (1981) have suggested that people with low self-esteem may be more self-protective than people with high self-esteem. Roth and colleagues presented evidence consistent with the idea that high self-esteem individuals are more likely to use a self-enhancing strategy than low self-esteem individuals; high self-esteem individuals were more likely to present themselves in an unrealistically positive manner than were low self-esteem individuals (Roth et al., 1988; Roth et al., 1986).

Some behaviors combine both self-protection and self-enhancement. Self-handicapping, for instance, normally accomplishes both self-protection and self-enhancement with the same ploy. (Self-handicapping will be treated in more detail later in this chapter; for now, it can be understood as creating barriers to one's own performance that are recognized as making failure more likely.) One may handicap oneself by getting drunk or failing to prepare before an important evaluation, for example. Drunkenness and lack of effort both provide external attributions that reduce the responsibility for failure, but they also augment the prestige of success should one succeed despite the handicap.

Attempting to improve one's performance at any given task is another example of a behavior that combines both the self-protective and the self-enhancing motivation. Improving performance (e.g., raising one's SAT scores, improving one's tennis serve) can be self-protective; after improvement, one has less chance of embarrassing oneself with a humiliating failure. An improvement in performance can also be self-enhancing, however, because a better performance is more likely to stand out as an exceptional success. High and low self-esteem people may thus be concerned with the same behavior (improving their performance on various tasks) for different reasons. High self-esteem people may be interested in identifying their strengths and cultivating them so as to stand out, which is consistent with a self-enhancing orientation. Low self-esteem people, on the other hand, may focus on their failures and weaknesses and seek to remedy them in order to protect the self against failure, rejection, humiliation, or anxiety.

Despite the frequent overlap, self-protection and self-enhancement can be conceptually and empirically distinguishable, as Arkin (1981) pointed out. In some circumstances, people must choose between pursuing a relatively risky strategy that has the potential to enhance one's public image and pursuing a safer, less attention-seeking strategy that avoids the potential to embarrass or humiliate the self publicly. Performing in public, for example, increases one's potential for enhancing one's public image, because it means exposing oneself to opportunities to gain esteem by impressing others with one's performance. Performing in public, however, also risks embarrassment and humiliation; should one perform badly, one might lose esteem. A person who is oriented toward self-enhancement will often seek out opportunities to perform publicly because of the chance these opportunities offer for increasing his or her public image. A person who is oriented toward self-protection, on the other hand, might avoid such opportunities because of the risk of public embarrassment.

Similarly, seeking competitive situations pits self-enhancement against self-protection motivations. A person who is oriented toward enhancing self-esteem (a high self-esteem person) may tend to seek out competition because it increases one's potential for enhancing one's public image, in that one exposes oneself to the chance of winning the competition and gaining esteem for one's success. A person who is oriented toward protecting self-esteem (a low self-esteem person), however, will probably avoid competition, because a competitive failure could result in a loss of self-esteem.

SELF-HANDICAPPING

As I indicated above, self-handicapping normally accomplishes both attributional goals (protection and enhancement) with one strategy. Putting barriers in the way of one's own success both provides a protective excuse for failure and enhances credit for success. Most researchers using the term *self-handicapping* have included in their definitions both the self-protective and self-enhancement benefits of the strategy (e.g., Berglas & Jones, 1978; Harris & Snyder, 1986; E. Jones & Berglas, 1978; Shepperd & Arkin, 1989a,b; Snyder, 1990; Snyder, Smith, Augelli, & Ingram, 1985). Although theory has asserted the existence of both motives for self-handicapping, however, empirical work has generally focused only on self-protection and ignored self-enhancement (see Hirt, 1989; Snyder, 1990; Tice, 1991, for reviews).

Although some individuals may self-handicap for both motives—that is, they desire both the enhancement and protection benefits of the strategy—I suggested (Tice, 1991) that an individual may engage in self-handicapping behavior primarily for one of the two motives; he or she simply receives the benefits of the other as a bonus. In a set of studies, I attempted to demonstrate that self-handicapping occurs for both motivations, that the two motivations may be separated in the laboratory, and that self-esteem is the key to predicting which motive is likely to be the main one in any individual case.

Self-handicapping presumably occurs because of threats to self-esteem on important, self-relevant dimensions. What self-handicapping specifically protects, or enhances, is self-esteem (e.g., Arkin & Baumgardner, 1985; Berglas & Jones, 1978; Harris & Snyder, 1986; E. Jones & Berglas, 1978; Snyder, 1990; Snyder & Smith, 1982; Snyder et al., 1985). Thus, there was ample reason to predict that individual differences in self-esteem should affect the tendency to self-handicap. And, sure enough, preliminary research indicated that personality differences in self-esteem could indeed be powerful predictors of self-handicapping tendencies (Tice & Baumeister, 1990).

To set up my main series of studies on self-handicapping, I reasoned from my understanding of the motivational basis of self-esteem. People with high self-esteem want to increase their credit for success, so they should engage in self-handicapping mainly when the situation is structured so that self-handicapping enhances one's credit for success but does not necessarily protect one from failure. In contrast, if people with low self-esteem are primarily motivated by self-protection, they should engage in self-handicapping mainly when the situation is structured so that self-handicapping protects one from the esteem-threatening implications of failure but does not necessarily enhance success.

In my first study in this series (Tice, 1991), self-handicapping was operationalized as lack of practice before an important evaluation, as has often been done in previous work (e.g., Harris & Snyder, 1986; Rhodewalt, Saltzman, & Wittmer, 1984; Tice & Baumeister, 1990). Participants were allowed to decide how much they wanted to practice a task in preparation for a performance. The situation was structured so that self-handicapping (i.e., not practicing) either enhanced success but did not protect against the threat of failure, or provided protection for the threat of failure but did not enhance success. This was done by describing the test as suitable only for finding extreme scores in one direction. Half the participants were told that the test would only identify exceptional, genius-level performances (so one could gain esteem but not lose it), whereas the rest were told that the test would only identify exceptionally poor, unintelligent individuals (so that one could lose esteem but not gain it). Participants were asked to take a test and were given an opportunity to practice before the evaluation. As predicted, I found that high self-esteem people self-handicapped when the situation was structured so that self-handicapping enhanced credit for success but did not protect against failure. Low self-esteem people showed the opposite pattern: They self-handicapped when the situation was structured so that self-handicapping provided protection from the esteem-threatening implications of failure but did not enhance success.

In addition to the conditions described above, in which the anticipated evaluation was described as important, another set of conditions was run in which the anticipated evaluation was described as relatively unimportant. Characterizing a task or evaluation as important and ego relevant versus inconsequential had been shown to influence self-handicapping behavior (e.g., DeGree & Snyder, 1985; Pyszczynski & Greenberg, 1983; Rhodewalt et al., 1984; Shepperd & Arkin, 1989a,b; Smith, Snyder, & Handelsman, 1982; Smith, Snyder, & Perkins, 1983; Snyder, Smith, Augelli, & Ingram, 1985; see also Snyder, 1990) such that self-handicapping occurs only when the task is important or self-relevant. Thus, I predicted and found that when the evaluation was described as relatively unimportant (a test of hand-eye coordination and fine motor control), participants were not motivated to engage in strategic ploys such as self-handicapping to maximize the attributional benefits of performance. Instead, the behavior of participants in the unimportant conditions was typical of their usual approach to everyday, nonthreatening tasks. On an unimportant task, individuals seemed to be more concerned with the actual task performance (test score) than with what that test score might say about them, because an unimportant task could not say very much about them anyway. Consistent with a self-enhancement orientation, high self-esteem participants practiced more if there was a chance of looking outstanding on an unimportant evaluation. Consistent with a self-protection orientation, low self-esteem participants practiced more if there was a chance of failing. These results were thus the reverse of what was found when the task was important and a great deal was at stake.

The most plausible interpretation of all these findings is that low self-esteem participants in both important (self-handicapping) and unimportant conditions were concerned with protection. In the unimportant conditions, they attempted to protect their images by preparing a great deal in order to decrease their chances of failing. When the task was more self-relevant, they used the strategic ploy of reduced practice, which, although increasing their chances of receiving a failing score, also increased the attributional ambiguity of the score. Thus, it would not be clear that a low score reflected low ability, because the failure could be attributed to the handicap rather than to the individual's ability. Meanwhile, when the potential implications of the test were unimportant, people with high self-esteem sought to maximize their performance if there was a chance to appear outstanding; but when the outcome could mean something highly important, they focused instead on maximizing their possible credit for success.

My second study was a conceptual replication of the high-importance conditions of first study, with a different operationalization of self-handicapping. All subjects were told that they were going to be given a nonverbal intelligence test. Again, half the subjects were told that only a high score was meaningful (so that enhancement of success was the only benefit of self-handicapping), and half the subjects were told that only a low score was meaningful (so that protection from failure was the only benefit of self-handicapping).

The operationalization of self-handicapping for the second study was adapted from Shepperd and Arkin (1989a); self-handicapping was operationalized by allowing participants to choose distracting, performance-impairing music to play during their evaluation. High and low self-esteem participants were told that they would be taking a computerized nonverbal intelligence test while music played in the background. Participants were given a chance to select the music that played during their evaluation from a selection of tapes identified as likely to enhance or detract from their scores on the test. Choosing a detracting tape constituted self-handicapping, as it was likely to decrease performance score while providing an excuse in the case of failure and enhancing success should the participant succeed despite the handicap.

The results of the second study replicated the results from the high-importance conditions of the first. Low self-esteem people were more likely than high self-esteem people to self-handicap by selecting a performance-inhibiting tape if the situation was structured so that self-handicapping protected them from the esteem-threatening implications of failure, but did not enhance success. High self-esteem people were more likely to self-handicap if the situation was structured so that self-handicapping enhanced credit for success but did not protect against failure.

Studies 3 and 4 (Tice, 1991) were designed to measure the subjective processes of individuals engaging in self-handicapping behavior. As described above, Studies 1 and 2 identified situations in which high and low self-esteem individuals self-handicap; Studies 3 and 4 were attempts to elucidate more directly the *motivations* behind the self-handicapping observed in Studies 1 and 2.

Studies 3 and 4 measured the attributions made by high and low self-esteem individuals who had a chance to self-handicap (they were about to practice before taking a nonverbal intelligence test). Before practicing, participants were asked to rate how true of themselves were statements explicitly defining the protective benefits of low practice (i.e., failure after low practice can be blamed on the handicap rather than lack of ability) and the enhancement benefits of low practice (i.e., success following low practice suggests exceptional ability). Both Studies 3 and 4 supported the findings of Studies 1 and 2 by demonstrating that high self-esteem people were more likely to endorse and agree with a statement describing the enhancement of success benefits of self-handicapping than were low self-esteem people. Low self-esteem people were found to be more likely to endorse and agree with a statement describing the protection from failure benefits of self-handicapping.

The set of studies just described (Tice, 1991) is consistent with some of my earlier work on self-handicapping. A colleague and I had previously found that high self-esteem participants self-handicapped more frequently than low self-esteem participants when the task was described as identifying the extreme upper range of nonverbal intelligence (Tice & Baumeister, 1990). The more recent set of findings (Tice, 1991) provided a conceptual replication of the earlier studies (which suggested that high self-esteem people are motivated by self-enhancement) and extended the findings by suggesting that low self-esteem people are motivated to be self-protective.

In summary, my work on self-handicapping has provided some evidence that low self-esteem people are concerned with self-protection and will self-handicap in order to protect their self-esteem and reputations. High self-esteem people, on the other hand, are concerned with self-enhancement and will self-handicap in order to enhance their self-esteem and reputations. Low self-esteem people seem to be motivated by self-protective goals to self-handicap, whereas high self-esteem people seem motivated by self-enhancement goals.

SELF-PRESENTATION

Recent research on self-presentation provides further evidence about the social motivations associated with trait self-esteem. By inducing people to present themselves in various ways, it is possible to examine how they respond. If the view of low self-esteem as self-hatred or feelings of worthlessness is largely correct, then they should find it natural to present themselves in a modest, negative, self-effacing style, just as people with high self-esteem would find it natural to present themselves in a positive, self-enhancing style. On the other hand, if low self-esteem is instead guided by neutrality and self-protection, these people should find it natural to present themselves in intermediate, moderate ways. Recent studies by my colleagues and myself examined how people responded to self-presentational demands as a function of their level of self-esteem.

In the first set of studies (Baumeister, Hutton, & Tice, 1989), we examined the allocation of cognitive resources by requiring people to present themselves either positively or negatively and then measuring their recall for the social interaction. In that study, some subjects were instructed to respond to a series of questions during a subsequent group interview in either a very favorable or relatively modest fashion. These subjects were told not to lie or distort the truth, but rather to present themselves at their best, as if they were having a very good day, or at their worst, as on a very bad day. Other subjects did not receive any special instructions prior to the interview, and they tended spontaneously to conform their self-presentations to those of the instructed subjects. Thus, the partners of self-enhancers became self-enhancing themselves, whereas the partners of modest self-presenters became modest as well.

Our main goal was to study how well people remembered what was said in the interaction. Most subjects showed very good memory for what was said in the interaction, with the exception of subjects who had been instructed to be self-deprecating. We interpreted those results to mean that the instructions to be modest and self-deprecating formed an unusual demand and required subjects to allocate more cognitive resources to managing their self-presentation in a controlled, deliberate fashion, and that the cognitive demands of this task reduced their ability to process the interaction fully (hence the impaired memory).

Hutton (1991) extended the design of the investigation described above by examining how trait self-esteem would affect the results. She reasoned that presenting oneself in a positive, self-enhancing fashion would only be natural and familiar for people high in self-esteem, and so only they would show the improved memory for the interaction. Her results conformed to that pattern: People with high self-esteem recalled the interaction better when they had been boastful than when they had been modest. Furthermore, their recall of the interaction surpassed that of people with low self-esteem who had received the same instructions to be boastful.

Meanwhile, Hutton had competing predictions about how people low in self-esteem would respond. If low self-esteem really constituted self-dislike, a sense of worthlessness, and an otherwise negative image of self, then they should find the modest, self-deprecating style to be natural and familiar, so they should recall the interaction best in that condition. On the other hand, if our hypothesis about the neutral, non-committal nature of low self-esteem was correct, then these individuals should find both boastfulness *and* modesty difficult, and so their memory for the interaction should be impaired in both conditions. Hutton's findings supported the latter prediction; people with low self-esteem showed equally poor memory for their partners' statements in both conditions. Apparently, it is relatively difficult for people with low self-esteem to adopt either a self-enhancing *or* a self-derogating style of presenting themselves, and the difficulty requires them to invest more of their cognitive resources in managing their own self-presentation— leaving less capacity to process what their partner is saying.

Hutton also measured how well people could recall their own statements during the interviews. Self-presentational style made little difference on this measure, but self-esteem had a strong effect: People with low self-esteem were relatively poor at recalling their own verbal behavior. Their poor performance fits Campbell's view (1990) that low self-esteem is associated with a relatively impoverished knowledge structure about the self. Without a well-defined self-concept, they found it more difficult to process and recall what they had said about themselves.

Hutton's findings do not bear on the issue of self-protection, but they do contradict a view of people with low self-esteem as habitual self-derogators. Instead, these results support the view of low self-esteem as people who lack a firm, elaborate self-concept and who therefore find it difficult to present themselves in either a strongly positive or negative fashion. People with high self-esteem, in contrast, appear to be habitual self-enhancers. Boasting comes easily and naturally to them, leaving them able to process the social interaction fully and, hence, able to remember it well later on. Modest self-derogation, however, is apparently more difficult for them.

PERSISTENCE AND CHOICE OF TASK

Another way to look at the protection-enhancement hypothesis is to postulate that everyone aims to be a little better than he or she is. People with low self-esteem think they are vulnerable to failure and have various shortcomings, so they should focus on remedying these deficiencies in order to come up to a passable, acceptable level. People with high self-esteem think they are already quite passable and acceptable, so they should seek to reach levels of outstanding excellence.

With a colleague, I tested this reasoning some years ago by having people perform a task, giving them feedback about their level of ability, and surreptitiously measuring whether they later chose to spend some of their free time working on the same task (Baumeister & Tice, 1985). Each subject's initial performance was recorded and then described as either an outstanding, exceptional success or as a surprisingly miserable failure. Moreover, some people were allowed to save face after failure by making excuses, whereas others were humiliated by being invited to make excuses, hearing their excuses rejected and discounted, and then hearing a reiteration of how badly they had done. The latter manipulation was included because in everyday life not all failures are the same; the social context allows one to salvage some dignity and esteem from some failures, whereas other contexts defy and thwart such face-saving efforts, making it much harder to shake off the blow to esteem.

People were then left alone on the pretext that the experimenter needed to obtain another questionnaire. Each individual was left sitting in a room with the opportunity to continue working on the same task. Meanwhile, a confederate secretly observed the subject through a concealed observation window, recording how much time (if any) was spent on the focal task. There was no implicit demand to work on the task any more; nothing was said, and no further performance was anticipated. Indeed, the subject had been told that all that remained was to fill out a last questionnaire.

High self-esteem people were likely to continue working on the task when they had succeeded and to avoid the task after failure, especially if the failure was humiliating and did not allow them to save face. Low self-esteem people, on the other hand, tended to avoid the task if they had been told that they had performed exceptionally well on it, whereas they tended to persist at the task after a humiliating failure. Thus, high self-esteem people seemed to glory in their successes and avoid situations in which they had failed. Low self-esteem people appeared concerned with remedying their deficiencies in order to reach a passable level of performance. Consistent with a self-enhancing orientation, high self-esteem people focus on their good points and seek to cultivate them so as to stand out. Once low self-esteem people reach competence levels at a task, they may be less concerned with the task, for their primary concern seems to be to correct deficiencies in order to protect themselves against humiliating failures, which is consistent with a self-protective strategy.

CONCLUSION

The studies described in this chapter support a broad conclusion about the social motivations associated with high and low self-esteem. People with high self-esteem are no mystery: They think they are good at most things, they want others to recognize their fine qualities, and they want to achieve outstanding, exceptional things. But what about people with low self-esteem? Apparently they are neither pathetic self-haters nor reckless, nothing-to-lose self-enhancers. Instead, they appear to be cautious, uncertain people who desire success but fear failure—and the fear often outweighs the desire, resulting in an attitude of self-protection. Encountering a new or demanding situation, their first concern apparently is to prevent disaster, and so they act in ways designed to protect themselves from the dangers of failure, social rejection, and other humiliations.

Self-enhancement and self-protection are not always in conflict, and some forms of behavior may fit both motivations. In such cases, people may act the same regardless of their level of self-esteem. Ironically, however, such similarity may be superficial and misleading, because people may do the same thing for different reasons. This appears to be the case with self-handicapping. The self-handicapping strategy of creating obstacles to one's own performance appeals to people with different levels of self-esteem for quite different reasons. People with high self-esteem will engage in self-handicapping in order to boost their credit for success, because they may receive extra credit for succeeding despite obstacles and handicaps. People with low self-esteem, in contrast, engage in self-handicapping to protect themselves from the potential implications of failure.

The same may be true for improving performance at a given task or ability. Both high and low self-esteem people may be concerned with improving their performance levels, but they may be concerned with improvement for different reasons, and they may attempt to improve different performances or abilities. High self-esteem people may be interested in identifying their good points and strengths and cultivating them so as to stand out, which is consistent with their self-enhancing orientation. Low self-esteem people, consistent with their self-protective orientation, may focus on their weaknesses and failures and seek to remedy them in order to protect themselves from failure and humiliation.

People with low self-esteem do not portray themselves negatively in their responses on self-esteem scales; they are essentially neutral in their self-descriptions, attributing neither strongly positive nor strongly negative traits to themselves. They are low in self-esteem only in a relative sense, in comparison to the very flattering way that people with high self-esteem portray themselves. Thus, low self-esteem does not seem to be equivalent to self-hatred, but rather it is typically a matter of regarding and presenting oneself in a neutral, noncommittal, and self-protective fashion.

REFERENCES

Arkin, R. M. (1981). Self-presentational styles. In J. T. Tedeschi (Ed.), *Impression management theory and social psychological research* (pp. 311–333). New York: Academic Press.

Arkin, R. M., & Baumgardner, A. H. (1985). Self-handicapping. In J. H. Harvey & G. Weary (Eds.), *Attribution: Basic issues and applications* (pp. 169–202). New York: Academic Press.

Aronson, E., & Carlsmith, J. M. (1962). Performance expectancy as a determinant of actual performance. *Journal of Abnormal and Social Psychology, 65,* 178–182.

Aronson, E., & Mettee, D. (1968). Dishonest behavior as a function of differential levels of induced self-esteem. *Journal of Personality and Social Psychology, 9* 121–127.

Baumeister, R. F. (1982). Self-esteem, self-presentation, and future interaction: A dilemma of reputation. *Journal of Personality, 50,* 29–45.

Baumeister, R. F., Hutton, D. G., & Tice, D. M. (1989). Cognitive processes during deliberate self-presentation: How self-presenters alter and misinterpret the behavior of interaction partners. *Journal of Experimental Social Psychology, 25*, 59–78.

Baumeister, R. F., & Tice, D. M. (1985). Self-esteem and responses to success and failure: Subsequent performance and intrinsic motivation. *Journal of Personality, 53*, 450–467.

Baumeister, R. F., Tice, D. M., & Hutton, D. G. (1989). Self-presentational motivations and personality differences in self-esteem. *Journal of Personality, 57*, 547–579.

Berglas, S., & Jones, E. E. (1978). Drug choice as a self-handicapping strategy in response to non-contingent success. *Journal of Personality and Social Psychology, 36*, 405–417.

Brock, T. C., Edelman, S. K., Edwards, D. C., & Schuck, J. R. (1965). Seven studies of performance expectancy as a determinant of actual performance. *Journal of Experimental Social Psychology, 1*, 295–310.

Campbell, J. D. (1990). Self-esteem and the clarity of the self-concept. *Journal of Personality and Social Psychology, 59*, 538–549.

Cohen, A. R. (1959). Some implications of self-esteem for social influence. In C. I. Hovland & I. L. Janis (Eds.), *Personality and persuability* (pp. 102–120). New Haven, CT: Yale University Press.

Crocker, J., & Schwartz, I. (1985). Prejudice and ingroup favoritism in a minimal intergroup situation: Effects of self-esteem. *Personality and Social Psychology Bulletin, 11*, 379–386.

DeGree, C. E., & Snyder, C. R. (1985). Adler's psychology (of use) today: Personal history of traumatic life events as a self-handicapping strategy. *Journal of Personality and Social Psychology, 48*, 1512–1519.

Dinner, S., Lewkowicz, B., & Cooper, J. (1972). Anticipatory attitude change as a function of self-esteem and issue familiarity. *Journal of Personality and Social Psychology, 24*, 407–412.

Harris, R. N., & Snyder, C. R. (1986). The role of uncertain self-esteem in self-handicapping. *Journal of Personality and Social Psychology, 51*, 451–458.

Hirt, E. R. (1989). *Self-handicapping: Antecedents and consequences.* Paper presented at the annual convention of the Midwestern Psychological Association, Chicago, IL.

Hutton, D. G. (1991). *Self-esteem and memory for social interaction.* Unpublished dissertation, Case Western Reserve University, Ohio.

Jones, E. E., & Berglas, S. C. (1978). Control of attributions about the self through self-handicapping strategies: The appeal of alcohol and the role of underachievement. *Personality and Social Psychology Bulletin, 4*, 200–206.

Jones, S. C. (1973). Self- and interpersonal evaluations: Esteem theories vs. consistency theories. *Psychological Bulletin, 79*, 185–199.

Maracek, J., & Mettee, D. (1972). Avoidance of continued success as a function of self-esteem, level of esteem certainty, and responsibility for success. *Journal of Personality and Social Psychology, 22*, 98–107.

McFarlin, D. B., & Blascovich, J. (1981). Effects of self-esteem and performance feedback on future affective preferences and cognitive expectations. *Journal of Personality and Social Psychology, 40*, 521–531.

Pyszczynski, T., & Greenberg, J. (1983). Determinants of reduction in intended effort as a strategy for coping with anticipated failure. *Journal of Research in Personality, 17*, 412–422.

Rhodewalt, F., Saltzman, A. T., & Wittmer, J. (1984). Self-handicapping among competitive athletes: The role of practice in self-esteem protection. *Basic and Applied Social Psychology, 5*, 197–209.

Roth, D. L., Harris, R. N., & Snyder, C. R. (1988). An individual differences measure of attributive and repudiative tactics of favorable self-presentation. *Journal of Social and Clinical Psychology, 6,* 159–170.

Roth, D. L., Snyder, C. R., & Pace, L. M. (1986). Dimensions of favorable self-presentation. *Journal of Personality and Social Psychology, 51,* 867–874.

Shepperd, J. A., & Arkin, R. M. (1989a). Determinants of self-handicapping: Task importance and the effects of preexisting handicaps on self-generated handicaps. *Personality and Social Psychology Bulletin, 15,* 101–112.

Shepperd, J. A., & Arkin, R. M. (1989b). Self-handicapping: The moderating roles of public self-consciousness and task importance. *Personality and Social Psychology Bulletin, 15,* 252–265.

Shrauger, J. S. (1975). Responses to evaluation as a function of initial self-perceptions. *Psychological Bulletin, 82,* 581–596.

Smith, T. W., Snyder, C. R., & Handelsman, M. M. (1982). On the self-serving function of an academic wooden leg: Test anxiety as a self-handicapping strategy. *Journal of Personality and Social Psychology, 42,* 314–321.

Smith, T. W., Snyder, C. R., & Perkins, S. C. (1983). The self-serving function of hypochrondriacal complaints: Physical symptoms as self-handicapping strategies. *Journal of Personality and Social Psychology, 44,* 787–797.

Snyder, C. R. (1990). Self-handicapping processes and sequelae: On the taking of a psychological dive. In R. L. Higgins, C. R. Snyder, & S. Berglas, *Self-handicapping: The paradox that isn't* (pp. 107–150). New York: Plenum.

Snyder, C. R., & Smith, T. W. (1982). Symptoms as self-handicapping strategies: The virtues of old wine in a new bottle. In G. Weary & H. Mirels (Eds.), *Integrations of clinical and social psychology* (pp. 104–127). New York: Oxford University Press.

Snyder, C. R., Smith, T. W., Augelli, R. W., & Ingram, R. E. (1985). On the self-serving function of social anxiety: Shyness as a self-handicapping strategy. *Journal of Personality and Social Psychology, 48,* 970–980.

Swann, W. B., Griffin, J. J., Predmore, S. C., & Gaines, B. (1987). The cognitive-affective crossfire: When self-consistency confronts self-enhancement. *Journal of Personality and Social Psychology, 52,* 881–889.

Tice, D. M. (1991). Esteem protection or enhancement? Self-handicapping motives and attributions differ by trait self-esteem. *Journal of Personality and Social Psychology, 60,* 711–725.

Tice, D. M., & Baumeister, R. F. (1990). Self-esteem, self-handicapping, and self-presentation: The strategy of inadequate practice. *Journal of Personality, 58,* 443–464.

Wolfe, R. N., Lennox, R. D., & Cutler, B. L. (1986). Getting along and getting ahead: Empirical support for a theory of protective and acquisitive self-presentation. *Journal of Personality and Social Psychology, 50,* 356–361.

CHAPTER 4

SELF-ESTEEM AND SELF-SERVING BIASES IN REACTIONS TO POSITIVE AND NEGATIVE EVENTS
AN INTEGRATIVE REVIEW

BRUCE BLAINE AND JENNIFER CROCKER

The *self-serving bias* refers to the tendency of people to interpret and explain outcomes in ways that have favorable implications for the self. The term *bias* often implies distorted or inaccurate perception that can be shown to be erroneous according to some objective standard. But according to the Random House *College Dictionary* (1975), a bias is also "a tendency or inclination of outlook; a subjective point of view" (p. 131). Similarly, the *Webster's New Collegiate Dictionary* (1976) defines a bias as "an inclination of temperament or outlook; esp. a highly personal and unreasoned distortion of judgment" (p. 106). In this chapter, we regard self-serving biases as judgments or interpretations of oneself, one's behavior, and the behavior of others in ways that are favorable to the self, without requiring that such judgments be accurate according to some objective standard. We also begin with no assumptions that biases nec-

BRUCE BLAINE AND JENNIFER CROCKER • Department of Psychology, State University of New York at Buffalo, Amherst, NY 14260.

Self-Esteem: The Puzzle of Low Self-Regard, edited by Roy F. Baumeister. Plenum Press, New York, 1993.

essarily reflect motivated distortions in reasoning, rather than normal cognitive processes.

Research provides unequivocal support that self-serving biases are widespread (for review, see Bradley, 1978; Miller & Ross, 1975; Taylor & Brown, 1988; Zuckerman, 1979). For example, people tend to take credit for success and deny responsibility for failure (Miller & Ross, 1975). Married individuals take more responsibility for a jointly produced outcome than their spouses give them credit for, even when both parties' contributions are equal (Ross & Sicoly, 1979). People tend to attribute a series of favorable random outcomes to ability, whereas an unfavorable outcome is seen as an unlucky break, thus creating an illusory sense of control over purely random events (Gilovich, 1983). Students who perform well on an exam describe it as a valid measure of their knowledge, whereas poor performers tend to criticize the exam as not being indicative of their ability (Arkin & Maruyama, 1979). People compare themselves with others in a self-serving manner by strategically selecting the target and dimension of comparison that makes their outcome appear more favorable (Wills, 1981). Taylor (1983) reports that even the critically and terminally ill forge self-serving social comparisons by contrasting their admittedly dire circumstances with hypothetical targets who are worse off than they are. Finally, people are more likely to ascribe positive personality traits to themselves than to others, whereas negative traits are seen as more descriptive of others than of the self (Brown, 1986; Tabachnik, Crocker, & Alloy, 1983).

These self-serving biases also extend to outcomes associated with one's friends, acquaintances, and groups. Individuals tend to associate and identify more with the successful performance of a favored other, yet distance themselves from a poor performance by the same person (Cialdini et al., 1976). People overestimate the extent to which their opinions and shortcomings also characterize others (Campbell, 1986). Also, athletic team members generally explain a poor team performance by citing external factors, such as the weather or poor officiating, whereas a good team effort is attributed to ability (Lau & Russell, 1980). Finally, people in groups take personal credit for successful group outcomes and deny responsibility for unsuccessful group efforts (Schlenker & Miller, 1977).

The focus of the present chapter concerns the relation between global self-esteem and the use of self-serving biases. Global self-esteem refers to a generalized sense of self-worth, or a generally positive self-evaluation (see Rosenberg, 1979). Theoretically, there are four possibilities for the effect of self-esteem on the use of self-serving biases. First, people who are low in self-esteem may be *more* likely to use self-serving biases, because their need for self-esteem is greater (Wills, 1981). Second, people who are low in self-esteem may be *less* likely to use self-serving biases; indeed, the failure to use self-serving biases may be a cause of low self-esteem (see Crocker, Thompson, McGraw, & Ingerman, 1987). Third, it is theoretically possible that there are no differences between high and low self-esteem people in their use of self-serving biases. Finally, it is possible that high and low self-esteem individuals both use self-serving biases, but under different circumstances.

Empirical research on this issue has yielded conflicting results. Many studies have demonstrated that high self-esteem persons are more likely to show self-serving biases than are low self-esteem persons. Some studies have found the opposite pattern, however, other studies have shown no differences between high and low self-esteem persons, and still others have found that high and low self-esteem people use self-serving biases under different circumstances.

Theoretical explanations for these various empirical results are equally mixed. Some researchers have suggested that people who are low in self-esteem have a greater need for self-enhancement (Wills, 1981). Others have suggested that people who are low in self-esteem lack the motivation for self-enhancement (Alloy & Abramson, 1979; Brockner, 1983). Some have suggested that low self-esteem individuals have self-concepts and expectations that do not support self-serving biases (Shrauger, 1972). Still others have suggested that low self-esteem individuals will engage in self-serving biases when the self-enhancement is indirect rather than direct (Brown, Collins, & Schmidt, 1988), or when it is passive rather than active (Gibbons & McCoy, 1990). Others have suggested that people who are high in self-esteem are oriented toward self-enhancement, whereas people who are low in self-esteem are oriented toward self-protection, leading them to use self-serving biases under different circumstances (Baumeister, Tice, & Hutton, 1989).

Our goal in this chapter is to review this literature, identifying the types of biases that are shown by people high and low in self-esteem and the circumstances under which they are susceptible to these biases. We will attempt to integrate these conflicting findings into an overall framework of the relations between self-esteem and self-serving biases. To anticipate our position, we will argue that the apparently contradictory results regarding self-esteem and self-serving biases can be understood by considering the motivational and cognitive aspects of the self-concepts of high and low self-esteem individuals. Specifically, research suggests that people who are high in self-esteem have more positive self-concepts and more certain self-concepts than do those who are low in self-esteem, but high and low self-esteem individuals do not differ in the importance they place on having positive and not having negative attributions. These self-concept differences, we will argue, can account for the various conflicting findings on self-esteem and self-serving biases.

In our review, we will draw not only on self-esteem research, but also on research pertaining to depression and the use of self-serving biases. According to the diagnostic manual (DSM-IIIR) of the American Psychiatric Association, low self-esteem is a key symptom of depression. Furthermore, low self-esteem and depression co-occur with estimates of the correlation between the two ranging from .40 to .60 (Crandall, 1973). Theoretically, researchers have suggested that low self-esteem and depression are manifestations of the same underlying basic trait, the predisposition to experience negative affect (see Campbell & Fehr, 1990). Finally, self-esteem and depression appear to predict the use of self-serving biases equally well (Campbell, 1986; Tennen & Herzberger, 1987), and evidence suggests that it is self-esteem that accounts for the effects of depression on the use of self-serving biases (Tennen, Herzberger, & Nelson, 1987). Some caution must also be used in extrapolating from the literature on depression and self-serving biases to that of self-esteem and self-serving biases, however, because depression and self-esteem are not identical, and accordingly not all people who are depressed are also low in self-esteem.

Our focus in this chapter is on self-serving reactions to positive and negative feedback. Because of space constraints, other types of self-serving biases (e.g., biases in the self-concept, biases in social comparisons, biases in self-handicapping, and biases in public self-presentation) will not be reviewed here (but see Crocker & Blaine, 1992). In the review to follow, each self-serving bias effect is defined, and some examples of the effect are presented. Second, research documenting self-esteem differences on the self-serving bias effect is reviewed. Third, theoretical explanations for the effect are presented and evaluated. In this final section of the chapter, we attempt to account for self-serving biases within a single framework.

When positive and negative events occur, people may react in a number of ways. They may draw inferences about those events, they may make judgements about the degree of control they have over those events, they may have cognitive reactions such as evaluating the believability or credibility of the information, and they may have affective reactions to the information or the source of the information. These reactions may be self-serving in that they lead to interpretations of those events that have favorable implications for the self.

SELF-SERVING ATTRIBUTIONS

Self-serving attributions refer to the tendency for individuals to make internal attributions for positive outcomes and/or external attributions for negative outcomes. An internal attribution explains an outcome in terms of traits, abilities, or efforts; an external attribution explains the outcome in terms of other people's traits or behavior, environmental contingencies or circumstances, or even luck (see Heider, 1958; Weiner, 1985). For example, after narrowly avoiding an auto accident one is likely to credit one's quick reflexes or driving skill, whereas being involved in an accident tends to evoke blaming the other driver, the poor weather conditions, or bad luck. Self-serving biases in attributions may take the form of either self-enhancing or self-protective biases. According to Miller and Ross (1975), the tendency to internalize responsibility for positive outcomes is a self-enhancing bias. Conversely, the tendency to externalize or deny responsibility for negative outcomes is a self-protecting bias.

Self-serving attributional biases are well documented (Bradley, 1975; Miller & Ross, 1978). Most people will usually take credit for success and deny responsibility for failure. Attributions for success and failure, however, are not always self-serving. Under some conditions, such as when the attributions are made in public and can be compared to the attributions that observers make for the same event, people will accept responsibility for failure (Bradley, 1978; Miller & Ross, 1975; Weary, 1979).

SELF-ESTEEM AND SELF-SERVING ATTRIBUTIONS

Self-serving attributional biases are stronger in people who are high rather than low in self-esteem, although the data are inconsistent with regard to whether high self-esteem people are more self-enhancing, more self-protective, or both. In an early demonstration, Fitch (1970) had high and low self-esteem subjects undergo a success or failure experience and measured attributions for the outcome. He found that high self-esteem subjects attributed failure more to external factors than did low self-esteem subjects, but high self-esteem subjects did not attribute a successful outcome internally any more than low self-esteem subjects. In other words, high self-esteem people showed a clear self-protecting bias compared to low self-esteem people, but were not more self-enhancing.

Using a similar procedure, Ickes and Layden (1978) found that positive outcomes were attributed to internal causes more by high than by low self-esteem subjects. Negative outcomes were attributed to internal causes by low self-esteem subjects, however, whereas high self-esteem subjects attributed them to external causes. Thus, high self-esteem people exhibited both self-enhancing and self-protective biases, whereas low self-esteem people showed a self-deprecating bias—the tendency to blame oneself for negative outcomes.

Self-serving attributional biases extend to groups with which one is associated. In a study by Schlenker, Soraci, and McCarthy (1976), high and low self-esteem subjects generated ideas for the solution of a group task. Following the manipulation of group failure or success, attributions for the outcome were measured by having subjects rate how much they felt their ideas were influenced by other group members. When the group was successful, high self-esteem subjects took credit for the outcome by saying that their ideas were not influenced by the other group members. When the group failed, however, high self-esteem subjects claimed that their ideas had been influenced by the other group members. Low self-esteem subjects reported their ideas being influenced by other group members equally in success and failure conditions (see also Schlenker & Miller, 1977). This pattern of results indicates both self-enhancing and self-protective attributional biases among high self-esteem subjects; low self-esteem subjects reacted to both success and failure in an evenhanded manner.

Self-esteem differences also emerge in attributions for hypothetical or imagined events. The Attributional Styles Questionnaire (Seligman, Abramson, Semmel, & von Baeyer, 1979) assesses the tendency to attribute good and bad hypothetical events to causes that are internal to the self versus external, stable over time versus unstable, and global in their effects versus specific to particular circumstances or situations. People who are high in self-esteem tend to attribute positive events to internal, stable, and global causes, and negative events to external, unstable, and specific causes. That is, high self-esteem people are both self-protective and self-enhancing in their attributions for hypothetical events. People who are low in self-esteem, on the other hand, are relatively evenhanded in their attributions for positive and negative events, although more extremely low self-esteem people appear to show a self-deprecating attributional style (Tennen & Herberger, 1987; see also Cohen, van den Bout, van Vliet, & Kramer, 1989; Feather, 1989).

Because low self-esteem is highly correlated with depression, it is not surprising that a similar pattern of results has been obtained in studies of the attributions that depressed and nondepressed people make for positive and negative outcomes. Compared to nondepressed persons, depressed persons tend to attribute negative outcomes to causes that are internal, global, and stable, and positive outcomes to causes that are external, specific, and unstable (Peterson, Schwartz, &

Seligman, 1981; Rizley, 1978; for a review see Sweeney, Anderson, & Bailey, 1986). It should be noted that as a group, depressed individuals' attributions are relatively evenhanded—they are equally likely to attribute positive and negative events to internal causes, whereas nondepressed people's attributions show a strong self-serving bias (Alloy, 1982; Raps, Reinhard, Peterson, Abramson, & Seligman, 1982; Sackheim & Wegner, 1986). Cohen et al. (1989), however, have reported that severely depressed persons may not be evenhanded, but show a self-deprecating attributional style.

EXPLANATIONS

Motivational Explanations

Until the mid-1970s, most explanations for self-serving biases in attributions centered on the role of motivational forces. Specifically, it was hypothesized that people want to feel good about themselves by taking credit for success and avoiding blame for failure, and consequently these wishes and desires lead to distortions in attributions for events (see Bradley, 1978, for a review). For example, Heider (1958) claimed that "since one's idea includes what 'ought to be' and 'what one would like to be' as well as 'what is,' attributions and cognitions are influenced by the mere subjective forces of needs and wishes as well as by the more objective evidence presented in the raw material" (pp. 120–121).

Both theories of emotion as well as empirical research indicate that attributions for success and failure do have consequences for affect and feelings of self-esteem. For example, Weiner's attributional model of achievement motivation and emotion suggests that making internal attributions for success results in increased feelings of pride, self-satisfaction, and state self-esteem relative to external attributions for those same events. Similarly, external attributions for failure result in higher feelings of self-esteem than internal attributions for those same events (Weiner, 1985, 1986). Empirical research is consistent with this view (McFarland & Ross, 1978). Thus, research on the affective and state self-esteem consequences of self-serving attributions suggests that they can have self-enhancing and self-protective consequences, consistent with the view that people might be motivated to distort attributions to serve self-esteem needs. Also consistent with motivational interpretations, studies using the misattribution paradigm have demonstrated that when subjects are given a cue to which they can misattribute their negative affect following failure feedback, self-serving biases in attributions disappear (Fries & Frey, 1980; Gollwitzer, Earle, & Stephan, 1982; Stephan & Gollwitzer, 1981). Brown and Rogers (1991) recently demonstrated that self-serving attributions are particularly strong among subjects who show high levels of arousal following failure feedback, again implicating motivation in self-serving attributions. Thus, these studies suggest that self-serving biases for negative events are driven by the experience of negative affect.

In a review of the literature, Bradley (1978) suggested that two types of esteem needs—public and private—might affect the tendency to make self-serving attributions. Private esteem needs refer to the need or desire to feel good about oneself, or avoid feeling badly about oneself. Public esteem needs refer to the desire to be regarded favorably by others. Bradley suggested that public esteem needs could sometimes best be served by self-serving biases, and at other times could best be served by self-deprecating biases. People make self-serving (enhancing) attributions in public to make a favorable impression on whomever the "public" might be: the experimenter, an evaluator, or an audience. But studies also show that people make self-effacing, or counterdefensive, attributions in public situations to avoid making a negative impression on an audience by appearing too boastful (Greenberg, Pyszczynski, & Solomon, 1982; Weary et al., 1982). Thus, Bradley suggested that both studies that obtain the self-serving bias effect in causal attributions *and* studies that fail to obtain this effect can be explained by a consideration of which type of esteem needs are in operation.

Greenberg, Pyszczynski, and Solomon (1982) addressed this issue by pitting these two motivational models against each other in a study measuring outcome attributions. In their study, subjects received favorable or unfavorable performance feedback in either a public condition (where the experimenter scored their test) or a private condition (in which subjects scored their own tests). The results showed that the public/private manipulation did not qualify the effect of feedback. As expected, subjects internalized favorable performances and externalized unfavorable efforts, but they did so to the same extent in public and private conditions. This study shows that even in conditions where concerns about public image are ruled out, people still make self-serving attributions. Thus, people need to see themselves as good, competent, and worthy, regardless of how others view them, and this need explains the use of self-serving attributional biases. Greenberg et al. showed that self-esteem and public-esteem concerns have independent effects on attributions; both motives produced similar attributional patterns in subjects, even when the other motive was ruled out.

If self-serving biases are motivated by the desire to maintain, enhance, or protect public and private self-esteem, then why do people who are low in self-esteem or depressed fail to show these biases? Although Bradley's analysis does not specifically review studies testing self-esteem differences in causal attributions, based on her analysis one would suggest that the fact that high self-esteem individuals engage in self-serving biases more must reflect that they have more motivation to enhance the self. It is not clear, however, why people who are low in self-esteem would be less motivated to enhance or protect self-esteem. Perhaps people who are low in self-esteem lack the defenses necessary to convince themselves that they are worthy (Sackheim, 1983), or perhaps the motive to enhance the self is in conflict with the motive to be consistent (Swann, 1987; Brown, this volume). Alternatively, Bradley's analysis leaves open the possibility that low self-esteem people are equally motivated to enhance the self in private, but are more modest in presenting themselves to the experimenter (Baumeister et al., 1989).

Cognitive Explanations

The most cogent case for cognitive explanations for self-serving biases in attributions was outlined by Miller and Ross (1975) in their seminal article. They argued that the tendency for most people to attribute positive outcomes to their own efforts could be explained as a function of the tendency of most people to expect their behavior to produce success. Generally, unexpected outcomes, whether success or failure, tend to be attributed to external causes (Feather, 1969; Feather & Simon, 1971a,b; Gilmor & Minton, 1974). Presumably, expectancies are often based on assessments of our abilities. When outcomes are consistent with expectancies, then abilities provide an obvious and available explanation for those outcomes. When outcomes are inconsistent with expectancies, then some external factor must have played a role. Miller and Ross (1975) also suggest that people who consistently expect and achieve success may observe a covariation between the application of their skill or effort with successful outcomes. As a result, they often assume that their efforts or ability caused the outcome.

Miller and Ross suggest that differences in the causal attributions of high and low self-esteem persons may be explained by differences in their expectancies for success. There is ample evidence that people who are high in self-esteem have generally positive self-conceptions (Baumgardner, 1990; Brown, 1986; Crocker et al., 1987; Marsh, 1986; Pelham & Swann, 1989), think they compare favorably to others (Brown, 1986), and expect to succeed at a variety of tasks (Shrauger, 1972; Brockner, 1983). Each of these aspects of self-knowledge could contribute to the tendency of people who are high in self-esteem to show greater self-serving biases than do those who are low in self-esteem. Thus, Miller and Ross's analysis (1975) suggests that self-esteem effects on attributions for positive and negative events can be accounted for strictly in terms of the information-processing effects of self-knowledge, without reference to motivational forces such as the need or desire to maintain, enhance, or protect self-esteem.

The difficulty of teasing apart cognitive and motivational explanations for self-serving biases is evident in the debate that continued between Miller and Weary (Miller, 1978; Miller & Porter, 1988; Weary, 1979). Both cognitive and motivational explanations for the biases appear to be compelling and consistent with other literature. As Tetlock and Levi (1982) noted, it is virtually impossible to design a study that entirely rules out either cognitive or motivational explanations. Manipulations intended to have cognitive effects (e.g., providing information about past successes) may have motivational or affective consequences (increasing the need or desire for self-esteem), and manipulations intended to have motivational effects (e.g., a prior failure) may also have cognitive consequences (changing the information available to the subject). Indeed, the attempt to pit motivational and cognitive explanations against each other is likely to be inconclusive and misleading, given that motivational and cognitive systems interact (Kruglanski, 1990; Kunda, 1990; Pyszczynski & Greenberg, 1987; Tetlock & Levi, 1982).

REACTIONS TO FEEDBACK FROM OTHERS

Self-serving biases can also be evidenced as biased reactions to others' perceptions of oneself. These reactions can be measured in several ways. Shrauger (1975) has suggested that people's reactions to performance feedback comprise six phases: (a) reception of, and memory for, evaluations; (b) assessing the validity of the evaluation source; (c) attributions for evaluative feedback; (d) changes in self-evaluations; (e) like or dislike for the evaluation; and (f) motivation for subsequent performances. Because much of this literature has been reviewed by Shrauger (1975), we will only briefly consider research covered in his review, focusing on studies that have been conducted since his review that address each of these issues. Because self-esteem differences in self-serving attributions have been reviewed in the previous section, they will not be discussed further here.

Self-Esteem and Reactions to Evaluative Feedback

Studies of self-esteem differences in reactions to evaluative feedback have yielded mixed results. Studies of recall for positive and negative feedback generally show that feedback is more accurately retained when it is consistent with one's initial self-evaluations (see Shrauger, 1975, for a review). For example, Crary (1966) found that subjects high in perceived confidence (and presumably self-esteem) overestimated their performance when outperformed by another, whereas subjects low in perceived competence (and presumably low in self-esteem) underestimated their performance, regardless of how they had actually performed relative to another. Although self-esteem was not actually measured in this study, the results are consistent with the hypothesis that high self-esteem people enhance themselves following negative feedback, whereas low self-esteem people are self-deprecating. Studies with depression as the individual difference variable yield similar results. For example, a study by Nelson and Craighead (1977) found that depressed college students accurately recalled the frequency of negative feedback on a laboratory task, whereas nondepressed students underestimated the frequency of negative feedback (see also DeMonbreun & Craighead, 1977).

A recent study by Crocker (1991) shows that self-enhancement may also take the form of recalling negative information about others. In this study, high and low self-esteem subjects were given a test of social sensitivity, and they received feedback that they had scored either very well or very poorly on the test. Under the guise of a second unrelated experiment, subjects then were read a list of 20 sentences describing positive and negative behaviors of hypothetical other people (e.g., "John received an A on the chemistry exam"). Subjects then took a surprise recall test. Subjects who were high in self-esteem remembered three times as many negative sentences about others when they had failed the social sensitivity test compared to when they had succeeded. Low self-esteem subjects remembered somewhat fewer negative sentences when they had failed the social sensitivity test. Recall of positive sentences showed no effects of the self-esteem of subjects. Although the self-enhancing effects of recalling negative information about others were not directly assessed in this study, recalling negative behaviors of others following failure may be self-enhancing because it provides a comparison that suggests that one is not so bad after all, when compared to others. Thus, even on this indirect measure of self-enhancement, high self-esteem subjects were apparently self-enhancing following failure, and low self-esteem subjects were not.

A recent study using depressed and nondepressed college students as subjects illustrates that even people who are low in self-esteem (or depressed) will react to feedback in a self-serving manner when they are unconstrained by the "reality" imposed by the self-concept. The self-concept acts as a filter through which information relevant to the self is interpreted. Thus, high self-esteem individuals should perceive self-relevant information through the filter of their positive self-concept, and low self-esteem individuals should interpret such information through the filter of their relatively negative self-concepts. Information that is irrelevant to the self-concept, however, should not be distorted by schematic processing. In a test of this idea, depressed and nondepressed subjects were given ambiguous or unambiguous positive or negative feedback on a dot-counting task (Dykman, Abramson, Alloy, & Hartlage, 1989). The task was characterized to subjects in one of two ways. In the schema-discriminating condition, the task was described as a measure of motivation and probability of success, a dimension on which the self-schemas of depressed and nondepressed persons were known to differ. In the schema-nondiscriminating condition, the task was described as a measure of politeness or courteousness, a dimension on which depressive and nondepressive self-schemas do not typically differ. The feedback was ambiguous in the sense that subjects were given two ratings (e.g., very successful and somewhat successful, or somewhat rude and very rude) and were asked to choose which of the two was their "true" feedback.

Results showed that both depressed and nondepressed subjects showed positive and negative biases in their choice of their "true" feedback; the direction of the bias depended on relevance of the feedback to their self-concepts, as well as the particular match of the positivity of the feedback with the positivity of subjects' self-schema. In the schema-discriminating conditions, depressed subjects' choices were more negative than were nondepressed subjects' choices. Nondepressed subjects consistently distorted the feedback in a positive direction. Only when the ambiguous feedback was very positive, such as the choice between "very motivated" and "moderately motivated," were nondepressed subjects unbiased or accurate in their judgments. Depressed subjects, on the other hand, distorted positive feedback in a negative direction, choosing the less positive of the pair. As the feedback became more moderate and aligned more closely with their self-ratings, depressed subjects showed unbiased, accurate judgments. When the feedback became negative, those subjects exhibited positive bias. In the schema-nondiscriminating conditions, however, both depressed and nondepressed subjects tended to distort their choices in a positive direction.

This study demonstrates that distortions in processing information about the self depend on the relevance of the information to a self-schema. When ambiguous information is relevant to the self-concept, it will be distorted in the direction of the self-concept—in a positive direction for nondepressed (and, we assume, high self-esteem) people, and toward a neutral direction for depressed (and, we assume, low self-esteem) people. When the information is not relevant to a self-schema, however, both depressed and nondepressed people distorted in a positive direction. This suggests that all people, both depressed and nondepressed, will distort information in a self-serving manner when unconstrained by what they believe to be true of themselves.

Studies of the ratings of evaluator credibility tend to show a somewhat different pattern. Typically, high self-esteem subjects find the source of feedback more credible or valid when the feedback is positive than when it is negative. Low self-esteem subjects, however, rate the feedback or the evaluator as equally credible whether they have received positive or negative feedback (see Shrauger, 1975, for a review). For example, Shrauger and Lund (1975) had a clinician interview high and low self-esteem subjects and give either a positive or negative personality evaluation to subjects. High self-esteem subjects who received a positive evaluation thought the feedback was more valid and the clinician more competent than when they received a negative evaluation. Low self-esteem subjects' ratings were not affected by the positivity of the evaluation (see also Korman, 1968). Thus, in these studies, people who are high in self-esteem appear to be self-enhancing, whereas those who are low in self-esteem are neither self-enhancing nor self-deprecating.

Studies of changes in self-evaluation in response to positive and negative feedback tend to show that self-evaluations change in the direction of feedback only when the feedback is moderately (rather than extremely) discrepant from initial self-evaluations, and only when the feedback is in the direction of one's general level of self-evaluation. For example, Shrauger and Rosenberg (1970) gave high and low self-esteem subjects either positive or negative feedback on a test that supposedly measured subjects' social sensitivity. The subjects did not differ in actual social sensitivity at the beginning of the study, but when changes in subjects' views as a result of the feedback were unobtrusively measured, they found that high self-esteem subjects rated themselves more socially sensitive after positive feedback, whereas low self-esteem subjects lowered their self-ratings of social sensitivity after negative feedback. High and low self-esteem subjects who received, respectively, negative and positive feedback did not alter their self-views (see also Harvey & Clapp,

1965). Thus, high self-esteem people appear to change their self-conceptions in a self-enhancing direction following positive feedback, whereas low self-esteem subjects appear to change their self-conceptions in a self-deprecating direction following negative feedback.

Studies of satisfaction with positive and negative feedback tend to show quite a different pattern. Typically, high and low self-esteem subjects do not differ in their satisfaction with positive and negative feedback, both types of subjects tend to be more satisfied with positive feedback than with negative feedback (see Shrauger, 1975, for a review). When the feedback exceeds expectancies by the same amount for both high and low self-esteem subjects, high self-esteem subjects tend to be more satisfied than low self-esteem subjects, because their performance is higher. When the feedback is identical for high and low self-esteem subjects, low self-esteem subjects tend to be more satisfied, because the feedback exceeds their expectancies to a greater degree (Shrauger, 1975). Both high and low self-esteem subjects, however, are more satisfied with positive than with negative feedback.

In sum, studies of reactions to positive and negative feedback show an inconsistent pattern of results. Studies of recall for feedback and studies of changes in self-evaluation tend to show that people who are high in self-esteem are self-enhancing, whereas people who are low in self-esteem are self-deprecating. Studies of evaluations of the credibility of feedback tend to show that people who are high in self-esteem are self-enhancing, whereas people who are low in self-esteem are neither self-enhancing nor self-deprecating, a pattern also found in attributions for positive and negative outcomes. Finally, studies of satisfaction have tended to find that both high and low self-esteem people are self-enhancing in that they are more satisfied with positive than with negative feedback.

EXPLANATIONS

Shrauger (1975) evaluated the ability of self-consistency theory and self-enhancement theory to explain this pattern of results. According to self-consistency theory, people are motivated to maintain consistent attitudes about themselves (Shrauger, 1975; Swann, 1983, 1985). Therefore, they prefer evaluative feedback that confirms or is consistent with important elements of their self-concepts. Further, evaluative feedback that is *not* self-consistent should be attributed more to external factors, found less credible, and disliked more than feedback about the self that *is* consistent with one's self-concept. Self-enhancement theory, on the other hand, argues that people are motivated to achieve and maintain favorable, positive attitudes about themselves (Shrauger, 1975; Smith, 1968; Wills, 1981). Therefore, they should both believe and like positive self-relevant feedback more than negative feedback. Both self-enhancement and self-consistency theories are motivational in nature—that is, they frame reactions to feedback in terms of whether people *want* feedback that is consistent with their self-conceptions or *want* feedback that is positive.

The key point of difference between the two theories is their predictions regarding high and low self-esteem individuals. For high self-esteem people, both self-consistency and self-enhancement theories predict that positive self-evaluative feedback should be much preferred over negative feedback. For low self-esteem persons, however, the models make differing predictions. According to a self-consistency perspective, low self-esteem people should not prefer positive self-relevant feedback, because their self-concepts are not positive. From a self-enhancement perspective, low self-esteem people should desire such feedback about themselves.

Shrauger (1975) suggested that the relationship between self-esteem and self-serving biases depends on how reactions to evaluative feedback are measured. He showed that what one *thinks* about evaluative feedback is different from how one *feels* about it. Both low self-esteem and high self-esteem persons demonstrate biased affective reactions to evaluations; they report liking positive evaluations and evaluators better than negative. Low self-esteem individuals, however, have trouble thinking or believing that favorable evaluations are accurate. Therefore, they are more inclined to accept negative evaluations or to find them more credible, because such feedback is consistent with their self-views. High self-esteem persons respond to virtually all evaluative feedback in self-serving ways; positive feedback about the self is both liked *and* believed more than negative feedback.

Of course, Shrauger's elegant interpretation of previous studies was post hoc. More compelling evidence for this theory would be provided if self-consistency on cognitive measures and self-enhancement on affective measures could be demonstrated within a single study. In a test of Shrauger's ideas, Moreland and Sweeney (1984) conducted a field study in which undergraduate students completed a series of questionnaires 1 week prior to and 1 week following a genuine classroom examination. The first testing session measured subjects' self-esteem and expectancies specific to the upcoming exam. The second session included measures of cognitive and affective reactions to performance feedback. The results showed that affective reactions conformed to self-enhancement predictions for all subjects but were the strongest among low self-esteem subjects. That is, all subjects felt more satisfied about a good (versus a poor) performance and felt more optimistic about subsequent evaluations, but this was more true for low self-esteem subjects than for high self-esteem subjects. Cognitive reactions were less clear and were not the same for high self-esteem and low self-esteem subjects. There was a tendency for high self-esteem subjects to be self-enhancing on cognitive measures, such as rating the validity of the test as higher and the results as more attributable to internal factors if they did well as opposed to poorly. There was also a tendency for low self-esteem subjects to react cognitively in a manner consistent with the test feedback. Of the eight cognitive reactions measured by Moreland and Sweeney, however, only three supported self-consistency predictions. Self-enhancing responses were actually observed on the measure of the fairness of the test in that both high and low self-esteem subjects judged the test to be more fair following success than following failure.

One drawback of Moreland and Sweeney's study is that subjects were not randomly assigned to receive positive or negative performance feedback. This raises the possibility that, in the natural course of events, high self-esteem subjects would tend to experience more positive evaluations, whereas low self-esteem subjects might be more likely to experience negative evaluations. In fact, Moreland and Sweeney's data showed this pattern. This could have influenced the results such that the reactions of high self-esteem subjects were attenuated in negative feedback conditions. Perhaps the inconsistent results on cognitive measures, where self-enhancing patterns were expected, resulted from the fact that high self-esteem people, who would be most likely to react to cognitive measures in a self-enhancing way, were underrepresented in negative feedback cells. Furthermore, because subjects were chosen for the conditions based on extreme self-esteem scores, some regression to the mean could have occurred in which high self-esteem subjects performed a little worse than expected and low self-esteem subjects did a little better than they expected. Thus, the lack of predicted self-esteem differences on cognitive measures could be an artifact of statistical regression.

In a study designed to address the drawbacks of Moreland and Sweeney's study, Swann, Griffin, Predmore, and Gaines (1987) randomly assigned high and low self-esteem subjects to receive either a bogus positive or negative performance evaluation. Following the evaluation, subjects completed questionnaires assessing both their cognitive and affective reactions. Overall, cognitive reactions conformed to self-consistency predictions. High self-esteem subjects were more likely to say the feedback was accurate, the rater was competent, and the technique diagnostic when they received a positive (as compared to a negative) evaluation. This pattern of reactions was largely reversed for low self-esteem subjects, who rated the accuracy and diagnosticity of the evaluation and the evaluator's competence as higher when they received negative feedback. Affective reactions conformed to self-enhancement predictions, with both high and low self-esteem subjects feeling less depression, hostility, anxiety, and more attraction to the evaluator after a positive evaluation than after a negative evaluation.

Although not intended as a test of Shrauger's model, a study by Crocker et al. (1987) also yielded consistent results. In this study, high and low self-esteem subjects were given either success or failure feedback regarding their performance on a test. Subjects then rated their satisfaction with their performance and how much they wished they had done better on the test. Crocker et al. also rated above-average scorers and below-average scorers on the test on positive and negative personality dimensions related to the test. The results showed that both high and low self-esteem subjects were less satisfied with their scores, and wished they had scored high, when they failed relative to when they succeeded on the test. When rating above- and below-average scorers, however, high self-esteem subjects rated above-average scorers more positively and below-average scorers more negatively when they themselves had succeeded, showing a self-enhancing pattern. Low self-esteem subjects, on the other hand, rated above- and below-average scorers the same regardless of their own performance on the test. Thus, on the affective measures of satisfaction with performance, both high and low self-esteem subjects were self-enhancing, but on the cognitive measures of how good above- and below-average scorers really are, only high self-esteem subjects were self-enhancing.

Thus, the data seem generally consistent with Shrauger's conclusion that on cognitive measures, the data fit a self-consistency framework, whereas on affective measures, the data fit a self-enhancement framework. It should be noted that for high self-esteem people, however, the data can be interpreted equally well in terms of the desire for self-consistency and the desire for self-enhancement, for across all types of measures, high self-esteem people appear to be self-serving.

One criticism on Shrauger's framework is that, although it nicely summarizes the existing pattern of results, it does not *explain* that pattern. In Swann's terms (1985), the framework fails to specify "why the consistency motive should control cognitive responses and the enhancement motive should control affective responses" (p. 107). To further muddy the waters, it should also be noted that although both self-consistency and self-enhancement theories are framed in motivational terms, data consistent with self-consistency theory can also be interpreted in cognitive terms. That is, instead of claiming that people *want* feedback that is consistent with the self-concept, one could argue (as Miller and Ross did for attributions for success and failure) that people believe information that is consistent with their self-concepts strictly for information-processing reasons. For example, people who are quite sure that they are competent might reasonably infer that a test on which they fail is not a very good test. Similarly, people who are unsure of their competence might reasonably infer that a test on which they fail is relatively accurate. Thus, one need not assume a *motive* for self-consistency; one need only assume that reasonable, logical thought processes can lead high and low self-esteem people to different conclusions regarding positive and negative feedback. Of course, as we noted in our discussion of self-serving attributions, it is not particularly fruitful to pit cognitive and motivational interpretations against one another. We merely want to acknowledge that cognitive interpretations of consistency effects are plausible.

SELF-SERVING JUDGMENTS OF CONTROL

Biased reactions to environmental events can also take the form of self-serving judgments of control. People often maintain illusions of control, even over chance-determined events such as lotteries (Langer, 1975). According to Gilovich (1991), many athletes and gamblers who experience "hot streaks" overestimate the probability that they will score on their next shot or win the next hand of cards. They erroneously assume that the string of good outcomes is attributable more to skill than to luck, and this provides an illusory sense of control over subsequent outcomes.

Depression and Judgments of Control

In research investigating depression differences in judgments of control, Alloy and Abramson (1979) had depressed and nondepressed college students perform a task that involved attempting to control the onset of a light. On each trial of the experiment, subjects could choose either to press or not to press a button, and the light either did or did not come on. Unbeknownst to subjects, the experimenter had programmed the light to turn on in 75% of the trials when the button was pressed, and 50%, 25%, or 0% of the trials when the button was not pressed, independent of the subjects' responses. Thus, according to Alloy and Abramson (1979), subjects had either 25%, 50%, or 75% control over the onset of the light by pressing the button. Subjects then judged the degree of control they had over the onset of the light. Nondepressives overestimated the control they had over the light onset, whereas depressives were accurate in their assessments that they in fact had no control. When the valence of the outcome was varied by associating monetary gains and losses with the outcome, nondepressed subjects underestimated the control they had in causing negative outcomes, but overestimated the amount of control they had over positive, but purely random outcomes. Outcome type did not affect depressed subjects' estimates of control over the outcome. Apparently accurate judgments of control can also be elicited when a depressed mood is experimentally induced in nondepressed subjects (Alloy, Abramson, & Viscusi, 1981).

EXPLANATIONS

Alloy and Abramson (1979) suggest that the biased judgments of control exhibited by nondepressed persons are attributable to the motivation to enhance self-esteem. Depressives fail to show self-serving biases in their judgments of control, they argue, because they are not motivated to maintain or enhance self-esteem. Thus, the researchers' reasoning is consistent with motivational explanations of self-serving biases in attributions of causality. They do not explain, however, why depressed individuals lack the motivation to maintain or enhance self-esteem. Thus, to some degree their reasoning seems circular: Because depressives do not show self-serving biases, they must lack the motivation to enhance self-esteem; because depressives lack the motivation to enhance self-esteem, they do not show self-serving biases.

Alternatively, one might suggest that the judgments of control expressed by nondepressed individuals are influenced by their expectations that they have control over important events, especially when those events are positive. As Miller and Ross (1975) suggested in their attempt to explain self-serving attributions in cognitive terms, these expectations of control over positive events may affect the degree of contingency that nondepressives perceive between their responses and their outcomes. Indeed, Alloy and Abramson showed that nondepressed subjects generate more complex hypotheses regarding their control over the onset of the light. For example, when a simple "press to turn on the light" strategy did not seem to work, nondepressed subjects would try more complex patterns of responding, such as "press twice, then don't press once." This generation of complex hypotheses to explain a contingency between their behavior and their outcomes is consistent with the notion that nondepressed subjects were attempting to reconcile the discrepancy between their expectancies and their outcomes.

One telling piece of evidence argues against the interpretation that nondepressives show an illusion of control because of their expectations that they control positive events. Specifically, in a later study, Alloy and Abramson (1982) found that the nondepressive illusion of control is eliminated when subjects are given a "pretreatment" of exposure to controllable noise. Presumably, such a pretreatment should only serve to increase nondepressives' expectations that they control important events, yet this manipulation eliminated self-serving judgments of control. Alloy and Abramson (1982) suggest that the pretreatment experience served to enhance the self-esteem of nondepressed persons, eliminating or reducing their need for further self-enhancement. The results of this study do not seem compatible with an interpretation based solely on self-concept or expectancy differences between depressed and nondepressed persons.

Summary

We have reviewed three relatively distinct literatures on reactions to positive and negative outcomes of high and low self-esteem people. Although there are some inconsistencies in the literature, there is also a fairly clear pattern of results. People who are high in self-esteem show self-serving biases in their attributions for positive and negative events; in their recall of information, in their assessments of the credibility of feedback, and in changes in their self-concepts following feedback; and in their judgments of control. People who are low in self-esteem do not show these self-serving biases. In about half of the studies reviewed, low self-esteem people are evenhanded or unbiased in their reactions to positive and negative events, whereas in the remaining studies, low self-esteem people showed self-deprecating biases. The main exception to this pattern appears in the affective reactions of high and low self-esteem people to positive and negative feedback. Both high and low self-esteem people appear to like positive feedback better than negative feedback.

Both cognitive and motivational explanations have been offered for these results. Cognitively, differences in the self-concepts of high and low self-esteem people may lead them to attend to and recall information differently, to make different inferences about the causes of events and the credibility of feedback, and to make different judgments regarding their control over events. Motivationally, people appear to desire self-enhancement, but low self-esteem people do not always act on this desire.

THE SELF-CONCEPT AND SELF-SERVING BIASES

We propose that differences in the use of self-serving biases among high and low self-esteem individuals can be understood in terms of their differing self-concepts. In this regard, our framework is similar to cognitive interpretations of self-serving biases that have been offered by others. However, we suggest that the self-concept also has motivational properties, and thus our analysis integrates both cognitive and motivational perspectives.

We begin with the assumption, shared by most psychologists, that people are motivated to experience positive affect and to avoid negative affect. It is this desire to experience positive affect and avoid negative affect, we argue, that underlies the more specific motivation to achieve a positive self-concept. Believing that one has positive qualities usually feels good, and believing that one has negative qualities usually feels bad. Our central thesis is that although high and low self-esteem people share the desire to experience positive affect and avoid negative affect, they differ in their self-concepts, and consequently, in their thoughts about the self and their strategies for regulating affect.

SELF-ESTEEM AND THE SELF-CONCEPT

A considerable amount of research has documented differences in the self-concepts of high and low self-esteem persons (for a review, see Crocker & Blaine, 1992). As one might expect, people who are high in self-esteem generally believe that positive attributes are characteristic of them, and that negative attributes are not. People who are low in self-esteem are not as biased in their self-evaluations. It is important to note, however, that the relatively positive self-concepts of high self-esteem people do not mean that people who are low in self-esteem have negative self-views. Rather, their self-views are simply less positive than are those of high self-esteem people (see Baumeister et al., 1979). People who are high in self-esteem are also more certain about which attributes do and do not describe them than are people who are low in self-esteem (see Baumgardner, 1990; Campbell, 1990; Campbell & Lavalee, this volume) and expect to succeed more than do low self-esteem people (Brockner, 1983; Shrauger, 1972).

Although high and low self-esteem people differ in how self-descriptive they think positive and negative traits are and differ in their certainty regarding those judgments, they do not appear to differ in the importance they place on positive and negative attributes (Harter, 1986). That is, high and low self-esteem people alike think it is important to be competent, intelligent, liked by others, and so on. Consequently, whereas high self-esteem people tend to think the attributes that characterize them are important and those that do not characterize them are not important, low self-esteem people place importance on attributes they believe they do not have (Harter, 1986; Marsh, 1986; Rosenberg, 1965, 1979).

Because people who are high and low in self-esteem place similar importance on having positive attributes, they both feel happier and more satisfied following positive feedback than following negative feedback, and in general should be motivated to engage in self-serving biases that would enable them to believe that they have positive attributes. We will consider first how this motive affects the use of self-serving biases among people who are high in self-esteem, and then consider how it plays out in people who are low in self-esteem.

High Self-Esteem and Self-Serving Biases

People who are high in self-esteem are confident that they have important positive qualities and that they do not have important negative qualities. When they do feel that they possess some negative attribute, they typically see it as relatively unimportant. Consequently, they approach evaluative situations with a high degree of confidence and are not particularly concerned about failure; they see evaluative situations as an opportunity to do well and to enhance the self. People who are high in self-esteem will handicap themselves (e.g., fail to practice) in evaluative situations when self-handicapping will result in further self-enhancement by succeeding in spite of obstacles or disadvantages (Tice, 1991).

When they do, in fact, succeed, people who are high in self-esteem naturally assume that their success is caused by their abilities, they find the positive feedback highly credible, and they feel that they have control over their outcomes. They might be modest in claiming these things to others, because they know that others might like them less if they are boastful. These favorable interpretations of events are no doubt partly a function of the self-concept. Research using the misattribution paradigm cited earlier, however, suggests that these self-serving interpretations are also motivated by the fact that it feels good to be able to take credit for one's successes. Following success, high self-esteem people will attempt to maintain that success and further enhance the self by spending free time practicing the task (Baumeister & Tice, 1985).

When they fail, however, people who are high in self-esteem are surprised, because this failure is inconsistent with their self-concepts (Fries & Frey, 1980; Gollwitzer et al., 1982; Stephan & Gollwitzer, 1981). No doubt, the discrepancy between the feedback and their self-concepts arouses negative affect, which motivates a search for explanations for the outcome that are consistent with their self concepts (Brown & Rogers, 1991). In addition to attributing the negative outcome to external causes, a number of other cognitive strategies may be available, such as devaluing the importance of the task, deciding that the evaluator is not credible, or focusing on negative information about other people. Eventually, one of these strategies will restore self-regard and positive affect.

Low Self-Esteem and Self-Serving Biases

People who are low in self-esteem approach evaluative situations with considerable uncertainty regarding whether they have positive attributes and do not have negative attributes. Nonetheless, they still care about having positive qualities and about not having negative qualities. Consequently, their concern in evaluative situations is both with obtaining confirmation that they do, in fact, have positive qualities, but also with avoiding confirmation of their fears that they have negative qualities. Therefore, they may begin to prepare for possible negative outcomes *prior to or during an evaluative task.* Thus, low self-esteem people are more likely to self-handicap (e.g., fail to practice) when self-handicapping would provide an excuse for failure (Tice, 1991, this volume; Tice & Baummeister, 1990). They may also think about the possibility of failure and reconcile themselves to it by devaluing the task or making other psychological preparations.

Should they actually succeed at the task, then, low self-esteem people should be quite pleased. They may be cautious about concluding that their success reflects their abilities, however, for two reasons. First, success is not entirely consistent with the self-concepts of low self-esteem people which contain a mix of positive and negative attributes. Therefore, success might not seem any more credible than failure. Similarly, because the self-concepts of low self-esteem people contain a mix of positive and negative attributes, success feedback is not more likely to be attributed to internal factors such as ability than is failure feedback. Thus, for low self-esteem people the use of self-serving biases may be constrained by what they believe to be true about the self. Second, one danger for people low in self-esteem is that even if they can convince themselves that they have a positive attribute or have succeeded at a task, they may be cognizant of the risk of failing at the same task in the future, perhaps leading to greater disappointment and more negative affect than if they had never entertained the possibility of being competent in the first place. Thus, for people low in self-esteem, successful regulation of affect involves acknowledging the possibility of future failure and other disconfirmations of one's attempts at self-enhancement.

Should they fail, low self-esteem people should not be especially surprised. Although undesired, failure is not particularly inconsistent with the mixed and uncertain self-concepts of low self-esteem people. Consequently, it is just as likely to be attributed to external causes as is success feedback and seems just as credible. Thus, low self-esteem people seem to make evenhanded attributions for success and failure and do not differ in their judgments of the credibility of success and failure feedback (Shrauger, 1975).

As we noted above, low self-esteem people may be more prepared in advance for the possibility of failure because they are uncertain about whether they have desired attributes or do not have undesired attributes. For example, they may have anticipated possible failure and generated excuses in advance. Thus, although they find failure unpleasant and unsatisfying, people who are low in self-esteem may be less aroused by the failure and hence less motivated to engage in self-serving biases. Furthermore, because they do not expect to do well in the future, low self-esteem people may not want to convince themselves that the present failure is completely externally caused, because to do so might set them up for disappointment should their illusions be disconfirmed. Consistent with this reasoning, Baumeister and Tice (1985) have found that low self-esteem individuals will spend more free time practicing at tasks at which they have failed than at tasks at which they have succeeded.

Thus, the "breakdown of the motivation for self-enhancement" that a number of researchers suggest might account for the absence of self-serving biases among people who are low in self-esteem or depressed might derive from several factors. First, low self-esteem people might not engage in self-serving biases because they are constrained by the less positive "reality" of the self-concept. Second, by anticipating possible failure, and creating or imagining excuses for failure, low self-esteem individuals may soften the blow of failure when it occurs. Thus, they may appear to lack the motivation to enhance the self *after* the event, because they have already adjusted to the idea of failure. Third, although they desire self-enhancement, for low self-esteem people this desire is tempered by the fear that self-enhancing claims (to the self or others) cannot be maintained in the future, leading to even greater disappointment and negative affect. Thus, a second source of the "breakdown in the motivation to enhance the self" is the anticipation of future disappointment.

This framework, which considers the positivity of the self-concept, the certainty of the self-concept, and the importance of positive and negative attributes, can account quite nicely for a number of findings in the literature. For example, it can account for the fact that both high and low self-esteem people are more satisfied with positive feedback and seem to want it, at least under most circumstances, because both high and low self-esteem people place importance on positive attributes. In addition, it explains the presence of self-serving biases in attributions, judgments of control, ratings of the credibility of the evaluator, and so on, in terms of the "reality" constraints placed on self-enhancement by the self-concept. These constraints involve not only what is credible to the self and to observers, but also what can be maintained over time.

This framework may also be able to account for self-esteem effects on other types of self-serving biases. For example, self-handicapping involves acquiring an impediment to performance that can excuse failure. As Tice (1991, this volume) has shown, low self-esteem people self-handicap to provide an excuse for failure, whereas high self-esteem people self-handicap to augment their successes. This analysis is similar to that proposed by Baumeister et al. (1989; see Tice, this volume), who suggest that high and low self-esteem people have different motivational orientations. Low self-esteem people are motivated to avoid failure, whereas high self-esteem people are motivated to seek success. We suggest that this difference stems from the fact that whereas high self-esteem people are quite certain that positive attributes do and negative attributes do not characterize them, low self-esteem people are not at all certain that they have positive and do not have negative attributes, although it is still important to them to have positive attributes. Thus, low self-esteem people are more oriented toward making sure that they do not fail.

Similarly, this framework may account for the tendency of people who are high in self-esteem to engage in direct forms of self-enhancement, whereas people who are low in self-esteem engage in indirect forms of self-enhancement (see Brown, this volume). Low self-esteem people may engage in indirect forms of self-enhancement (e.g., positively evaluating a product that their group, but not they themselves, produced) because although it is important to them to be competent, they are uncertain about their own competence. Thus, they attempt to enhance the self (and regulate affect) by enhancing their ratings of products with which they are only indirectly associated. Our framework differs from Brown's in that we suggest that the motive for self-enhancement is in conflict with the self-concept, whereas Brown argues that the motive for self-enhancement is in conflict with the motive for self-consistency. In our view, low self-esteem people do not desire self-consistency, but only to avoid negative affect. Sometimes negative affect is best avoided by abstaining from self-serving biases that are in direct conflict with the self-concept.

Finally, this framework is also compatible with Baumgardner, Kaufman, and Levy's suggestion (1989) that high self-esteem people seek self-enhancement intrapsychically, whereas low self-esteem people seek self-enhancement interpersonally. This may generally be true because people who are low in self-esteem have trouble believing their intrapsychic attempts at self-enhancement. Hence, they rely on eliciting positive reactions from others to enhance the self. The study by Dykman et al. (1989) cited above, however, suggests that when they are not constrained by the "reality" of the self-concept, even low self-esteem people will engage in intrapsychic self-enhancement.

CONCLUSIONS

We have argued that the contradictory evidence on the relationship between self-esteem and the use of self-serving biases may be understood by considering the self-concepts of high and low self-esteem people. High self-esteem people are quite certain that they have positive attributes and do not have negative attributes, and it is important to them to have positive attributes. Consequently, they are not particularly concerned about avoiding failure (because it seems so unlikely), but they are very interested in enhancing themselves through success. They find success feedback highly credible and attribute it to their abilities. This results both from the positive information included in the self-concept and from the motivation to enjoy the positive affect that success can induce.

Low self-esteem people, on the other hand, are unsure of their self-concepts. They are neither sure that they have positive qualities nor sure that they do not have negative qualities, although it is important to them to have positive and not have negative qualities. As a result, they approach and evaluate situations with an eye toward avoiding failure. They will create excuses for possible failure in advance of their performance. When failure comes, they are not surprised, they find it somewhat credible, and they find it to be equally likely that the failure was caused by their lack of ability as that it was caused by external circumstances. Because they are uncertain that they have positive qualities, low self-esteem people may be mistrustful of success. Although they desire success, they may be unsure they can maintain success in the future. Consequently, low self-esteem people may protect themselves from future disappointment by finding success feedback less credible, and attributing it less to their ability, than do low self-esteem people.

Thus, low self-esteem people are not such a puzzle after all. That is, they share the same motivations as people high in self-esteem, and the same information-processing systems. They differ, however, in the content of their self-concept, and it is these content differences that lead low self-esteem people to attempt to achieve a positive view of the self and positive affect via different routes than those used by people who are high in self-esteem.

REFERENCES

Alloy, L. B. (1982, August). *Depression: On the absence of self-serving cognitive biases.* Paper presented at the 90th annual meeting of the American Psychological Association, Washington, DC.

Alloy, L. B., & Abramson, L. Y. (1979). Judgment of contingency in depressed and non-depressed students: Sadder but wiser? *Journal of Experimental Psychology, 108,* 441–485.

Alloy, L. B., & Abramson, L. Y. (1982). Learned helplessness, depression, and the illusion of control. *Journal of Personality and Social Psychology, 42,* 1114–1126.

Alloy, L. B., Abramson, L. Y., & Viscusi, D. (1981). Induced mood and the illusion of control. *Journal of Personality and Social Psychology, 41,* 1129–1140.

Arkin, R. M., & Maruyama, G. (1979). Attribution, affect, and college exam performance. *Journal of Educational Psychology, 71,* 85–93.

Baumeister, R. F., & Tice, D. M. (1985). Self-esteem and responses to success and failure: Subsequent performance and intrinsic motivation. *Journal of Personality, 53,* 450–467.

Baumeister, R. F., Tice, D. M., & Hutton, D. (1989). Self-presentational motivations and personality differences in self-esteem. *Journal of Personality, 57,* 547–579.

Baumgardner, A. H. (1990). To know oneself is to like oneself: Self-certainty and self-affect. *Journal of Personality and Social Psychology, 58,* 1062–1072.

Baumgardner, A. H., Kaufman, C., & Levy, P. (1989). Regulating affect interpersonally: When low self-esteem leads to greater enhancement. *Journal of Personality and Social Psychology, 56,* 907–921.

Bradley, G. W. (1978). Self-serving biases in the attribution process: A reexamination of the fact or fiction question. *Journal of Personality and Social Psychology, 36,* 56–71.

Brockner, J. (1983). Low self-esteem and behavioral plasticity: Some implications. In L. Wheeler & P. Shaver (Eds.), *Review of personality and social psychology* (Vol. 4, pp. 237–271). Beverly Hills, CA: Sage.

Brown, J. D. (1986). Evaluations of self and others: Self-enhancement biases in social judgements. *Social Cognition, 4,* 353–375.

Brown, J. D., Collins, R., & Schmidt, G. (1988). Self-esteem and direct vs. indirect forms of self-enhancement. *Journal of Personality and Social Psychology, 55,* 445–453.

Brown, J. D., & Rogers, R. J. (1991). Self-serving attributions: The role of physiological arousal. *Personality and Social Psychology Bulletin, 17*, 501–506.

Campbell, J. D. (1986). Similarity and uniqueness: The effects of attribute type, relevance, and individual differences in self-esteem and depression. *Journal of Personality and Social Psychology, 50*, 281–294.

Campbell, J. D. (1990). Self-esteem and the clarity of the self-concept. *Journal of Personality and Social Psychology, 59*, 538–549.

Campbell, J. D., & Fehr, B. (1990). Self-esteem and perceptions of conveyed impressions: Is negative affectivity associated with greater realism? *Journal of Personality and Social Psychology, 58*, 122–133.

Cialdini, R. B., Borden, R. J., Thorne, A., Walker, M. R., Freeman, S., Sloan, L. R. (1976). Basking in reflected glory: Three (football) field studies. *Journal of Personality and Social Psychology, 34*, 366–375.

Cohen, L., van den Bout, J., van Vliet, T., & Kramer, W. (1989). Attributional asymmetries in relation to dysphoria and self-esteem. *Personality and Individual Differences, 10*, 1055–1061.

College Dictionary (Revised edition). (1975). New York: Random House.

Crandall, R. (1973). The measurement of self-esteem and related constructs. In J. Robinson & P. Shaver (Eds.), *Measures of social psychological attitudes*. Ann Arbor, MI: Institute for Social Research.

Crary, W. G. (1966). Reactions to incongruent self-experiences. *Journal of Consulting Psychology, 30*, 246–252.

Crocker, J. (1991). *Memory for information about others: Effects of self-esteem and performance feedback*. Unpublished manuscript.

Crocker, J., & Blaine, B. (1992). *Self-esteem and self-serving biases: An integrative review*. Unpublished manuscript.

Crocker, J., Thompson, L., McGraw, K., & Ingerman, C. (1987). Downward comparison, prejudice, and evaluations of others: Effects of self-esteem and threat. *Journal of Personality and Social Psychology, 52*, 907–916.

DeMonbreun, B. G., & Craighead, W. E. (1977). Distortion of perception and recall of positive and neutral feedback in depression. *Cognitive Therapy and Research, 1*, 311–329.

Dykman, B., Abramson, L. Y., Alloy, L. B., & Hartlage, S. (1989). Processing of ambiguous and unambiguous feedback by depressed and nondepressed college students: Schematic biases and their implications for depressive realism. *Journal of Personality and Social Psychology, 56*, 431–445.

Feather, N. T. (1969). Attribution of responsibility and valence of success and failure in relation to initial confidence and task performance. *Journal of Personality and Social Psychology, 13*, 129–144.

Feather, N. (1989). The rosy glow of self-esteem: Depression, masculinity, and causal attributions. *Australian Journal of Psychology, 39*, 25–41.

Feather, N. T., & Simon, J. G. (1971a). Attribution of responsibility and valence of outcome in relation to initial confidence and success and failure of self and other. *Journal of Personality and Social Psychology, 18*, 173–188.

Feather, N. T., & Simon, J. G. (1971b). Causal attributions for success and failure in relation to expectation of success based on selective or manipulative control. *Journal of Personality, 39*, 527–541.

Fitch, G. (1970). Effects of self-esteem, perceived performance, and choice on causal attribution. *Journal of Personality and Social Psychology, 16*, 311–315.

Fries, A., & Frey, D. (1980). Misattribution of arousal and the effects of self-threatening information. *Journal of Experimental Social Psychology, 16*, 405–416.

Gibbons, F. X., & McCoy, S. B. (1991). Self-esteem similarity, and reactions to active vs. passive downward comparison. *Journal of Personality and Social Psychology, 60,* 414–424.

Gilmor, T. M., & Minton, H. L. (1974). Internal versus external attribution of task performance as a function of locus of control, initial confidence and success-failure outcome. *Journal of Personality, 42,* 159–174.

Gilovich, T. (1983). Biased evaluation and persistence in gambling. *Journal of Personality and Social Psychology, 44,* 1110–1126.

Gilovich, T. (1991). *How we know what isn't so: The fallibility of human reason in everyday life.* New York: Free Press.

Gollwitzer, P. M., Earle, W. B., & Stephan, W. G. (1982). Affect as a determinant of egotism: Residual excitation and performance attributions. *Journal of Personality and Social Psychology, 43,* 702–709.

Greenberg, J., Pyszczynski, T., & Solomon, S. (1982). The self-serving attributional bias: Beyond self-presentation. *Journal of Experimental Social Psychology, 18,* 56–67.

Harter, S. (1986). Processes underlying the construction, maintenance, and enhancement of the self-concept in children. In J. Suls & A. Greenwald (Eds.), *Psychological perspectives on the self* (Vol. 3, pp. 137–181). Hillsdale, NJ: Lawrence Erlbaum.

Harvey, O., & Clapp, W. (1965). Hope, expectancy, and reactions to the unexpected. *Journal of Personality and Social Psychology, 2,* 45–52.

Heider, F. (1958). *The psychology of interpersonal relations.* New York: John Wiley.

Ickes, W., & Layden, M. A. (1978). Attributional styles. In W. Ickes & R. Kidd (Eds.), *New directions in attribution research* (Vol. 2, pp. 119–152). Hillsdale, NJ: Lawrence Erlbaum.

Korman, A. K. (1968). Task success, task popularity, and self-esteem as influences on task liking. *Journal of Applied Psychology, 52,* 484–490.

Kruglanski, A. W. (1990). Motivations for judging and knowing: Implications for causal attribution. In E. T. Higgins & R. M. Sorrentino (Eds.), *The handbook of motivation and cognition: Foundations of social behavior* (Vol. 2, pp. 333–368). New York: Guilford.

Kunda, Z. (1990). The case for motivated reasoning. *Psychological Bulletin, 108,* 480–498.

Langer, E. J. (1975). The illusion of control. *Journal of Personality and Social Psychology, 32,* 311–328.

Lau, R., & Russell, D. (1980). Attribution in the sports pages: A field test of some current hypotheses in attribution research. *Journal of Personality and Social Psychology, 39,* 39–48.

Marsh, H. W. (1986). Global self-esteem: Its relation to specific facets of self-concept and their importance. *Journal of Personality and Social Psychology, 51,* 1224–1236.

McFarland, C. & Ross, M. (1982). Impact of causal attributions on affective reactions to success and failure. *Journal of Personality and Social Psychology, 43,* 937–946.

Miller, D. T. (1978). What constitutes a self-serving attributional bias? A reply to Bradley. *Journal of Personality and Social Psychology, 36,* 1221–1223.

Miller, D. T., & Porter, C. A. (1988). Errors and biases in the attribution process. In L. Y. Abramson (Ed.), *Social cognition and clinical psychology: A synthesis* (pp. 3–32). New York: Guilford.

Miller, D. T., & Ross, M. (1975). Self-serving biases in attribution of causality: Fact or fiction? *Psychological Bulletin, 82,* 213–225.

Moreland, R. L., & Sweeney, P. (1984). Self-expectancies and reactions to evaluations of personal performance. *Journal of Personality, 52,* 156–176.

Nelson, R. E., & Craighead, W. E. (1977). Selective recall of positive and negative feedback, self-control behaviors, and depression. *Journal of Abnormal Psychology, 86,* 379–388.

Pelham, B. W., & Swann, W. B., Jr. (1989). From self-conceptions to self-worth: On the sources and structure of global self-esteem. *Journal of Personality and Social Psychology, 57,* 672–680.

Peterson, C., Schwartz, S. M., & Seligman, M. E. P. (1981). Self-blame and depression symptoms. *Journal of Personality and Social Psychology, 41,* 253–259.

Pyszczynski, T., & Greenberg, J. (1987). Toward an integration of cognitive and motivational perspectives on social inference: A biased hypothesis testing model. In L. Berkowitz (Ed.), *Advances in experimental social psychology* (Vol. 20, pp. 297–340). New York: Academic Press.

Raps, C. S., Reinhard, K. E., Peterson, C., Abramson, L. Y., & Seligman, M. E. P. (1982). Attributional style among depressed patients. *Journal of Abnormal Psychology, 91,* 102–108.

Rizley, R. (1978). Depression and distortion in the attribution of causality. *Journal of Abnormal Psychology, 87,* 32–48.

Rosenberg, M. (1965). *Society and the adolescent self-image.* Princeton, NJ: Princeton University Press.

Rosenberg, M. (1979). *Conceiving the self.* New York: Basic Books.

Ross, M., & Sicoly, F. (1979). Egocentric biases in availability and attribution. *Journal of Personality and Social Psychology, 37,* 322–337.

Sackheim, H. A. (1983). Self-deception, self-esteem, and depression: The adaptive value of lying to oneself. In J. Masling (Ed.), *Empirical studies of psychoanalytic theories* (Vol. 1, pp. 101–157). Hillsdale, NJ: Lawrence Erlbaum.

Sackheim, H. A., & Wegner, A. Z. (1986). Attributional patterns in depression and dysthymia. *Archives of General Psychiatry, 43,* 553–560.

Schlenker, B. R., & Miller, R. S. (1977). Egocentrism in groups: Self-serving biases or logical information processing? *Journal of Personality and Social Psychology, 35,* 755–764.

Schlenker, B. R., Soraci, S., Jr., & McCarthy, B. (1976). Self-esteem and group performance as determinants of egocentric perceptions in cooperative groups. *Human Relations, 29,* 1163–1176.

Seligman, M. E. P., Abramson, L. Y., Semmel, A., & von Baeyer, C. (1979). Depressive attributional style. *Journal of Abnormal Psychology, 88,* 242–247.

Shrauger, J. S. (1972). Self-esteem and reactions to being observed by others. *Journal of Personality and Social Psychology, 23,* 192–200.

Shrauger, J. S. (1975). Responses to evaluation as a function of initial self-perceptions. *Psychological Bulletin, 82,* 581–596.

Shrauger, J. S., & Lund, A. K. (1975). Self-evaluation and reactions to evaluations from others. *Journal of Personality, 43,* 94–108.

Shrauger, J. S., & Rosenberg, S. E. (1970). Self-esteem and the effects of success and failure feedback on performance. *Journal of Personality, 38,* 404–417.

Smith, M. B. (1968). The self and cognitive consistency. In R. B. Abelson et al., (Eds.), *Theories of cognitive consistency: A sourcebook* (pp. 366–372). Chicago: Rand McNally.

Stephan, W. G., & Gollwitzer, P. M. (1981). Affect as a mediator of attributional egotism. *Journal of Experimental Social Psychology, 17,* 443–458.

Swann, W. B., Jr. (1983). Self-verification: Bringing social reality into harmony with the self. In J. Suls & A. Greenwald (Eds.), *Social psychological perspectives on the self* (Vol. 2, pp. 33–66). Hillsdale, NJ: Lawrence Erlbaum.

Swann, W. B., Jr. (1985). The self as architect of social reality. In B. Schlenker, (Ed.), *The self and social life* (pp. 100–125). New York: McGraw-Hill.

Swann, W. B., Jr. (1987). Identity negotiation: Where two roads meet. *Journal of Personality and Social Psychology, 53,* 1038–1051.

Swann, W. B., Jr., Griffin, J., Predmore, S., & Gaines, B. (1987). The cognitive-affective crossfire: When self-consistency confronts self-enhancement. *Journal of Personality and Social Psychology, 52,* 881–889.

Sweeney, P. D., Anderson, K., & Bailey, S. (1986). Attributional style in depression: A meta-analytic review. *Journal of Personality and Social Psychology, 50,* 974–991.

Tabachnik, N., Crocker, J., & Alloy, L. B. (1983). Depression, social comparison, and the false-consensus effect. *Journal of Personality and Social Psychology, 45,* 688–699.

Taylor, S. E. (1983). Adjustment to threatening events: A theory of cognitive adaptation. *American Psychologist, 38,* 1161–1173.

Taylor, S. E., & Brown, J. D. (1988). Illusion and well-being: A social psychological perspective on mental health. *Psychological Bulletin, 103,* 193–210.

Tennen, H., & Herzberger, S. (1987). Depression, self-esteem, and the absence of self-protective attributional biases. *Journal of Personality and Social Psychology, 52,* 72–80.

Tennen, H., Herzberger, S., & Nelson, H. (1987). Depressive attributional style: The role of self-esteem. *Journal of Personality, 55,* 631–660.

Tetlock, P. E., & Levi, A. (1982). Attribution bias: On the inconclusiveness of the cognition-motivation debate. *Journal of Experimental Social Psychology, 18,* 68–88.

Tice, D. M. (1991). Esteem protection or enhancement? Self-handicapping motives and attributions differ by trait self-esteem. *Journal of Personality and Social Psychology, 60,* 711–725.

Tice, D. M., & Baumeister, R. F. (1990). Self-esteem, self-handicapping, and self-presentation: The strategy of inadequate practice. *Journal of Personality, 58,* 443–464.

Weary, G. (1979). Self-serving attributional biases: Perceptual or response distortions? *Journal of Personality and Social Psychology, 37,* 1418–1420.

Weary, G., Harvey, J. H., Schwieger, P., Olson, C. T., Perloff, R., & Pritchard, S. (1982). Self-presentation and the moderation of self-serving biases. *Social Cognition, 1,* 140–159.

Webster's New Collegiate Dictionary (8th ed.). (1976). New York: Merriam-Webster.

Weiner, B. (1985). An attributional theory of achievement motivation and emotion. *Psychological Review, 92,* 548–573.

Weiner, B. (1986). *An attributional theory of motivation and emotion.* New York: Springer-Verlag.

Wills, T. A. (1981). Downward comparison principles in social psychology. *Psychological Bulletin, 90,* 245–271.

Zuckerman, M. (1979). Attribution of success and failure revisited, or the motivational bias is alive and well in attribution theory. *Journal of Personality, 47,* 245–287.

CHAPTER 5

CAUSES AND CONSEQUENCES OF LOW SELF-ESTEEM IN CHILDREN AND ADOLESCENTS

SUSAN HARTER

"When I look in the mirror, I don't like what I see; I don't like who I am as a person."
"I'm usually down on myself; I just don't like who I am."
"I'm a nothing; I have no personality."
"I don't like myself because I'm ugly."
"I'm not living up to the kind of person I want to be."
"If nobody else likes you, how can you like yourself?"
"Let's face it, I have low self-esteem."

The preceding comments from studies of young people by myself and colleagues are personally very distressing. Theoretically, they are perplexing. It is commonly asserted in the literature that the self-concept is a theory, a cognitive construction, and that its architecture—by evolutionary design—is extremely functional (see Allport, 1961; Bartlett, 1932; Brim, 1976; Damon & Hart, 1988; Epstein, 1973, 1981, 1991; Greenwald, 1980; Harter, 1983; Kelly, 1955; Lecky, 1945; Lynch, 1981; Markus, 1980; Piaget, 1965; Rogers, 1951; Sarbin, 1962). One such widely touted function is to maintain high self-esteem. Considerable evidence now exists

SUSAN HARTER • Department of Psychology, 2155 South Race Street, Denver, CO 80208.

Self-Esteem: The Puzzle of Low Self-Regard, edited by Roy F. Baumeister. Plenum Press, New York, 1993.

that most people do exhibit a modest self-enhancing bias (Taylor & Brown, 1988).

Given this functional scenario, why should the system falter, leading certain individuals to experience and so clearly express their feelings of low self-esteem? What can go awry to undermine the supposed protective function of the self? In order to address this question, one first needs to examine the processes governing the construction of self-esteem. In delving into the causes of self-esteem, it will be necessary to adopt a developmental perspective as a backdrop against which individual differences can be understood. These issues will be explored within the context of our own research program investigating the causes and consequences of self-esteem in children and adolescents.

Self-esteem or self-worth, within our framework, has been conceptualized as the level of global regard that one has for the self as a person (Harter, 1985a, 1986, 1990), a definition that has much in common with Rosenberg's conception (1979, 1986) of self-esteem. Although the studies by myself and colleagues have addressed individuals exhibiting the entire range of self-esteem, in the present chapter I will focus on those individuals reporting low self-esteem, including their propensity for depression and suicidal thinking, a major mental health concern in the 1980s and 1990s.

ORIGINAL MODEL OF THE CAUSES OF SELF-ESTEEM

In developing our original model of self-esteem, my colleagues and I turned to two historical scholars of the self, James (1892) and Cooley (1902), for theoretical guidance. Each of these theorists was explicit on the point that one possesses a global concept of self over and above more specific self-evaluations. Their formulations, however, put forth very different determinants of this global sense of one's worth as a person.

For James, global self-esteem was captured by the ratio of one's successes to one's pretensions. According to this formulation, individuals do not scrutinize their every action or attribute; rather, they focus primarily on ability in domains of importance, where one has aspirations to succeed. Thus, if one perceives oneself as competent in domains where one aspires to excel, one will have high self-esteem. Conversely, if one falls short of one's ideals by being unsuccessful in domains where one aspires to be competent, low self-esteem will result. It is critical to appreciate that from a Jamesian perspective, lack of competence in domains deemed unimportant to the self will *not* adversely affect self-esteem. For example, an individual may judge himself or herself to be unathletic; however, if athletic prowess is not an aspiration, then self-esteem will not be negatively affected. The high self-esteem individual is able to discount the importance of domains in which he or she is not competent, whereas the low self-esteem individual appears unable to devalue success in domains of incompetence.

In contrast to James, who focused primarily on the individual's cognitive evaluation of his or her adequacy, Cooley (1902) postulated that the origins of self-esteem were primarily social in nature, and he adopted a mirror metaphor in describing his concept of the "looking-glass self." For Cooley, the self was constructed by casting one's gaze into the social mirror to ascertain the opinions of significant others toward the self. These opinions, the reflected appraisals of others, were then incorporated as the self. Mead (1934) elaborated on this theme in his concept of the "generalized other," which represented the pooled or collective judgments of the significant others in one's life. From such a perspective, if others hold the self in high regard, one's own sense of self-esteem will be high. Conversely, if others have little regard for the self, one will incorporate these negative opinions in the form of low self-esteem.

FINDINGS IN SUPPORT OF JAMES'S FORMULATION

Our model of the nature of self-evaluations in older children and adolescents lent itself to a Jamesian analysis. My colleagues and I had previously determined that children, beginning at approximately age 8, develop domain-specific evaluations of their competence or adequacy in addition to a more global concept of their worth as a person (Harter, 1982, 1985a, 1986). The most relevant domains, which were incorporated into our Self-Perception Profile for Children (Harter, 1985a), are scholastic competence, athletic competence, social acceptance, physical appearance, and behavioral conduct. Our instrument allows us to obtain a profile of self-concept scores across the specific domains, as well as a separate index of the child's sense of global self-esteem or self-worth.

In our earliest examination of individual profiles, we were puzzled by comparisons of children with very similar profiles across the five specific domains, but very different global self-esteem scores. For example, in Figure 1, child C and child D feel relatively poorly about their scholastic and athletic competence, whereas they rate themselves more highly in the other three domains (social acceptance, behavioral conduct, and physical appearance). Yet the global self-esteem of child C is

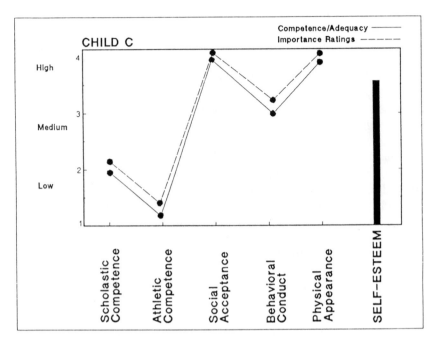

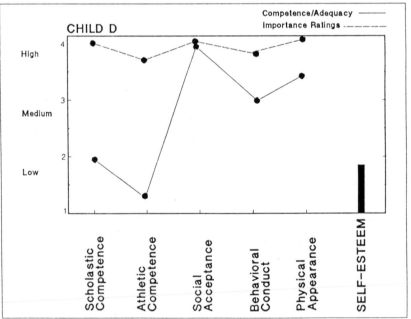

FIGURE 1. Profiles of two young adolescents with similar scores for specific domains but very different levels of self-esteem.

quite high, whereas the self-esteem of child D is quite low. James came to the conceptual rescue here by alerting us to the need to consider the *importance* of success in these domains. Thus, we constructed parallel importance items, allowing us to examine directly James's contention that competence or adequacy in domains of importance contributes to one's level of self-esteem. (Scores on both instruments can range from a low of 1 to a high of 4.)

Our findings have revealed precisely what James hypothesized. By way of illustration, in Figure 1, it can be seen that child C, with high self-esteem, judged scholastic and athletic competence to be relatively unimportant. Thus, such a child can discount the importance of areas in which he or she is not competent while touting the importance of domains in which he or she is doing well. Conversely, child D is unable to discount the importance of scholastic and athletic competence, leading to a vast discrepancy between very high importance judgments and very low competence/adequacy evaluations in these two domains. It appears to be this discrepancy, therefore, that takes its toll on self-esteem.

We have since documented this pattern systematically, with group data from older children, adolescents, college students, and adults in the worlds of work and family (Harter, 1990). We have employed two data-analytic strategies, both of which tell the same story. One can construct actual discrepancy scores between importance ratings and competence judgments in each domain. Averaging these across domains, initially, we have determined that the larger the discrepancy (i.e., the more one's importance ratings exceed one's perceived adequacy or competence), the lower one's self-worth. Across numerous studies, these correlations typically range from .60 to .72. Employing a second procedure, in which we have examined self-esteem as a function of the average absolute competence/adequacy judgments for *only* those domains rated very important or sort of important, a systematic, linear relationship emerges (see Figure 2). Noteworthy is the finding that relatively low self-esteem is reported for those acknowledging that they lack competence or adequacy in domains for which they have aspirations of success. Employing correlational approaches, the relationship between competence in important domains and self-esteem ($r = .70$) far exceeds the correlation between competence in unimportant domains and self-esteem ($r = .30$).

This pattern of findings is not unique to our own data, but converges with other literature that has focused on the discrepancy between one's ideal and real selves (see Glick & Zigler, 1985; Higgins, 1987, 1991; Markus & Nurius, 1986; Rosenberg, 1979; Tesser, 1988; Tesser & Campbell, 1983). As shall become evident in a subsequent section, such dis-

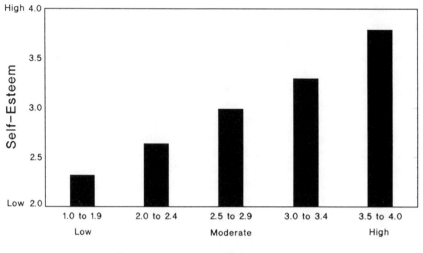

Competence in Important Domains

FIGURE 2. Self-esteem as a function of competence in important domains.

crepancies are not only predictive of self-esteem, but of such associated affects as depression and anxiety (Higgins, 1987, 1989). From a developmental perspective, it should be noted that the these discrepancy models do not apply to younger children. Competence does not appear to be as critical to young children's self-esteem (Harter, 1990), nor are young children cognitively able to compare two concepts such as importance ratings and self-evaluations simultaneously (Fischer, 1980; Harter, 1990; Higgins, 1991).

WHY SHOULD CERTAIN OLDER CHILDREN AND ADOLESCENTS MANIFEST LOW SELF-ESTEEM?

If the psychological system is adaptively programmed to reduce discrepancies between importance and perceived incompetence, beginning in middle childhood, why do they exist (and persist) among low self-esteem individuals? Both Jamesian and recent self-discrepancy formulations have now identified the relevant processes that could potentially be engaged to enhance self-esteem. James clearly asserted that for the low self-esteem individual, there are two routes to self-esteem enhancement: either raise one's level of competence or lower one's aspirations. Both of these serve to reduce the discrepancy between competence and importance, which should, in turn, increase one's level of self-esteem.

Although such interventions are theoretically compelling, how plausible are these strategies in the actual lives of children and adolescents? Several factors would appear to mitigate against their utilization and, therefore, their potential effectiveness. One can identify two psychological roadblocks to discounting the importance of the specific domains we have selected, even in the face of perceived inadequacy. First and foremost, these domains were initially selected because children and adolescents, in interviews, identified these areas as very important. That is, we are living in a society where scholastic competence, athletic competence, physical attractiveness, social acceptance, and appropriate behavioral conduct are highly valued and sought after by the majority of youths in the cultural mainstream. Thus, aspirations and standards in these domains are typically quite high, making it difficult for those feeling inadequate to discount their importance. (Note that such an argument pertains only to those choosing to remain within the cultural mainstream.)

Secondly, these domains are valued by *others*, notably parents and peers. Our own findings reveal that children and adolescents judge scholastic competence and behavioral conduct to be most important to parents, and social acceptance, physical appearance, and athletic competence to be most important to peers. Moreover, importance to others is highly correlated with importance to self, and competence in domains important to others is just as highly correlated with self-esteem as is competence in domains important to the self (Harter & Marold, 1991). Thus, it would appear to be extremely difficult for children and adolescents to discount the importance of domains that represent standards set by significant others whom one wishes to please (see also Baumeister, 1990), despite feelings of inadequacy in these areas. Thus, for both of these related reasons, the discrepancy between high importance and low competence/adequacy will be very difficult to reduce by lowering one's aspirations.

Increasing one's competence evaluations as a strategy for reducing this discrepancy would also appear to be problematic for many youths. There are undoubtedly natural limits on the extent to which one can increase actual competence or adequacy. Although a given child or adolescent may be highly motivated to improve his or her scholastic performance, athletic ability, or physical appearance, there may be little that an inadequate individual can realistically do, given certain ceilings on intellectual and physical potential.

There may also be limitations placed on one's perceived competence, given the standards imposed by social comparison. Studies have shown that the process of comparing the self to others for the purpose of self-evaluation begins in middle childhood and increases as one matures (Ruble, 1983; Suls & Sanders, 1982). Our own research has demonstrated that the use of social comparison is rampant in the five domains that we have selected. Moreover, children within regular classroom settings can rank order, with great precision, the competence level of every member of their class. Interestingly, my colleagues and I have also documented the use of social comparison among learning-disabled children (Renick & Harter, 1989), as well as intellectually talented children within segregated classes for the gifted (Zumpf & Harter, 1991). Beginning in middle childhood, therefore, one adopts the cultural preoccupation with how individuals are different from one another—with competition, with who is the "best," with who ascends to the top. Thus, how one measures up to one's peers, to societal standards, becomes the filter through which judgments about the self pass.

One may well espouse the value of social comparison, because it presumably provides us with the necessary guidelines or standards by which to evaluate ourselves and to improve our performance. Supposedly it offers a welcome anchor to ground us in reality. Because most of life's activities are graded on a curve, however (particularly the domains we have selected), relatively few individuals can occupy the prestigious positions at the top of the ladder. Thus, even if an individual who is motivated to improve does demonstrate actual gains compared to his or her own past performance, he or she will likely fall short relative to the punishing peer standards that provide the metric for self-evaluation. As a result, it becomes difficult to greatly increase one's perceptions of competence, relative to others, as a potential route to reducing the discrepancy between importance and competence that contributes to low self-esteem.

In addition, there are two general reasons, articulated by Epstein (1991), for why judgments of such personal constructs as perceived competence or the importance attached to success in particular domains may be resistant to change, even though their discrepancy produces low self-esteem. Epstein has cogently addressed the issue of why maladaptive beliefs are maintained, despite conditions that could favor their modification or abandonment. Two of these mechanisms are particularly pertinent. First, he notes that higher-order schemas or postulates in a hierarchically organized conceptual system such as one's self-theory (e.g., feelings of competence, esteem, and general value judgments) are far more resistant to modification than lower-order, situation-specific constructs. Such higher-order beliefs have typically been acquired early in development and are often derived from emotionally significant experiences to which the individual may have little conscious access, making the beliefs difficult to alter.

Second, Epstein (1991) states that "people have a vested interest in maintaining the stability of their personal theories of reality, for they are the only systems they have for making sense of their world and guiding their behavior" (p. 97). Threats to the stability of one's personal theory, producing disorganization in the conceptual system, will lead to anxiety and are therefore to be avoided. Epstein further identifies several strategies that individuals employ to maintain the integrity of their basic beliefs despite what would appear to be disconfirming evidence: (a) One can frame one's personal theory in a manner that renders it untestable, (b) one can select only information that supports one's theory, or (c) one can seek out experiences and shape events so that they confirm one's existing beliefs (see also Epstein & Erskine, 1983; Swann, 1983). Thus, because higher-order constructs about the self are resistant to change, one can further understand why a low self-esteem individual is likely to maintain his or her low self-regard.

THE INEXTRICABLE LINK BETWEEN APPEARANCE AND SELF-ESTEEM

In study after study, at any developmental level my colleagues and I have examined, including older children, adolescents, college students, and adults (Harter, 1990), we have repeatedly discovered that self-evaluations in the domain of physical appearance are inextricably linked to global self-esteem. The correlations between perceived appearance and self-esteem are staggeringly high and robust across the life span, typically between .70 and .80. Moreover, we find this relationship to be just as high in such special populations as the intellectually gifted (Zumpf & Harter, 1991) and the learning disabled (Renick & Harter, 1989), where one might anticipate that scholastic performance would bear a stronger relationship to self-esteem. (The lower correlations between scholastic competence and self-esteem are not attributable to a restricted range of scores for scholastic competence in these special groups; the standard deviations approximate those of our normative samples.) In the same vein, the correlation between appearance and self-esteem is equally high among adolescents identified as behaviorally disruptive (Junkin, Harter, & Whitesell, 1991), exceeding that of the correlation between behavioral conduct and self-esteem. Among all of these groups, the evaluation of one's looks takes precedence over every other domain as the number one predictor of self-esteem, causing us to question whether self-esteem is only skin-deep.

Why should one's outer, physical self be so tied to one inner, psychological self? One possibility is that the domain of physical appearance is qualitatively different from the other arenas we have tapped, in that it is an omnipresent feature of the self, always on display for others or for the self to observe. In contrast, one's adequacy in such domains as scholastic or athletic competence, peer social acceptance, conduct, or morality is more context specific; moreover, one has more control over whether, when, and how it will be revealed.

Studies reveal that others being to react to the ever-present display of the physical self when one is an infant and toddler (Langlois, 1981; Macoby & Martin, 1983). Those who are attractive, by societal standards, are responded to with more positive attention than those who are judged to be less physically attractive. Thus, from a very early age, the physical or outer self appears to be a highly salient dimension that provokes evaluative psychological reactions that may well be incorporated into the emerging sense of one's inner self.

Clearly, a critical contributing factor involves the emphasis that contemporary society places on appearance at every age (see Elkind, 1979; Hatfield & Sprecher, 1986). Movies, television, magazines, rock videos, and advertising all tout the importance of physical attractiveness, glamorizing the popular role models males and females should emulate. Standards regarding desirable bodily characteristics such as thinness have become increasingly unrealistic and demanding for women within the past two decades (see Garner, Garfinkel, Schwartz, & Thompson, 1980; Heatherton & Baumeister, 1991). An examination of such contemporary women's magazines such as *Family Circle, Woman's Day,* and *First for Women* reveals that the standards are paradoxical and punishing for women. All of these magazines relentlessly insist that women (a) attend fiercely to their appearance (hair, face, and particularly weight) at the same time as they (b) cook a vast array of fattening foods for themselves and their family! Moreover, articles and ads specifically preach that altering one's looks, often in the form of an invasive cosmetic overhaul to approximate rather narrowly defined cultural stereotypes of beauty, will enhance one's self-esteem.

Although the media are also increasingly emphasizing the importance of appearance for men, it would appear that there is more latitude in the standards of attractiveness for men. Moreover, for men there is not the singular focus on looks at the pathway to acceptance and esteem that one finds for women. For men, intelligence, job competence, athletic ability, wealth, and power are all routes to positive evaluation in the eyes of others as well as the self.

The difficulty for females of meeting the cultural stereotypes for appearance appears to be brought home over the course of development (i.e., the closer one comes to adopting one's role as a woman in this society). Our own data (see Figure 3) reveal that for females, perceptions of physical attractiveness decline systematically with grade level, whereas there is no such drop for males. In middle childhood, girls and boys feel equally good about their appearance, but by the end of high school, females' scores are dramatically lower than those of males.

Gender differences in self-esteem also increase with development, paralleling the trajectories for physical appearance. Beginning in junior high school and continuing into high school, self-esteem is consistently lower for females as compared to males. Decreased perceptions of attractiveness among females would appear to contribute to the lowered self-esteem of females, as other investigators have also suggested (Allgood-Merten, Lewinsohn, & Hops, 1990; Nolen-Hoeksema, 1987; Simmons & Blyth, 1987). In our own data, however, females' self-esteem

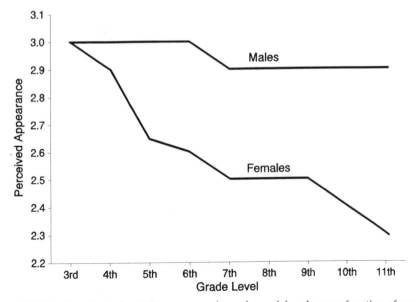

FIGURE 3. Perceived physical appearance for males and females as a function of grade level.

does not decline as dramatically with age as does perceived physical appearance. Rather there is another mediating factor, namely, the *directionality* of the link between appearance and self-esteem.

THE DIRECTIONALITY OF THE LINK BETWEEN APPEARANCE AND SELF-ESTEEM

The robust relationship between perceived appearance and self-esteem raised for us an intriguing question: Which comes first? Does one's appearance influence one's sense of self-esteem? Does the evaluation of it precede, that is, *determine* one's sense of worth as a person? Or, conversely, does one's self-esteem influence the evaluation of one's appearance, such that if one feels worthy as a person, one will evaluate one's looks favorably?

We have begun to research this issue by putting the question directly to young adolescents (Zumpf & Harter, 1989). That is, we have asked them to indicate which of these two options best describes the nature of the link between their appearance and their self-esteem. Our findings reveal that one group of adolescents acknowledges that their evaluation of appearance precedes or determines their sense of self-esteem, whereas an equal number endorse the opposite orientation, reporting that their sense of self-esteem determines how much they like the way they look. Converging evidence indicates that those in the first group (whose appearance determines their self-esteem) also report that appearance is more important, that they are more preoccupied with appearance, and that they worry more about how they look, compared to the group whose self-esteem precedes judgments of appearance (Harter & Waters, 1991).

Moreover, there is a particularly distressing pattern for the group basing their self-esteem on their appearance, a pattern that is more pronounced for girls. Adolescent females reporting that appearance determines their sense of worth as a person feel worse about their appearance, have lower self-esteem, and also report feeling more affectively depressed, compared to females for whom self-esteem precedes judgments of appearance (Zumpf & Harter, 1989; Harter & Waters, 1991). Thus, those adolescent females espousing the Jamesian model, in which self-evaluations in domains of importance determine one's self-esteem, are more at risk for low self-esteem and associated maladaptive outcomes. Sadly, this is the orientation that is underscored by our society, especially by the media. The irony, therefore, is that endorsement of a Jamesian perspective with regard to the domain of physical appearance represents a psychological liability for females in particular, undermining their evaluation of both the outer and inner self.

FINDINGS IN SUPPORT OF COOLEY'S FORMULATION

For Cooley (1902), self-esteem was a social construction. According to his looking-glass-self formulation, social support, in the form of positive regard from significant others, was the critical determinant of self-esteem. Thus, approval or disapproval from others becomes incorporated into one's own esteem for the self. Developmentally, the internalization of parental approval or disapproval is particularly crucial to the self-esteem formation of young children (Harter, 1987, 1990).

In order to examine Cooley's formulation empirically among older children and adolescents, my colleagues and I identified four sources of potential support: parents, teachers, classmates, and close friends. We then created self-report items (see the Social Support Scale for Children and Adolescents; Harter, 1985b) tapping the extent to which one feels that these others approve of or value the self. In creating such items, we can then directly examine the link between the perceived regard from others and the perceived regard for the self.

Across numerous studies with older children and adolescents, as well as with college students and adults, we have found that the correlations between perceived support from significant others and self-esteem range from .50 to .65 (Harter, 1990b). As anticipated from Cooley's model, those with the lowest levels of support report the the lowest self-esteem, those with moderate support have moderate levels of self-esteem, and those receiving the most support hold the self in the highest regard. Among the four sources of support that we have examined, we have repeatedly demonstrated that for older children and adolescents, perceived classmate and parent approval are the best predictors. Thus, Cooley's looking-glass-self model on the origins of self-esteem appears to be clearly documented with regard to the link between one's *perceptions* of the approval of others and one's self-esteem. To date, we have not examined whether *others'* reports of their approval they provide predicts self-esteem. Interesting, the literature suggests that there is no consistent agreement between people's self-perceptions and how they are actually viewed by others (Shrauger & Schoeneman, 1979).

Moreover, our findings reveal that both James' and Cooley's formulations, taken together, provide a powerful explanation for the level of self-esteem displayed by older children and adolescents (Harter, 1987).

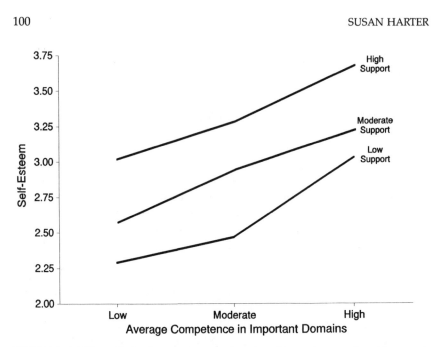

FIGURE 4. Additive effects of competence in domains of importance and social support on self-esteem.

As can be seen in Figure 4, the effects of these two determinants are additive. At each level of social support (representing the average of classmate and parent approval), greater competence in domains of importance leads to higher self-esteem. Similarly, at each level of competence in domains of importance, the more support one garners from classmates and parents, the higher one's self-esteem. Those individuals with the lowest self-esteem, therefore, are those who report both incompetence in domains of importance and the absence of supportive approval from others.

LIMITATIONS ON THE EXTENT TO WHICH ONE CAN INCREASE THE SUPPORT FROM OTHERS

Given that approval from significant others has such a major impact on self-esteem, and given that for many children and adolescents such support is often not available, it becomes understandable why these individuals suffer from low self-esteem. Yet why are these children and adolescents unable to obtain the needed support? Why is self-enhancing

approval not forthcoming? The answers would appear to lie at the inter-
face of the characteristics of the significant others, as well as attributes of
the children and adolescents themselves. With regard to parental support, there is now a growing literature on various factors, including
parental depression and stressful conditions within the family, that lead
to parents' inability to provide self-enhancing support (see Downey &
Coyne, 1990; Hammen & Goodman-Brown, 1990).

Our own research has identified another critical facet of support,
which we have labeled *conditionality* (Harter, Marold, & Whitesell, 1992).
Conditionality of support is defined as the extent to which one feels that
support is only forthcoming if one meets high parental or peer standards; we have contrasted it to unconditional positive regard (see Rogers
& Dymond, 1954), in which one is loved or supported for who one is as a
person, not for whether one fulfills the expectations of others. Level of
support and conditionality of support are correlated with one another,
such that parents and peers who provide little support typically adopt
the stance that they will only offer their support contingent upon the
display of behaviors and attitudes that they demand. We have also demonstrated the negative effects of conditionality on self-esteem, however,
when level of support is controlled. At relatively high as well as relatively low levels of support, the more conditional the support, the lower
one's self-esteem. Therefore, we are speculating that conditionality,
even at relatively high levels of support, undermines self-esteem because it does *not* validate or signify approval of the self, but rather
specifies behavioral contingencies through which one can please parents
or peers. As such, it is undoubtedly perceived as controlling rather than
enhancing.

From a behavioral perspective, the contingencies specified by conditional support may well shape the desired performance in question. It is
likely to lead to more negative self-perceptions, however, if the message
to the recipient is that he or she is less worthy as a person for not
performing the behaviors desired by others. This does not imply that
parents, teachers, counselors, and others should avoid the use of contingencies. Rather, the contingencies should specify particular consequences linked to the behavior (e.g., loss of privileges), without deni-
grating the individual's worth as a person. Here one is reminded of the
message that parents are encouraged to give to their child in the face of
the latter's misbehavior: "I'm punishing you because I don't like your
behavior, even though I still love you as my child."

The extent to which a parent or peer engages in conditionality undoubtedly represents, in part, a style that the parent or peer brings to
the relationship. Therefore, the child or adolescent may be at the mercy

of a style that undermines his or her own self-esteem. Conditionality also has as its target, however, particular domains of behavior that are displayed by the child or adolescent, domains in which the parent or peer has specific standards of performance. Hypothetically, then, the child or adolescent has only to meet these standards in order to obtain the needed support that will promote high self-esteem. Why, then, should low self-esteem exist or persist?

Our answer to this question lies in an analysis of the particular domains that peers and parents identify as critical performance arenas for children and adolescents. To obtain such information, we have asked our child and adolescent subjects to rate the importance that classmates and parents attach to the five domains we have explored. Our raters report that *peers* place the most importance on the physical appearance, likability, and athletic competence of others their age. In contrast, our raters report that their *parents* place more importance on the scholastic competence and behavioral conduct of their children. Thus, in order to obtain the approval of one's peers, one has to be good-looking, likable, and athletically talented. In order to obtain the approval of one's parents, one has to excel at schoolwork and manifest commendable conduct.

REVISED MODEL OF THE CAUSES OF SELF-ESTEEM

These links have now been incorporated into our most recent model on the antecedents and correlates of self-esteem (Figure 5). In previous models examining James's and Cooley's formulations (see Harter, 1986, 1987), competence in domains of importance and social support were treated as independent contributors to self-esteem, and thus paths from the self-concept variables to social support were not included. A plausible hypothesis given the importance ratings discussed above, however, is that one's level of competence or adequacy directly influences the amount of support one receives from significant others. Thus, in our most recent model testing, we predicted that the cluster defined by physical appearance, peer likability, and athletic competence would bear a stronger relationship to peer support than to parent support. Conversely, we hypothesized that the cluster comprised of scholastic competence and behavioral conduct would bear a stronger relationship to parent support than to peer support. Employing path-analytic techniques, our findings strongly support the model presented in Figure 5 (see Harter et al., in press), which captures these links between domain-specific

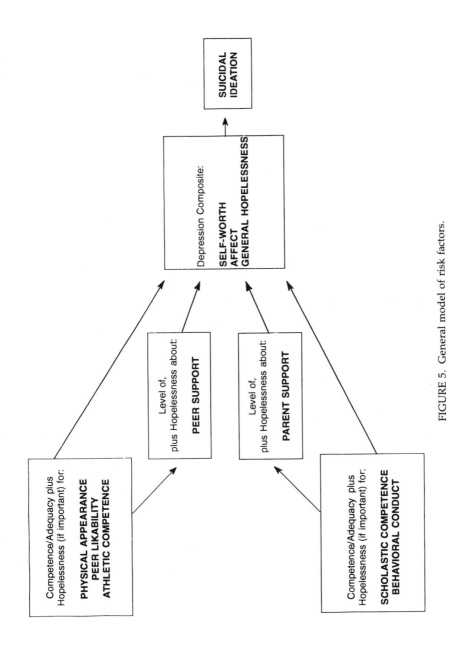

FIGURE 5. General model of risk factors.

103

self-concepts and support from peers and parents. Domain-specific self-concepts and support, in turn, affect global self-esteem.

This more comprehensive model suggests why some individuals develop and maintain low self-esteem. If approval from peers and parents is contingent upon manifesting competence or adequacy in these domains, and if one is unable to meet these standards, then self-enhancing support will not be forthcoming. I have already discussed several reasons why reducing the discrepancy between the importance of these domains and one's feelings of incompetence or inadequacy may be difficult. It is hard to discount the importance of domains that are touted as critical by parents, peers, society, and therefore by the self. Elevating one's actual level of competence may meet with roadblocks, given natural limits on one's ability. Even in the face of effort and some demonstrable and absolute level of improvement, social comparison standards may preclude dramatically enhanced perceptions of one's relative competence or adequacy. Finally, it was noted that constructs about the self are extremely resistant to change, and threats to one's personal theories are likely to cause anxiety-producing disorganization (Epstein, 1991). Thus, factors militating against change in one's domain-specific self-concepts will, in turn, limit the extent to which changes in the level and conditionality of social support are possible. In such circumstances, one's level of self-esteem, therefore, will also remain relatively constant, making it difficult for the low self-esteem individual, in particular, to elevate his or her regard for the self.

WHY SHOULD ONE CARE ABOUT SELF-ESTEEM?

In the past three decades, considerable attention has been devoted to an analysis of the determinants of self-esteem in the lives of children and adolescents (see Coopersmith, 1967; Harter, 1986, 1987, 1990; Rosenberg, 1979, 1986; Wylie, 1979). Yet why should one be concerned about self-esteem, unless it can be demonstrated that self-esteem plays a role in individuals' lives—unless we can demonstrate that it performs some critical function? What are some likely candidates? What, of any significance, might self-esteem influence? A major candidate is one's mood, along the dimension of cheerful to depressed. Recent theory and research have placed increasing emphasis on cognitions that give rise to or accompany depression; cognitions involving the self have found particular favor.

There is clear historical precedent for including negative self-evaluations as one of a constellation of symptoms experienced in depression, beginning with Freud's observations (1968) of the low self-esteem displayed by adults suffering from depressive disorders. Those within the psychoanalytic tradition have continued to accord low self-esteem a central role in depression (Bibring, 1953; Blatt, 1974). More recently, a number of theorists who have addressed the manifestations of depression in children and adolescents, as well as in adults, have focused heavily on cognitive components involving the self. For example, attention has been drawn to the role of self-deprecatory ideation and hopelessness in depression (Abramson, Metalsky, & Alloy, 1989; Baumeister, 1990; Beck, 1975; Hammen & Goodman-Brown, 1990; Kovacs & Beck, 1977, 1978, 1986), to attributional style (Abramson, Seligman, & Teasdale, 1986; Nolen-Hoeksema, Girgus, & Seligman, 1986; Seligman, 1975; Seligman & Peterson, 1986) and to cognitive and sociocognitive influences and self-discrepancies (Baumeister, 1990; Higgins, 1987, 1989; Kaslow, Rehm, & Siegel, 1984; McCauley, Mitchell, Burke, & Moss, 1988). Higgins's work is particularly relevant, as he finds that discrepancies between what one would *like* to be and what one *perceives* oneself to be produce such dejection-related emotions as depression.

My colleagues and I consistently find that among older children and adolescents, self-esteem is highly related to affect along a continuum of cheerful to depressed (with correlations ranging from .72 to .80). These findings are consistent with those of other investigators (Battle, 1987; Beck, 1975; Kaslow et al., 1984). Of particular relevance to this chapter is our finding that those older children and adolescents reporting low self-esteem consistently report depressed affect (Renouf & Harter, 1990). Thus, the two causal constructs in our model, competence in domains of importance and social support, not only serve to influence one's level of self-esteem, but provoke a powerful emotional reaction that, for the low self-esteem child or adolescent, results in a chronic mood state of depression.

Following the lead of Beck (1967, 1975, 1987) and his colleagues (Kovacs & Beck, 1977, 1978), we further broadened our network to include hopelessness, because hopelessness and helplessness have now been clearly implicated in depressive reactions (see also Seligman, 1975). We have found self-esteem and affect to be highly correlated not only to each other, but to general hopelessness as well. These three variables are so highly related that it is impossible statistically to model their sequence or directionality. As a result, these three variables have been combined in our most recent model (Figure 5) and are labeled the *depression composite*. For the interested reader, we have determined, through interview procedures into the phenomenological experience of these components, that some adolescents report that low self-esteem precedes or causes their depressive reaction, whereas others report that depressed affect occurs first and then ushers in feelings of low self-esteem (Harter & Marold, 1991; Harter, Marold, & Jackson, 1991).

As Figure 5 indicates, we have extended our inquiry to suicidal ideation. The incidence of suicide among older children and adolescents has tripled in recent decades, leading to efforts to identify the determinants of this major mental health threat to our youth (see Maris, 1985; Pfeffer, 1986, 1988). Evidence to date reveals a constellation of social/psychological correlates that are predictive of suicidal behaviors, including the variables in our model, namely: lack of social support, low self-esteem, depressed affect, and hopelessness (see Baumeister, 1990; Carlson & Cantwell, 1982; Cicchettit & Schneider-Rosen, 1986; Pfeffer, 1986; Pfeffer, Conte, Plutchick & Jerrett, 1979; Rutter, 1988; Rutter, Izard, & Reed, 1985).

From a developmental perspective, these particular risk factors become increasingly salient as one moves into adolescence (see Emery, 1983). Self-awareness, self-consciousness, introspectiveness and preoccupation with one's self-image dramatically increase (see review by Harter, 1990). Self-esteem becomes more vulnerable (Rosenberg, 1986), and adolescents become more aware of the relationship between self-esteem, social support, and depressed affect (Harter, Marold, & Jackson, 1991). With regard to the support system, peer approval becomes more critical (Brown, 1990; Savin-Williams & Berndt, 1990). Although young adolescents are beginning to make bids for autonomy from parents, they are nevertheless struggling to remain connected (Cooper, Grotevant, & Condon, 1983; Grotevant & Cooper, 1986; Steinberg, 1990), and thus parent support continues to be critical. Depressive symptomatology itself increases in adolescence (see Cantor, 1987; Carlson & Cantwell, 1982; Hawton, 1986; Pfeffer, 1988; Shaffer, 1974, 1985; Shaffer & Fischer, 1981).

In extending our model to include suicidal ideation, my colleagues and I have begun to address the links between these constructs, including self-esteem, in asking the question of what provokes many youths to consider terminating their lives. What cognitive and socioemotional processes conspire to convince an adolescent that life is not worth living? What role do self-representations play in this intrapsychic plot, which has such a potentially tragic outcome? What features of adolescents' socialization histories cause them to question their worth as a person and the worth of their lives?

The sequential model in Figure 5 provides a number of clues. Feelings of incompetence or inadequacy with regard to one's appearance and one's likability, domains judged important to the self as well as to one's peers, lead to lack of peer support. Both of these affect the depression composite, leading to low self-esteem, depressed affect, and general hopelessness. Feelings of scholastic incompetence, along with inadequacy with regard to one's behavioral conduct, provoke lack of parent support; both also influence the depression composite. The constellation of low self-esteem, depressed affect, and hopelessness, in turn, provoke many to consider suicide as a solution, as a form of escape from the painful cognitions and affects concerning the self and the reactions of others (see also Baumeister, 1990).

The following poignant self-disclosure by one of the adolescents in our studies provides a personal cameo of the model that has evolved in our research:

> I look in the mirror and most days I don't like what I see, I don't like how I look, I don't like myself as a person. So I get depressed, bummed out. Plus, my family has rejected me, and that makes me feel pretty lousy about myself. My mother is really on my case because I'm not living up to what she wants me to be. If I get A's in school, she's nice and is proud of me, but if I don't, she doesn't approve of me; you could say how she treats me is conditional on how I do. Mostly she tells me I'm a failure, and I'm beginning to believe it. Doing well in school has always been important to me, but now I feel like I'll never amount to anything. There's no way I'll ever be able to please her; it's pretty hopeless. I don't get much support from other kids, either. I probably never will, because I'm an introvert, I don't even try to make friends. So a lot of the time I get depressed, really bummed out. I feel so depressed that I often think about just killing myself. Life is worthless. But so is death. So what's the use?

Our adolescent narrator identifies each of the features in our sequential process model that predispose him to thought of suicide. He is dissatisfied with his appearance (his outer self), leading him to denigrate himself as a person, to question his essential worth as a human being. As an introvert, he questions his likability, acknowledging that he receives little support from peers. He is dissatisfied with his scholastic performance, a domain that he values—as does his mother, who considers him a failure. He has begun to internalize his mother's view, leading him to devalue himself further. Interestingly, he labels her reactions, which contribute to his feelings of worthlessness, as "conditional." This constellation of precursors ushers in very intense feelings of depression and hopelessness. The toll exacted is tortuous, as he wrestles with the question of whether to to kill himself and with the uselessness of both his life and possible death.

IS LOW SELF-ESTEEM AMENABLE TO CHANGE?

The self-disclosures of adolescents experiencing such a constellation of perceptions of self and others are painful to witness, particularly if one has doubts about their modifiability. Yet from a mental health perspective, it is essential that the field develops intervention strategies that will prevent depression and the tragic loss of life among such youths. What are the implications of our research in this regard? Is low self-esteem, in particular, amenable or resistant to change? There are those (e.g., Epstein, 1991) who have emphasized the stability of such personal constructs, arguing that low self-esteem individuals are reluctant to modify or abandon these seemingly maladaptive beliefs. Our own position is somewhat more sanguine, based upon our findings revealing patterns of change. In fact, during the formative developmental periods of later childhood and adolescence, self-concept change, if not volatility, is relatively common (see Rosenberg, 1986).

A model identifying the determinants of self-esteem has the potential for not only predicting one's level of self-esteem at any given point in time, but for specifying interventions that may lead to such modifications in self-esteem. Although childhood experiences, particularly approvals that validate the self, are critical to the establishment of one's initial level of self-esteem (Harter, 1987, 1990), the self is not set in psychological cement; that is, alterations in the identified determinants should produce changes in one's level of self-esteem. Therefore, building upon our model derived from the formulations of James and Cooley, changes in competence for domains judged important, as well as shifts in approval or disapproval from significant others, should lead to corresponding changes in self-esteem.

Our own longitudinal findings demonstrate that over a one-year period in the lives of older children and adolescents, one-third to one-half of the individuals manifest significant self-esteem changes. The typical pattern is for three groups to be identified: those who show substantial gains in self-esteem; those who display significant decreases in self-esteem; and those who manifest no change, whose self-esteem remains stable over time (see Harter, 1986).

Moreover, we have demonstrated that the two determinants derived from James and Cooley (competence in domains of importance and approval from significant others, respectively) are directly related to changes in self-esteem. Those whose self-esteem increases over time show corresponding increases in competence in domains deemed important (and/or decreases in the importance of domains in which one is inadequate), as well as enhanced support from significant others. Conversely, those whose self-esteem decreases over time show corresponding decreases in competence and support. Finally, as anticipated, those reporting no change in self-esteem also report no change in either competence or support.

In exploring these issues, our research has found that self-esteem change is most likely to occur during times of transition—for example, the shift from an elementary to a junior high or middle school (Harter, 1986), or the transition from high school to college (Harter & Johnson, 1991). A reevaluation of one's self-esteem is more likely during such educational transitions, because they typically bring with them (a) changes in one's perceptions of competence, given new developmental tasks to be mastered and new reference groups with whom one compares the self; (b) alterations in one's hierarchy of aspirations concerning which domains are the most important in the new environment; and (c) the need to establish new social networks that will come to serve as sources of approval or disapproval. Thus, changes in one's environment set the stage for changes in one's self-theory, leading to increases in self-esteem for some individuals and decreases for those moving into a less favorable setting.

These observations may seem somewhat at odds with earlier suggestions concerning the plight of the low self-esteem child or adolescent whose feelings of worthlessness may be difficult to elevate. There are certainly numerous factors militating against self-esteem increases for youths handicapped by the lack of natural abilities or attributes in the face of harsh social comparison standards, by a difficult temperamental style, and/or by a social environment composed of neglecting or disapproving significant others. To the extent that such a situation remains constant, low self-esteem will inevitably persist. Conscious intervention efforts to reduce the discrepancy between competence and importance, however, and to provide support that validates the self or propitious alterations in the child's environment toward these same ends, can lead to increases in self-esteem if the individual is still open and motivated to change.

Our findings suggest that there are certain ranges of scores that are more amenable to change than others. Older children and adolescents with the very lowest levels of self-esteem (between 1.0 and 1.75 on our 4-point scale) are the least likely to show gains, given dramatically large competence/importance discrepancies and exceedingly low levels of support. Those low self-esteem individuals within the 2.0 to 2.5 range (still below the midpoint) are more likely to have the potential for self-esteem enhancement if placed in more favorable environments that foster the attributes they do possess and that provide validating, less conditional approval.

SUMMARY

Theorists have increasingly emphasized that the self is a theory—a cognitive construction, functionally designed to assimilate the data of reality in a manner designed to maintain or provoke high self-esteem for the individual. Yet the presence of numerous individuals professing low self-esteem causes us to ask what has gone awry to disrupt the protective nature of the self system. In addressing this question, our model of the antecedents of self-esteem, derived from the formulations of James and Cooley, serves as a conceptual and empirical backdrop. The findings from our laboratory clearly reveal that competence in domains deemed important (from James), as well as approval from significant others (from Cooley and Mead), are highly predictive of self-esteem in older children and adolescents. Thus, the low self-esteem individual is one who feels incompetent or inadequate in domains where success is valued, leading to a large discrepancy between high importance and low competence. Low self-esteem children and adolescents also report low levels of approval, and/or support that is conditional upon meeting the high standards of parents and peers.

For individuals who hold themselves in low regard, self-esteem enhancement may be unlikely given the difficulty of discounting the importance of the domains we have selected (scholastic competence, behavioral conduct, likability, physical appearance, and athletic competence) because they are typically valued by the society, by either parents or peers, and therefore by the self. Physical appearance is by far the most predictive domain, and females in particular, who base their self-esteem on evaluations of appearance, are especially at risk for low self-esteem. Moreover, there may be natural limits that pose challenges to increasing one's adequacy or competence across these domains, as well as roadblocks in the form of harsh standards of social comparison that may preclude one from evaluating the self positively. In addition, characteristic styles of parents or peers, as well as the inability to meet their expectations, may limit the availability of support that validates or enhances the self. Finally, resistance to alterations in one's personal theory concerning others as well as the self may preclude attitudinal changes that are considered threatening to the coherence of one's cognitive construction of reality.

In addressing the question of why one should care about self-esteem, it was noted that low self-esteem individuals are critically at risk for depressive reactions, including suicidal ideation; both constitute a major mental health threat to our youth. My colleagues and I have extended our sequential model, demonstrating pathways from competence/adequacy in domains of importance to a constellation that we have labeled the depression composite, comprising low self-esteem, depressed affect, and general hopelessness. Inadequacy with regard to a cluster of domains that includes appearance, likability, and athletic competence provokes low levels of peer support, and both lead to the combination of low self-esteem, depressed affect, and hopelessness. Inadequacy with regard to a cluster of scholastic competence and behavioral conduct diminishes the level of parent support, and these both also provoke the constellation of depressive reactions. These reactions, in turn, are highly predictive of suicidal ideation.

Despite this rather pessimistic profile, the potential for self-esteem change was also explored. Our own findings reveal that changes in the determinants of self-esteem (competence in domains of importance and social support) produce corresponding changes in self-esteem. Although change appears challenging for those with exceedingly low self-esteem, there is more potential for enhancement among those with moderately low self-esteem, to the extent that the competence/ importance discrepancy can be reduced and more self-enhancing approval can be provided. Thus, a theory-based model holds promise as a framework within which both to understand and possibly to alter the life-threatening low self-esteem that plagues many of our youth.

ACKNOWLEDGMENTS

Support for the research reported in this chapter was provided by NICHD and the Grant Foundation.

REFERENCES

Abramson, L. Y., Metalsky, G. I., & Alloy, L. B. (1989). Hopelessness depression: A theory-based subtype of depression. *Psychological Review, 96,* 358–372.

Abramson, L. Y., Seligman, M. E. P., & Teasdale, J. D. (1986). Learned helplessness in humans: Critique and reformulation. In J. C. Coyne (Ed.), *Essential papers on depression.* New York: New York University Press.

Allgood-Merten, B., Lewinsohn, P. M., & Hops R. (1990). Sex differences and adolescent depression. *Journal of Abnormal Psychology, 99,* 55–63.

Allport, G. W. (1961). *Pattern and growth in personality.* New York: Holt, Rinehart & Winston.

Bartlett, F. C. (1932). *Remembering.* Cambridge, MA: Cambridge University Press.

Battle, J. (1987). Relationship between self-esteem and depression among children. *Psychological Reports, 60,* 1187–1190.

Baumeister, R. F. (1990). Suicide as escape from self. *Psychological Review, 97,* 90–113.

Beck, A. T. (1967). *Depression: Clinical, experimental and theoretical aspects.* New York: Hoeber.

Beck, A. T. (1975). *Depression: Causes and treatments.* Philadelphia: University of Pennsylvania Press.

Beck, A. T. (1987, May). *Hopelessness as a prediction of ultimate suicide.* Paper presented at the joint meeting of the American Association of Suicidology and the International Association for Suicide Prevention, San Francisco.

Bibring, E. (1953). The mechanism of depression. In P. Greenacre (Ed.), *Affective disorders: Psychoanalytic contribution to their study.* New York: International Universities Press.

Blatt, S. J. (1974). Levels of object representation in anaclitic and introjective depression. *Psychoanalytic Study of the Child, 29*, 107–157.

Brim, O. G. (1976). Life span development of the theory of oneself: Implications for child development. In H. W. Reese (Ed.), *Advances in child development and behavior, vol. 11.* New York: Academic Press.

Brown, B. (1990). Peer groups and peer cultures. In S. S. Feldman & G. R. Elliot (Eds.), *At the threshold: The developing adolescent* (pp. 171–196). Cambridge, MA: Harvard University Press.

Bynner, J. M., O'Malley, P. M., & Bachman, J. C. (1981). Self-esteem and delinquency revisited. *Journal of Youth and Adolescence, 10*, 407–441.

Cantor, P. (1987). *Young people in crisis: How you can help.* Film presentation of the National Committee on Youth Suicide Prevention and American Association of Suicidology, in consultation with Harvard Medical School, Department of Psychiatry, Cambridge Hospital.

Carlson, G. A., & Cantwell, D. P. (1982). Suicidal behavior and depression in children and adolescents. *Journal of the American Academy of Child Psychiatry, 21*, 361–368.

Carlson, G. A., & Gerber, J. (1986). Developmental issues in the classification of depression in children. In M. Rutter, C. E. Izard, & P. B. Read (Eds.), *Depression in young people: Developmental and clinical perspectives* (pp. 399–434). New York: Guilford.

Cicchetti, D., & Schneider-Rosen, K. (1986). An organizational approach to childhood depression. In M. Rutter, C. E. Izard, & P. Read (Eds.), *Depression in young people: Clinical and developmental perspectives* (pp. 71–134). New York: Guilford.

Cooley, C. H. (1902). *Human nature and the social order.* New York: Scribner's.

Cooper, C. R., Grotevant, H. D., & Condon, S. M. (1983). Individuality and connectedness: Both father and adolescent identity formation and role taking skills. In H. D. Grotevant & C. R. Cooper (Eds.), *Adolescent development in the family: New directions for child development.* San Francisco: Jossey-Bass.

Coopersmith, S. (1967). *The antecedents of self-esteem.* San Francisco, CA: W. H. Freeman.

Damon, W., & Hart, D. (1988). *Self understanding in childhood and adolescence.* New York: Cambridge University Press.

Downey, G., & Coyne, J. C. (1990). Children of depressed parents: An integrative review. *Psychological Bulletin, 108*, 50–76.

Elkind, D. (1979). Growing up faster. *Psychology Today, 12*, 38–45.

Emery, P. E. (1983). Adolescent depression and suicide. *Adolescence, 18*, 245–258.

Epstein, S. (1973). The self-concept revisited, or a theory of a theory. *American Psychologist, 28*, 405–416.

Epstein, S. (1981). The unity principle versus the reality and pleasure principles, or the tale of the scorpion and the frog. In M. D. Lynch, A. A. Norem-Hebeisen, & K. Gergen (Eds.), *Self concept: Advances in theory and research.* Cambridge, MA: Ballinger.

Epstein, S. (1991). Cognitive-experiential self theory: Implications for developmental psychology. In M. R. Gunnar & L. A. Sroufe (Eds.), *Self processes and development: The Minnesota symposium on child development*, vol. 23. Hillsdale, NJ: Lawrence Erlbaum.

Epstein, S., & Erskine, N. (1983). The development of personal theories of reality. In D. Magnusson & V. L. Allen (Eds.), *Human development: An interactional perspective.* New York: Academic Press.

Fischer, K. W. (1980). A theory of cognitive development: The control and construction of hierarchies of skills. *Psychological Review, 87*, 477–531.

Freud, S. (1968). Mourning and melancholia. In J. Strachey (Ed.). *The standard edition of the complete works of Sigmund Freud* (Vol. 14). London: Hogarth Press (Original work published in 1917).

Furman, W. (1989). The development of children's social networks. In D. Belle (Ed.), *Children's social networks and social supports.* New York: John Wiley.

Garner, D. M., Garfinkel, P. E., Schwartz, D., & Thompson, M. (1980). Cultural expectations of thinness in women. *Psychological Reports, 47,* 483–491.

Glick, M., & Zigler, E. (1985). Self-image: A cognitive-developmental approach. In R. Leahy (Ed.), *The development of the self.* New York: Academic Press.

Greenwald, A. G. (1980). The totalitarian ego: Fabrication and revision of personal history. *American Psychologist, 7,* 603–618.

Grotevant, H. D., & Cooper, C. R. (1986). Individuation in family relationships. *Human Development, 29,* 83–100.

Hammen, C., & Goodman-Brown, T. (1990). Self-schemas and vulnerability to specific life stress in children at risk for depression. *Cognitive Therapy and Research, 14,* 215–227.

Hammen, C., Burge, D., & Stansbury, K. (1990). Relationship of mother and child variables to child outcomes in a high-risk sample: A causal modeling analysis. *Developmental Psychology, 26,* 24–30.

Harter, S. (1982). The Perceived Competence Scale for Children. *Child Development, 53,* 87–97.

Harter, S. (1983). Developmental perspectives on the self-system. In E. M. Hetherington (Ed.), *Handbook of child psychology, vol. 4: Socialization, personality, and social development* (pp. 275–386). New York: John Wiley.

Harter, S. (1985a). *The Self-Perception Profile for Children* (manual). Denver, CO: University of Denver.

Harter, S. (1985b). *The Social Support Scale for Children and Adolescents* (manual). Denver, CO: University of Denver.

Harter, S. (1986). Processes underlying the construction, maintenance, and enhancement of the self-concept in children. In J. Suls & A. G. Greenwald (Eds.), *Psychological perspectives on the self,* vol. 3 (pp. 137–181). Hillsdale, NJ: Lawrence Erlbaum.

Harter, S. (1987). The determinants and mediational role of global self-worth in children. In N. Eisenberg (Ed.), *Contemporary issues in developmental psychology* (pp. 219–242). New York: John Wiley.

Harter, S. (1989). Causes, correlates and the functional role of global self-worth: A life-span perspective. In J. Kolligan & R. Sternberg (Eds.), *Perceptions of competence and incompetence across the life span* (pp. 43–70). New York: Springer-Verlag.

Harter, S. (1990). Adolescent self and identity development. In S. S. Feldman & G. R. Elliot (Eds.), *At the threshold: The developing adolescent* (pp. 352–387). Cambridge, MA: Harvard University Press.

Harter, S., & Johnson, C. (1991). *Patterns of self-esteem change during the transition to college.* Unpublished manuscript, University of Denver.

Harter, S., & Marold, D. B. (1991). A model of the determinants and mediational role of self-worth: Implications for adolescent depression and suicidal ideation. In G. Goethals & J. Strauss (Eds.), *The self: An interdisciplinary approach.* New York: Springer-Verlag.

Harter, S., Marold, D., & Jackson, B. (1991). *The directionality of the link between self-esteem and depressed affect as experienced by adolescents.* Paper presented at the Society for Research in Child Development, Seattle, WA.

Harter, S., Marold, D. B., & Whitesell, N. R. (1992). A model of psychosocial risk factors leading to suicidal ideation in young adolescents. *Development and Psychopathology 4,* 167–188.

Harter, S., & Waters, P. (1991). *Correlates of the directionality of perceived physical appearance and global self-worth.* Unpublished manuscript, University of Denver.

Hatfield, E., & Sprecher, S. (1986). *Mirror, mirror: The importance of looks in everyday life.* Albany: State University of New York Press.

Hawton, K. (1986). *Suicide and attempted suicide among children and adolescents.* Beverly Hills, CA: Sage.

Heatherton, T. F., & Baumeister, R. F. (1991). Binge eating as escape from self-awareness. *Psychological Bulletin, 110,* 86–108.

Higgins, E. T. (1987). Self-discrepancy: Theory relating self and affect. *Psychological Review, 94,* 319–340.

Higgins, E. T. (1989). Self-discrepancy theory: What patterns of self-beliefs cause people to suffer? In L. Berkowitz (Ed.), *Advances in experimental social psychology,* vol. 22. New York: Academic Press.

Higgins, E. T. (1991). Development of self-regulatory and self-evaluative processes: Costs, benefits, and trade-offs. In M. R. Gunnar & L. A. Sroufe (Eds.), *Self processes in development: Twenty-third Minnesota Symposium on Child Psychology.* Hillsdale, NJ: Lawrence Erlbaum.

James, W. (1892). *Psychology: The briefer course.* New York: Henry Holt.

Junkin, L., Harter, S., & Whitesell, N. R. (1991). *Correlates of global self-worth among normally achieving, learning disabled, and behaviorally disordered adolescents.* Unpublished manuscript, University of Denver.

Kaplan, H. B. (1975). *Self attitudes and deviant behavior.* Pacific Palisades, CA: Goodyear.

Kaslow, N. J., Rehm, L. P., & Siegel, A. W. (1984). Social-cognitive and cognitive correlates of depression in children. *Journal of Abnormal Child Psychology, 12,* 605–620.

Kelly, G. A. (1955). *The psychology of personal constructs.* New York: W. W. Norton.

Kendall, P. C., Cantwell, D. P., & Kazdin, A. E. (1989). Depression in children and adolescents: Assessment issues and recommendations. *Cognitive Therapy and Research, 13,* 109–146.

Kovacs, M., & Beck, A. T. (1977). An empirical-clinical approach towards a definition of childhood depression. In J. G. Schulterbrandt & A. Raskin (Eds.), *Depression in childhood: Diagnosis, treatment, and conceptual models.* New York: Raven.

Kovacs, M., & Beck, A. T. (1978). Maladaptive cognitive structures in depression. *American Journal of Psychiatry, 135,* 525–533.

Kovacs, M., & Beck, A. T. (1986). Maladaptive cognitive structures in depression. In J. C. Coyne (Ed.), *Essential papers on depression.* New York: New York University Press.

Langlois, J. H. (1981). Beauty and the beast: The role of physical attractiveness in the development of peer relations and social behavior. In S. S. Brehm, S. M. Kassin, & F. X. Gibbons (Eds.), *Developmental social psychology: Theory and research.* New York: Oxford University Press.

Lecky, P. (1945). *Self-consistency: A theory of personality.* New York: Island.

Lynch, M. D. (1981). Self-concept development in childhood. In M. D. Lynch, A. A. Norem-Hebeisen & K. Gergen (Eds.), *Self concept: Advances in theory and research.* Cambridge, MA: Ballinger.

Maccoby, E., & Martin, J. (1983). Socialization in the context of the family: Parent-child interaction. In E. M. Heatherington (Ed.), *Handbook of child psychology,* vol. 4: *Socialization, personality and social development.* New York: John Wiley.

Maris, R. (1985). The adolescent suicide problem. *Suicide and Life Threatening Behavior, 15,* 91–100.

Markus, H. (1980). The self in thought and memory. In D. M. Wegner & R. R. Vallacher, (Eds.), *The self in social psychology.* New York: Oxford University Press.

Markus, H., & Nurius, P. (1986). Possible selves. *American Psychologist, 41,* 954–969.

McCauley, E., Mitchell, J. R., Burke, P., & Moss, S. (1988). Cognitive attributes of depression in children and adolescents. *Journal of Consulting and Clinical Psychology, 56*, 903–908.

Mead, G. H. (1934). *Mind, self, and society.* Chicago: University of Chicago Press.

Nolen-Hoeksema, S. (1987). Sex differences in unipolar depression: Evidence and theory. *Psychological Bulletin, 101*, 259–282.

Nolen-Hoeksema, S., Girgus, J. S., & Seligman, M. E. P. (1986). Learned helplessness in children: A longitudinal study of depression, achievement, and explanatory style. *Journal of Personality and Social Psychology, 51*, 435–442.

Pfeffer, C. R. (1986). *The suicidal child.* New York: Guilford.

Pfeffer, C. R. (1988). Risk factors associated with youth suicide: A clinical perspective. *Psychiatric Annals, 18*, 652–656.

Piaget, J. (1965). *The child's conception of the world.* Paterson, NJ: Littlefield, Adams.

Renick, M. J., & Harter, S. (1989). Impact of social comparisons on the developing self-perceptions of learning disabled students. *Journal of Educational Psychology, 81*(4), 631–638.

Renouf, A. G., & Harter, S. (1990). Low self-worth and anger as components of the depressive experience in young adolescents. *Development and Psychopathology, 2*, 293–310.

Rogers, C. R. (1951). *Client-centered therapy.* Boston, MA: Houghton Mifflin.

Rogers, C. R., & Dymond, R. (1954). *Psychotherapy and personality change.* Chicago: University of Chicago Press.

Rosenberg, M. (1979). *Conceiving the self.* New York: Basic Books.

Rosenberg, M. (1986). Self-concept from middle childhood through adolescence. In J. Suls & A. G. Greenwald (Eds.), *Psychological perspectives on the self, vol. 3* (pp. 107–136). Hillsdale, NJ: Lawrence Erlbaum.

Ruble, D. (1983). The development of social comparison processes and their role in achievement-related self-socialization. In T. Higgins, D. Ruble, & W. Hartup (Eds.), *Social cognitive development: A social-cultural perspective.* Cambridge, MA: Cambridge University Press.

Rutter, M. (1988). Epidemiological approaches to developmental psychopathology. *Archives of General Psychiatry, 45*, 486–495.

Rutter, M., Izard, C., & Read, P. (Eds.). (1985). *Depression in childhood: Developmental perspectives.* New York: Guilford.

Sarbin, T. R. (1962). A preface to a psychological analysis of the self. *Psychological Review, 59*, 11–22.

Savin-Williams, R. C., & Berndt, T. (1990). Friendship during adolescence. In S. S. Feldman & G. R. Elliot (Eds.), *At the threshold: The developing adolescent.* Cambridge, MA: Harvard University Press.

Seligman, M. E. P. (1975). *Helplessness: On depression, development, and death.* San Francisco: Freeman.

Seligman, M. E. P., & Peterson, C. (1986). A learned helplessness perspective on childhood depression: Theory and research. In M. Rutter, C. E. Izard, & P. B. Read (Eds.), *Depression in young people: Developmental and clinical perspectives* (pp. 223–249). New York: Guilford.

Shaffer, D. (1974). Suicide in childhood and early adolescence. *Journal of Child Psychology and Psychiatry, 15*, 275–291.

Shaffer, D. (1985). Depression and suicide in children and adolescents. In M. Rutter & L. Hersov (Eds.), *Child and adolescent psychiatry: Modern approaches* (2nd ed.). Oxford: Blackwell Scientific.

Shaffer, D., & Fischer, P. (1981). The epidemiology of suicide in children and young adolescents. *Journal of the American Academy of Child Psychiatry, 21*, 545–565.

Shrauger, J. S., & Schoeneman, T. J. (1979). Symbolic interactionist view of self-concept: Through the looking glass darkly. *Psychological Bulletin, 86* (3), 549–573.

Simmons, R. G., & Blyth, D. A. (1987). *Moving into adolescence: The impact of pubertal change and social context.* New York: Aldine DeGruyter.

Sroufe, L. A., & Rutter, M. (1985). The domain of developmental psychopathology. *Child Development, 55,* 17–29.

Steinberg, L. (1990). Autonomy, conflict, and harmony in the family. In S. S. Feldman & G. R. Elliot (Eds.), *At the threshold: The developing adolescent* (pp. 255–276). Cambridge, MA: Harvard University Press.

Suls, J., & Sanders, G. (1982). Self-evaluation via social comparison: A development analysis. In I. Wheeler (Ed.), *Review of personality and social psychology* (Vol. 3). Beverly Hills, CA: Sage.

Swann, W. B., Jr. (1983). Self-verification: Bringing social reality into harmony with the self. In J. Suls & A. Greenwald (Eds.), *Social psychological perspectives on the self* (Vol. 2, pp. 33–66). Hillsdale, NJ: Lawrence Erlbaum.

Taylor, S. E., & Brown, J. D. (1988). Illusion and well-being: A social psychological perspective on mental health. *Psychological Bulletin, 103,* 193–210.

Tesser, A. (1988). Toward a self-evaluation maintenance model of social behavior. In L. Berkowitz (Ed.), *Advances in experimental social psychology; Social psychological studies of the self: Perspectives & programs* (Vol. 21). New York: Academic Press.

Tesser, A., & Campbell, J. (1983). Self-definition and self-evaluation maintenance. In J. Suls & A. G. Greenwald (Eds.), *Psychological perspectives on the self* (Vol. 2, pp. 1–32). Hillsdale, NJ: Lawrence Erlbaum.

Wylie, R. C. (1979). *The self concept (Vol. 2): Theory and research on selected topics.* Lincoln, NE: University of Nebraska Press.

Zumpf, C. L., & Harter, S. (1989). *Mirror, mirror on the wall: The relationship between appearance and self-worth in adolescent males and females.* Paper presented at the annual meeting for the Society for Research in Child Development, Kansas City, Missouri.

Zumpf, C. L., & Harter, S. (1991). *Social comparison processes among the gifted.* Unpublished manuscript, University of Denver.

Chapter 6

MOTIVATIONAL CONFLICT AND THE SELF

THE DOUBLE-BIND OF LOW SELF-ESTEEM

Jonathon D. Brown

Students of the self have long recognized two motives that influence self-processes. On the one hand, people want to feel good about themselves. They want to believe that they are competent, worthy, and loved by others. This desire for self-enhancement is regarded as so fundamental to human functioning that it was dubbed the "master sentiment" by William McDougall (1932) and "the basic law of human life" by the renowned anthropologist Ernest Becker (1971). Many other figures of historical (e.g., Allport, 1943; Cooley, 1902; Mead, 1934) and contemporary (e.g., Baumeister, 1991; Greenwald, 1980; Schlenker, 1985; Steele, 1988; Tesser, 1988) prominence have endorsed the belief that a drive to achieve a positive self-image is, in the words of William James (1890), a direct and elementary endowment of human nature.

Alongside the self-enhancement motive stands a drive toward self-consistency. Self-consistency refers to a desire to protect the self-concept against change (Lecky, 1945; Swann, 1983, 1987). Once formed, thoughts

Jonathon D. Brown • Department of Psychology, NI-25, University of Washington, Seattle, WA 98195.

Self-Esteem: The Puzzle of Low Self-Regard, edited by Roy F. Baumeister. Plenum Press, New York, 1993.

about the self function as conceptual tools; they enable individuals to predict and control important life experiences (Epstein, 1973). For this reason, people become invested in preserving their current self-views. Any experience that challenges or disturbs a person's self-concept is potentially threatening.

Self-enhancement and self-consistency motives operate in concert for people who think well of themselves. That is, for people with high self-esteem, the desire to enhance self-worth is compatible with the need to maintain a positive self-image. The two motives clash, however, among people with low self-esteem. For these individuals, the desire to promote a positive self-image conflicts with the need to protect a negative self-view against change. People with low self-esteem must therefore walk a fine line between these competing motive forces (Brown, Collins, & Schmidt, 1988; Jones, 1973; McFarlin & Blascovich, 1981; Shrauger, 1975; Swann, Griffin, Predmore, & Gaines, 1987).

SELF-ESTEEM, POSITIVE LIFE EVENTS, AND HEALTH

The precarious nature of low self-esteem is revealed by research on positive life events and physical well-being. Although numerous investigations have found that *negative* life experiences are commonly associated with ill health (for reviews, see Jemmott & Locke, 1984; Lazarus & Folkman, 1984), the effect of *positive* life experiences is much less clear. Some studies have found that positive life events impair health, some have found that positive life events reduce the adverse effects of negative events or facilitate well-being, and some have found no effect (Cohen & Hoberman, 1983; Siegel & Brown, 1988; Thoits, 1983a).

In an attempt to bring order to these findings, Brown and McGill (1989) proposed that the impact of positive life events on health is moderated by people's self-esteem levels. In particular, they suggested that positive life events adversely affect people with low self-esteem but do not harm people with high self-esteem. This prediction follows from Brown's identity disruption model of stress (Brown, 1987; Swann & Brown, 1990). According to the model, the pathogenic impact of some significant life changes stems, in part, from their capacity to initiate disturbances in the self-concept.

Identity change is problematic because self-conceptions serve several important functions. Foremost among these is an organizing one. Many theorists have asserted that the self-concept acts largely to organize and guide personal experience (Lecky, 1945; Swann, 1987). According to this view, effective action requires the development of a self-theory (Epstein, 1973) that provides individuals with a perspective from which their own behavior and the behavior of others can be understood. Without such a conceptual system, the world would be a welter of confusion, and meaningful behavior would be impossible (Kelly, 1963).

In more specific terms, at least four functions of firmly held self-conceptions can be delineated: They facilitate the processing of personal information (Markus, 1977); they furnish individuals with a basis for immediate action (Gergen, 1971) and a goal for future behavior (Baumeister, 1986; Markus & Nurius, 1986); they are linked to a heightened sense of existential security (Thoits, 1983b); and they serve an important interpersonal function insofar as others relate to us largely on the basis of the identities we project (Swann, 1987).

Taken together, well-defined and stable conceptions of the self serve many functions and provide many benefits. Individuals experiencing identity confusion are without these benefits. As a consequence, they may encounter a variety of cognitive, motivational, affective, and interpersonal deficits and conflicts (Baumeister, 1986; Erikson, 1956). Ultimately, these adjustive demands may strip the person of resources necessary to fight off illness and disease (Selye, 1956).

Applying these ideas to the domain of positive life changes, the identity disruption model holds that the more a positive life event changes the way a person views the self, the more likely the person should be to develop illness. A reasonable assumption is that favorable life events are more consistent with the self-image of people with high self-esteem than ones with low self-esteem. High self-esteem people are used to thinking of themselves in favorable terms; events of a positive nature should initiate few, if any, disturbances in their self-concept. Consequently, positive life experiences should not place people with high self-esteem at risk for illness, according to the identity disruption model.

This is not the case for people with low self-esteem. Almost by definition, these individuals are unaccustomed to thinking of themselves in positive terms. An accumulation of favorable events may therefore cause disturbances in the self-image of those with low self-esteem. In turn, disturbances in the self-concept should increase the likelihood of illness, according to the identity disruption framework

In an initial test of these ideas, Brown and McGill (1989) had a sample of female high school students complete Rosenberg's self-esteem scale (1965) and a standard life events inventory (Sarason, Johnson, & Siegel, 1978). The life events scale gathered information regarding recent experiences, both positive and negative, in the student's life. These subjects also completed a health checklist developed for use by Brown and Siegel (1988). The health checklist was readministered several months later, and changes in self-reports of illness were examined as a joint function of positive life events and self-esteem.

As anticipated, positive life events were linked with deteriorations in self-reports of health only among low self-esteem subjects. The more positive life events low self-esteem subjects reported experiencing, the more illness they reported during the course of the investigation. For high self-esteem subjects, high levels of positive life events were associated with fewer health complaints. These findings were subsequently replicated and extended in a second study that tracked visits to a medical facility over a 6-month period (Brown & McGill, 1989, Study 2). In this investigation, high levels of positive life events were associated with increased visits to a university health center among college students with low self-esteem but with fewer visits to the health center among college students with high self-esteem.

To summarize, these two investigations suggest that positive life events compromise the physical well-being of people with low self-esteem but not people with high self-esteem. Presumably, this occurs because positive life events are inconsistent with, and initiate disturbances in, the self-image of people with low self-esteem. These disturbances leave low self-esteem people unsure of themselves and without a firm basis for action. In turn, uncertainty (and an attendant loss of feelings of control) places people with low self-esteem at risk for illness.

Though demonstrating that positive events can have negative consequences for people with low self-esteem, Brown and McGill's findings (1989) do not indicate that low self-esteem people *prefer* negative life experiences over positive life experiences. Elsewhere, I have argued that all individuals, regardless of their chronic levels of self-esteem, strive to achieve high feelings of personal worth (Brown et al., 1988; Brown & Gallagher, 1991; Brown & Smart, 1991). Nothing in the data reported by Brown and McGill contradicts this assumption. Instead, the data underscore the extent to which people with low self-esteem must endure a compromise between their desire for self-enhancement and their requirement for self-consistency.

DIRECT VERSUS INDIRECT FORMS OF SELF-ENHANCEMENT

The preceding analysis suggests that the challenge researchers face in understanding the nature of low self-esteem lies in understanding how self-enhancement needs and self-consistency processes combine to influence the behavior of people with low self-esteem. In other words, how do those with low self-esteem manifest their need for self-enhancement in the face of pressures toward maintaining consistent self-views?

One approach to this issue has focussed on indirect forms of self-enhancement. Brown et al. (1988) proposed that, in an effort to satisfy competing demands between self-enhancement desires and the need for self-consistency, low self-esteem people enhance feelings of self-worth indirectly via association with others. This proposition builds on the notion of the extended self, an idea first articulated by William James more than a century ago. James (1890) noted that an interesting feature of the self-concept is its ability to incorporate people and objects that are not directly part of the self.

> A man's SELF is the sum total of all that he CAN call his, not only his body and his psychic powers, but his clothes and his house, his wife and children, his ancestors and friends, his reputation and works, his lands and horses, and yacht and bank-account. All these things give him the same emotions. If they wax and prosper, he feels triumphant; if they dwindle and die away, he feels cast down—not necessarily in the same degree for each thing but in much the same way for all. (pp. 291–292)

The ability of the self-concept to reach beyond the physical self suggests a way that low self-esteem people may satisfy their desire for self-enhancement without violating their requirement for self-consistency. Specifically, they may do so by embellishing the qualities of those with whom they share a connection.

This hypothesis was first tested in an investigation by Brown et al. (1988). These researchers used the minimal intergroup paradigm developed by Tajfel and colleagues (for a review, see Tajfel & Turner, 1986). Adapting this procedure, Brown et al. first arbitrarily divided subjects into two groups based on their alleged propensity to overestimate or underestimate the number of dots in a series of stimulus displays. Each of the groups was then split into two smaller groups, and these smaller groups worked on a group problem-solving task. Thus, there were four groups: two groups of (alleged) overestimators and two groups of (alleged) underestimators. The task was a brainstorming task in which subjects were asked to generate numerous and unusual uses for a fly-swatter.

After the groups had generated their uses, subjects were asked to make comparative evaluations of the groups' answers. Half of the subjects were asked to compare the answers of their own group (i.e., the group they had actively participated in) with an out-group (i.e., a group of the opposite label); the rest of the subjects were asked to compare the answers of an in-group (i.e., a group of the same label, but not the group they had actively participated in) with an out-group.

Brown et al. (1988) anticipated that high self-esteem subjects would engage in direct forms of self-enhancement. In the present context, this would take the form of exaggerating the relative merits of the group in which these subjects had actively participated. This they could do by rating their own group's uses as especially exemplary compared to the uses an out-group had created. A different set of predictions was generated for subjects with low self-esteem. Subjects with low self-esteem were not expected to champion the quality of their own group's work. Instead, they were expected to engage in indirect forms of self-enhancement in which they inflated the merits of the group with which they were associated by name only. Low self-esteem subjects, then, were expected to exaggerate the relative quality of the uses generated by their fellow in-group members but not the quality of the uses generated by the group in which they had been an active participant.

These predictions were confirmed. Group favoritism among high self-esteem subjects was especially pronounced when these subjects compared their own group against an out-group. This is a direct form of self-enhancement insofar as these high self-esteem subjects were glorifying a product they had personally helped create. Low self-esteem subjects showed virtually no favoritism under these conditions. Instead, they showed favoritism only when evaluating the relative quality of the in-group's product. This is an indirect form of self-enhancement insofar as these low self-esteem subjects were lauding a product they had personally played no hand in creating. The entire pattern of findings thus supports the claim that high self-esteem people engage in forms of self-enhancement that directly implicate the self, whereas low self-esteem people seek to enhance self-worth indirectly via their association with others.

A critical assumption underlying this interpretation is that group favoritism stems from a desire to enhance feelings of personal worth. A second study was conducted to examine this issue more closely. Prior to engaging in the brainstorming task, subjects in Study 2 were given positive or negative feedback regarding their group's status. Some subjects were told that it was better to be an overestimator than an underestimator; others were led to believe that the opposite was true. These manipulations were expected to arouse temporarily different needs for self-enhancement. Subjects who had recently had self-esteem threatened through the receipt of negative feedback would presumably be more in need of self-enhancement than those who had recently had self-esteem bolstered through the receipt of positive feedback. Assuming that a desire to enhance self-worth motivates group bias in the minimal intergroup paradigm (Tajfel & Turner, 1986), the tendencies observed in Study 1 were expected to be exacerbated among subjects who had just received negative feedback and attenuated among subjects who had just received positive feedback.

The predicted pattern was observed. There was little evidence of self-enhancing group comparisons, either direct or indirect, among subjects who had received positive feedback. Group favoritism was very apparent, however, among those who had received negative feedback. Moreover, for high self-esteem subjects, this favoritism once again occurred when comparisons were made between one's own group and an out-group; for low self-esteem subjects, favoritism once again occurred when comparisons were made between an in-group and an out-group. These findings provide further evidence that high self-esteem people pursue direct forms of self-enhancement, whereas low self-esteem people favor forms of self-enhancement that do not directly implicate the self.

To summarize, the findings by Brown et al. (1988) suggest that people with low self-esteem seek self-enhancement vicariously via their associations with others. Rather than blowing their own horn, people with low self-esteem glorify those with whom they share some connection or association. Presumably, this strategy enables them to fulfill their desire for self-enhancement without sacrificing their need for self-consistency.

BENEFITS FROM ASSOCIATING WITH EXEMPLARY OTHERS

Although implied by the pattern of findings, the studies by Brown et al. (1988) provided no evidence that people with low self-esteem actually benefit more from their association with superior-performing others. A recent investigation by Brown, Novick, Lord, and Richards (1992 Study 4) provides evidence relevant to this assertion. In the context of an ostensive impression-formation task, female subjects were asked to view photographs of other women (targets). Some of these targets were very attractive; others were unattractive. Independent of the attractiveness manipulation, the psychological relationship between the subject and the target was also experimentally varied. This was accomplished by leading half of the subjects to believe that they shared the same birthday with the woman in the photograph; other subjects were given information indicating that they and the woman in the photograph were not born on the same day. After receiving this information, subjects rated their own attractiveness by answering some items that were embedded in a larger questionnaire.

Leading some subjects to believe that they were born on the same day as the woman in the photograph was intended to infuse a sense of psychological closeness between the subject and the other women (Cialdini & De Nicholas, 1989; Finch & Cialdini, 1989). Once established, feelings of relatedness were expected to lead subjects to take on or assume the characteristics of the other person (see Heider, 1958). Assuming that people with low self-esteem are most apt to seize upon their association with others in an attempt to inflate self-worth, Brown et al. (1992) predicted that low self-esteem subjects would be especially inclined to regard themselves as more attractive when they were subjectively joined with the attractive target. This proved to be the case. Low self-esteem subjects, but not high self-esteem subjects, subsequently rated themselves as more attractive when they believed that they were linked to an attractive person than when they believed they were linked to an unattractive person.

To summarize, it appears that low self-esteem people do derive feelings of self-worth through their associations with others. This suggests that other forms of self-enhancement that do not directly implicate the self may be especially prevalent among low self-esteem people. Cialdini and his associates (Cialdini et al., 1976; Cialdini & Richardson, 1980) have shown that people tend to unite themselves with other people or groups who are superior on some dimension and distance themselves from those who are inferior on some dimension. College students, for example, are more likely to use the pronoun *we* when discussing a football game their university team has won than when talking about a game their team has lost (Cialdini et al., 1976). This tendency is apt to be particularly characteristic of people with low self-esteem. Hero worship, intense national pride, and extreme allegiance to local sports teams may also be more common among low self-esteem people. By extolling the virtues of those with whom they are associated, or emphasizing their connection with those who exemplary in some way, people with low self-esteem appear capable of deriving benefit for their own feelings of self-worth without compromising their need for self-consistency.

COMPARISON WITH OTHER APPROACHES

The analysis presented in this chapter bears on previous accounts of the nature of low self-esteem. Self-enhancement needs have been conceived within a drive-reduction framework (Dittes, 1959; Jones, 1973). From this perspective, the need for self-enhancement increases the longer self-esteem needs go unfulfilled. Because they are chronically low in self-esteem, this position holds that people with low self-esteem experience more powerful needs for self-enhancement than do those with high self-esteem.

Very little support exists for this position. Study after study has found that people with low self-esteem are less, not more, likely to display self-enhancing behaviors than are persons with high self-esteem (for reviews, see Brown, 1991; Taylor & Brown, 1988). The clarity of this evidence strongly suggests that people with low self-esteem do not experience greater needs for self-enhancement than do those with high self-esteem.

The fact that people with low self-esteem are less apt to show signs of self-enhancement raises an alternative possibility: Perhaps people with low self-esteem experience a diminished need for self-enhancement, leading them to be disinterested in enhancing feelings of personal worth (see Alloy & Abramson, 1988 for an elaboration). The evidence to support this claim, however, is also sparse. Consider, for example, the findings reported in Study 2 by Brown et al. (1988). Group favoritism in the minimal intergroup paradigm has been shown to bolster feelings of self-worth (Lemyre & Smith, 1985; Oakes & Turner, 1980). The fact that low self-esteem subjects responded to negative feedback (a temporary threat to self-esteem) by engaging in group favoritism suggests that they were actively attempting to enhance self-worth. This implies that self-enhancement needs are an important source of motivation among people with low self-esteem.

A third possibility is that self-consistency needs overpower self-enhancement needs in people with low self-esteem; this position is similar to one taken by Swann (1983, 1987). Swann assumes that self-enhancement and self-consistency motives jointly influence behavior, but that self-consistency needs dominate. This leads to the prediction that people with low self-esteem prefer maintaining consistent negative self-views over improving feelings of personal worth. Guided by this assumption, Swann and his colleagues have amassed a great deal of evidence detailing ways in which people with low self-esteem maintain their negative self-views (Swann, 1983, 1987).

Though I agree that self-consistency is an important determinant of behavior, I do not believe that self-enhancement motives are subordinate to self-consistency concerns. People with low self-esteem may engage in behaviors that perpetuate their negative self-views, but this does not mean that they *want* to reinforce a negative self-image. Instead, this outcome may represent an unintended consequence of behavior directed toward other goals. Moreover, every year, scores of people with low self-esteem enter psychotherapy, purchase self-help books, or take other steps to improve their feelings of self-worth. These behaviors contradict the notion that people with low self-esteem are content to remain insecure and lacking in confidence. Self-consistency needs, it seems, temper but do not override people's desire to enhance feelings of personal worth.

In contrast to these previous analyses, the position I have outlined in this chapter assumes that people with low self-esteem are subject to the same needs for self-enhancement and self-consistency as are those with high self-esteem. What distinguishes the two self-esteem groups are the characteristic ways in which they try to satisfy these needs. High self-esteem people seek self-enhancement in ways that directly implicate the self; low self-esteem people seek self-enhancement in ways that do not directly involve the self (Brown et al., 1988; Brown et al., 1992).

This approach resembles one taken by Baumeister, Tice, and Hutton (1989). These theorists argued that self-esteem differences incorporate variations in interpersonal style. People with high self-esteem are assertive and risk oriented in social situations; those with low self-esteem are more conservative and risk averse in the interpersonal domain. Differences of this type also emerge under private conditions, when individuals believe they are accountable only to themselves (Brown, 1992; Brown & Gallagher, 1992).

Motivational ambivalence might underlie the conservatism of people with low self-esteem. Caught between an affectively based desire to enhance feelings of self-worth and a cognitively based need to maintain their existing self-conceptions (Shrauger, 1975; Swann et al., 1987), people with low self-esteem must fashion a compromise. This compromise takes the form of a conservative middle ground. From this perspective, the modesty low self-esteem people display represents an equilibrium point held in check by two competing forces (see Lewin, 1935).

CONCLUDING REMARKS

Self-approval is a basic human desire. From the earliest years of life, people embark on a journey to achieve a positive self-image. Yet not everyone achieves this goal. Some people are beset by doubts about themselves. They lack confidence that they can accomplish important life tasks; they agonize over a perceived moral deficiency; they despair over a presumed character flaw. How are we to account for this state of affairs? Do these people lack a desire for self-approval? These questions have occupied researchers who have sought to understand the nature of low self-esteem.

In this chapter, I have argued that all individuals experience a powerful need to enhance their feelings of personal worth, but that these needs are supplemented by a collateral need to maintain self-consistency. People with high self-esteem experience little or no conflict in satisfying these dual imperatives. For these individuals, the need to achieve a positive self-image is strengthened by the complementary need to protect favorable self-views against change.

A different state of affairs exists for people with low self-esteem. For these individuals, self-enhancement needs are countered by a need to maintain negative self-views. The joint impact of these competing motives appears to place low self-esteem people at risk when positive life events are experienced. These opposing forces also appear to lead people with low self-esteem to seek alternative routes to self-enhancement. Indirect forms of self-enhancement represent a suitable compromise. Tying self-worth to the achievements and outstanding qualities of others allows people with low self-esteem to feel good about themselves without drastically undermining their prevailing self-views.

ACKNOWLEDGMENTS

The preparation of this chapter and some of the research reported herein was supported by a Presidential Young Investigator Award from the National Science Foundation (BNS-8958211) and by a grant from the Wellness Behavior Northwest Foundation.

REFERENCES

Alloy, L. B., & Abramson, L. Y. (1988). Depressive realism: Four theoretical perspectives. In L. B. Alloy (Ed.), *Cognitive processes in depression* (pp. 223–265). New York: Guilford.

Allport, G. W. (1943). The ego in contemporary psychology. *Psychological Review, 50,* 451–478.

Baumeister, R. F. (1986). *Identity.* New York: Oxford University Press.

Baumeister, R. F. (1991). *Meanings of life.* New York: Guilford.

Baumeister, R. F., Tice, D. M., & Hutton, D. G. (1989). Self-presentational motivations and personality differences in self-esteem. *Journal of Personality, 57,* 547–579.

Becker, E. (1971). *The birth and death of meaning* (2nd ed.). New York: Macmillan.

Brown, J. D. (1987). *An identity disruption model of stress.* Unpublished manuscript, Southern Methodist University.

Brown, J. D. (1991). Accuracy and bias in self-knowledge. In C. R. Snyder & D. F. Forsyth (Eds.), *Handbook of social and clinical psychology: The health perspective* (pp. 158–178). New York: Pergamon.

Brown, J. D. (1992). *Accuracy and bias in the prediction of task performance: The role of self-esteem.* Manuscript submitted for publication.

Brown, J. D., Collins, R. L., & Schmidt, G. W. (1988). Self-esteem and direct versus indirect forms of self-enhancement. *Journal of Personality and Social Psychology, 55,* 445–453.

Brown, J. D., & Gallagher, F. M. (1992). Coming to terms with failure: Private self-enhancement and public self-effacement. *Journal of Experimental Social Psychology, 28,* 3–22.

Brown, J. D., & McGill, K. L. (1989). The cost of good fortune: When positive life events produce negative health consequences. *Journal of Personality and Social Psychology, 57,* 1103–1110.

Brown, J. D., Novick, N. J., Lord, K. A., & Richards, J. M. (1992). When Gulliver travels: Social context, psychological closeness, and self-appraisals. *Journal of Personality and Social Psychology, 60,* 717–727.

Brown, J. D., & Siegel, J. M. (1988). Exercise as a buffer of life stress: A prospective study of adolescent health. *Health Psychology, 7,* 341–353.

Brown, J. D., & Smart, S. A. (1991). The self and social conduct: Linking self-representations to prosocial behavior. *Journal of Personality and Social Psychology, 60,* 368–375.

Cialdini, R. B., Borden, R. J., Thorne, A., Walker, M. R., Freeman, S., & Sloan, L. R. (1976). Basking in reflected glory: Three (football) field studies. *Journal of Personality and Social Psychology, 34,* 366–375.

Cialdini, R. B., & De Nicholas, M. E. (1989). Self-presentation by association. *Journal of Personality and Social Psychology, 57,* 626–631.

Cialdini, R. B., & Richardson, K. D. (1980). Two indirect tactics of image management: Basking and blasting. *Journal of Personality and Social Psychology, 39,* 406–415.

Cohen, S., & Hoberman, H. (1983). Positive events and social support as buffers of life change stress. *Journal of Applied Social Psychology, 13,* 99–125.

Cooley, C. H. (1902). *Human nature and the social order.* New York: Scribner's.

Dittes, J. E. (1959). Attractiveness of group as a function of self-esteem and acceptance by group. *Journal of Abnormal and Social Psychology, 59,* 77–82.

Epstein, S. (1973). The self-concept revisited: Or a theory of a theory. *American Psychologist, 28,* 404–416.

Erikson, E. H. (1956). The problem of ego-identity. *Journal of the American Psychoanalytic Association, 4,* 56–121.

Finch, J. F., & Cialdini, R. B. (1989). Another indirect tactic of (self-)image management: Boosting. *Personality and Social Psychology Bulletin, 15,* 222–232.

Gergen, K. J. (1971). *The concept of self.* New York: Holt, Rinehart & Winston.

Greenwald, A. G. (1980). The totalitarian ego: Fabrication and revision of personal history. *American Psychologist, 35,* 603–618.

Heider, F. (1958). *The psychology of interpersonal relations.* New York: John Wiley.

James, W. (1890). *The principles of psychology, Vol. 1.* New York: Holt.

Jemmott, J. B., & Locke, S. E. (1984). Psychosocial factors, immunologic mediation, and human susceptibility to infectious diseases: How much do we know? *Psychological Bulletin, 95,* 78–108.

Jones, S. C. (1973). Self- and interpersonal evaluations: Esteem theories versus consistency theories. *Psychological Bulletin, 79,* 185–199.

Kelly, G. A. (1963). *A theory of personality: The psychology of personal constructs.* New York: W. W. Norton.

Lazarus, R. S., & Folkman, S. (1984). *Stress, appraisal, and coping.* New York: Springer.

Lecky, P. (1945). *Self-consistency: A theory of personality.* New York: Island.

Lemyre, L., & Smith, P. M. (1985). Intergroup discrimination and self-esteem in the minimal group paradigm. *Journal of Personality and Social Psychology, 49,* 660–670.

Lewin, K. (1935). *A dynamic theory of personality: Selected papers.* New York: McGraw-Hill.

Markus, H. (1977). Self-schemas and processing information about the self. *Journal of Personality and Social Psychology, 35,* 63–78.

Markus, H., & Nurius, P. (1986). Possible selves. *American Psychologist, 41,* 954–969.

McDougall, W. (1932). *The energies of men.* London: Methuen.

McFarlin, D. B., & Blascovich, J. (1981). Effects of self-esteem and performance feedback on future affective preferences and cognitive expectations. *Journal of Personality and Social Psychology, 40,* 521–531.

Mead, G. H. (1934). *Mind, self, and society.* Chicago: University of Chicago Press.

Oakes, P. J., & Turner, J. C. (1980). Social categorization and intergroup behavior: Does minimal intergroup discrimination make social identity more positive? *European Journal of Social Psychology, 10,* 295–301.

Rosenberg, M. (1965). *Society and the adolescent self-image.* Princeton, NJ: Princeton University Press.

Sarason, I. G., Johnson, J. H., & Siegel, J. M. (1978). Assessing the impact of life changes: Development of the Life Experiences Survey. *Journal of Consulting and Clinical Psychology, 46,* 932–946.

Schlenker, B. R. (1985). Identity and self-identification. In B. R. Schlenker (Ed.), *The self and social life* (pp. 65–99). New York: McGraw-Hill.

Selye, H. (1956). *The stress of life.* New York: McGraw-Hill.

Shrauger, J. S. (1975). Responses to evaluation as a function of initial self-perceptions. *Psychological Bulletin, 82,* 581–596.

Siegel, J. M., & Brown, J. D. (1988). A prospective study of stressful circumstances, illness symptoms, and depressed mood among adolescents. *Developmental Psychology, 24,* 715–721.

Steele, C. M. (1988). The psychology of self-affirmation: Sustaining the integrity of the self. In L. Berkowitz (Ed.), *Advances in experimental social psychology, vol. 21* (pp. 261–302). New York: Academic Press.

Swann, W. B., Jr. (1983). Self-verification: Bringing social reality into harmony with the self. In J. Suls & A. G. Greenwald (Eds.), *Psychological perspectives on the self, vol. 2* (pp. 33–66). Hillsdale, NJ: Lawrence Erlbaum.

Swann, W. B., Jr. (1987). Identity negotiation: Where two roads meet. *Journal of Personality and Social Psychology, 53,* 1038–1051.

Swann, W. B., Jr., & Brown, J. D. (1990). From self to health: Self-verification and identity disruption. In B. Sarason, I. Sarason, & G. Pierce (Eds.), *Social support: An interactional view* (pp. 150–172). New York: John Wiley.

Swann, W. B., Jr., Griffin, J. J., Predmore, S. C., & Gaines, B. (1987). The cognitive-affective crossfire: When self-consistency confronts self-enhancement. *Journal of Personality and Social Psychology, 52,* 881–889.

Tajfel, H., & Turner, J. C. (1986). The social identity theory of intergroup behavior. In S. Worchel & W. Austin (Eds.), *Psychology of intergroup relations* (pp. 7–24). Chicago: Nelson-Hall.

Taylor, S. E., & Brown, J. D. (1988). Illusion and well-being: A social psychological perspective on mental health. *Psychology Bulletin, 103,* 193–210.

Tesser, A. (1988). Toward a self-evaluation maintenance model of social behavior. In

L. Berkowitz (Ed.), *Advances in experimental social psychology, vol. 21* (pp. 181–227). New York: Academic Press.

Thoits, P. A. (1983a). Dimensions of life events that influence psychological distress: An evaluation and synthesis of the literature. In H. B. Kaplan (Ed.), *Psychosocial stress: Trends in theory and research* (pp. 33–103). New York: Academic Press.

Thoits, P. A. (1983b). Multiple identities and psychological well-being: A reformulation and test of the social isolation hypothesis. *American Sociological Review, 48,* 174–187.

CHAPTER 7

SELF-ESTEEM, SELF-PREDICTION, AND LIVING UP TO COMMITMENTS

TODD F. HEATHERTON AND NALINI AMBADY

In this chapter, we examine the role of self-esteem in complex self-regulation. Although high self-esteem generally is associated with superior self-regulation (Bandura, 1989; Taylor, 1989), we present evidence indicating that high self-esteem may interfere with self-regulation when self-esteem is threatened. We propose that an optimal level of self-esteem is important for successfully making and living up to commitments.

THE NEED FOR SELF-REGULATION

Self-regulation occurs when behavior is guided more by internal standards and expectations than by situational contingencies, cues, or guides (Bandura, 1989; Carver & Scheier, 1981; Kirschenbaum, Tomarken, & Humphrey, 1985). Individuals self-regulate when they set their own goals or standards and try to attain these goals and standards

TODD F. HEATHERTON AND NALINI AMBADY • Department of Psychology, Harvard University, 33 Kirkland St., Cambridge, MA 02138.

Self-Esteem: The Puzzle of Low Self-Regard, edited by Roy F. Baumeister. Plenum Press, New York, 1993.

(Scheier & Carver, 1988). Thus, complex self-regulation involves the making and keeping of commitments.

The attainment of goals and keeping of commitments depends upon an accurate knowledge of personal abilities and the setting of realistic goals (Sandelands, Brockner, & Glynn, 1988). Overestimating or underestimating one's abilities can impede self-regulation; a good analogy is the notion of bidding for a building project. The goal is to bid as close to actual costs as is possible, allowing for a modest profit. If one bids too low, the actual costs are likely to surpass the amount bid, resulting in a monetary loss (a striking example of this fallacious bidding strategy recently occurred at William James Hall at Harvard University when an asbestos abatement contractor had to forfeit a $25,000 deposit because the company realized—after winning the bid—that it would lose money if it actually performed the work). On the other hand, bidding too high is likely to result in more realistic competitors being granted the project, again resulting in monetary loss.

Similarly, setting goals that are far beyond one's abilities almost guarantees failure. Consider the apparent demise in the early 1990s of Donald Trump's financial empire. When entrepreneurs try to achieve the fiscally impossible, no degree of personal skill, luck, or persistence is likely to lead to a successful outcome. Trump's business goals may simply not have been viable for him or anyone else, and his risky attempts to achieve such unrealizable goals may have contributed to his monetary troubles. On the other hand, society encourages individuals to strive for superhuman proficiency, and history records many instances of individuals actually achieving what appeared to be objectively impossible. For example, White (1982) notes that many eminent individuals display a resilient sense of self, as observed in their sustained and persistent efforts, that appears impervious to rejection, and Bandura (1989) notes that many famous artists and musicians encountered years of criticism and failure before finally getting acclaim. Yet not all who follow this course succeed, and it remains to be seen whether the pursuit of grandiose goals is a viable strategy for the majority of individuals.

For most people, continued failures are likely to have a negative impact on self-esteem, which may subsequently lessen self-regulatory capacities by interfering with future goal setting and goal attainment, and thereby increasing the likelihood of future failure. Thus, the failure to judge one's abilities or the viability of one's goals contributes to poor self-regulation. Accurate self-knowledge about one's capabilities can indicate whether goals are attainable, and therefore whether a specific course of action is desirable and likely to be successful, or whether it is more efficient to pursue a different course of action.

SELF-ESTEEM AND SELF-REGULATION FAILURE

LOW SELF-ESTEEM (THE LITTLE ENGINE THAT CAN BUT WON'T)

Self-regulation failures among people with low self-esteem are most often related to their tendency to underestimate their capabilities and subsequently to set more humble goals for themselves. By attempting less challenging goals, they attain lesser outcomes (Campbell & Fairey, 1985; Coopersmith, 1967); such behavior must be considered inadequate self-regulation.

Individuals with low self-esteem attempt less challenging goals for a number of reasons. For example, low self-esteem individuals expect to perform worse than do those with high self-esteem (Brockner, 1979; McFarlin & Blascovich, 1981). These negative expectations may cause them to undertake less challenging goals, which they view as being better matched to their abilities. Similarly, low self-esteem individuals lack self-clarity, are less certain about their abilities and skills, and are therefore less confident that their efforts will lead to success (Baum-gardner, 1991; Campbell, 1990). This lack of self-clarity means that they are not sure about what they are capable of, and therefore they play it safe by keeping their aspirations modest.

Individuals with low self-esteem may be motivated to set lower goals for themselves because they are concerned with protecting them-selves from the image-damaging consequences of failure; high self-esteem individuals are more concerned with enhancing their public im-age (Baumeister & Tice, 1985; Baumeister, Tice, & Hutton, 1989). Hence, for self-protection, low self-esteem individuals use behavioral and psy-chological strategies (e.g., self-handicapping or making excuses) to min-imize the impact of failure on their self-image (Tice, 1991). By setting impediments in the way of success and by making excuses, low self-esteem individuals hope to escape public scrutiny about the inadequacy of their performance. At the same time, by setting goals that are easier to attain, they are less likely to fail and to suffer from embarrassment, humiliation, or other injuries to their self-images.

The attributions for behavioral outcomes made by low self-esteem individuals contribute to their motivation to set lower goals in order to minimize the likelihood of failure. Most individuals take credit for their successes and blame external factors for their failures (Cohen, van den Bout, van Vliet, & Kramer, 1989; Kuiper, 1978; Rizley, 1978; Zautra, Guenther, & Chartier, 1985). Low self-esteem individuals, however, are less likely to make these self-serving and self-protective attributions, and they tend to make internal attributions for failure (Fitch, 1970; Ickes &

Layden, 1978; Tennen & Herzberger, 1987). To avoid blaming themselves if they fail, they might set goals that are less demanding but have a high probability of success.

Thus, low self-esteem individuals consistently choose less risky and challenging actions because they are threatened by failure (Josephs, 1990). Failure reinforces the negative self-concept of low self-esteem individuals, partially because they tend to make internal attributions and blame themselves for failure, but also because they may not have the necessary coping strategies to overcome such experiences (Tennen & Herzberger, 1987). Therefore, they do not persist at difficult tasks or at tasks where they might fail (Brockner, 1983; Campbell & Fairey, 1985; Shrauger & Sorman, 1977).

In summary, self-regulation failure among low self-esteem individuals is related to their tendency to set less challenging goals for themselves. This could be because they lack a realistic knowledge of their own abilities, because they lack self-confidence, or because they try to avoid the image-damaging consequences of failure by pursuing and persisting at tasks where they are more likely to succeed.

High Self-Esteem (If the Little Engine Really Can't, It Shouldn't Try)

Individuals with high self-esteem generally undertake more challenging goals than do individuals with low self-esteem (Bandura, 1989). They expect to perform better (Brockner, 1979; McFarlin & Blascovich, 1981), and they usually do perform better than individuals with low self-esteem (Brockner 1979; 1983; Taylor, 1989). This can be considered efficient self-regulation, because a realistic knowledge of their potential capacities enables them to achieve their loftier goals.

Although these ambitions can often lead to superior performance, they are also likely to increase the number of failure experiences. High self-esteem individuals, however, generally use a variety of different methods to cope with such failures, such as making external attributions for failure, increasing their ratings on self-dimensions that are unrelated to the failure experience (Baumeister, 1982) in order to affirm their positive self-views (Steele, 1988) and derogating out-groups in response to ego threats in order to enhance self-esteem (Crocker, Thompson, McGraw, & Ingerman, 1987). Likewise, after failure, individuals with high self-esteem work harder and therefore tend to perform better than those with low self-esteem (Perez, 1973; Shrauger & Sorman, 1977). This reinforces the notion that hard work pays off, increases future task persistence, and bolsters existing levels of self-esteem.

Although individuals with high self-esteem generally outperform those with low self-esteem in self-regulatory tasks, certain circumstances might promote the opposite outcome. In these cases, self-regulatory failure among high self-esteem individuals is related to overconfidence. For instance, it is well documented that many people overestimate their ability to control outcomes over which they actually have little or no control (Langer, 1975; Taylor & Brown, 1988). These "positive illusions" are often associated with healthy psychological adjustment (partially because those who lack these illusions tend to be more depressed; Taylor & Brown, 1988), but they may become dysfunctional and maladaptive when they exceed optimal levels (Baumeister, 1989). People with high self-esteem risk setting overly ambitious goals and expecting too much from themselves, and therefore they often experience failure directly because of their overconfidence. Although an increase in the number of failures is probably "part of the territory" for those who set challenging goals, these failures are offset by the superior payoffs that occur when they do not fail. It is possible, however, that high self-esteem individuals set goals that are so challenging or so lofty that they will never be obtained. In these cases, there is no success to counteract the failure, and available coping mechanisms may not be sufficient to withstand the onslaught of repeated failure. Setting goals that are too ambitious may ultimately be more self-defeating than setting goals that are too easy, because failure is likely to result from the former, whereas success (even though it is diluted) is more likely to be the outcome of the latter course of action.

The tendency to make unrealistic commitments or set unrealistic goals, and therefore the tendency to experience self-regulatory failure, may be especially likely to occur when high self-esteem individuals feel personally threatened (Schlenker, Weigold, & Hallam, 1990). In this case, the need to affirm or enhance their egos may be likely to promote overconfidence or the setting of impossible goals or standards. For instance, Baumeister and Tice (1985) found that for subjects who had to repeat a task at which they had failed, subjects with high self-esteem performed best after a humiliating failure, whereas subjects with low self-esteem performed best when they could avoid self-blame by attributing failure to an external cause. Thus, those with high self-esteem are most highly motivated to perform or excel after they have experienced a failure for which external attributions are not possible.

Likewise, those with high self-esteem make more optimistic predictions regarding future performance after initial failure than after initial success, and they respond to failure with increased persistence (McFarlin & Blascovich, 1981). This increased persistence may not always pay off in superior performance. For example, if the task is unsolvable or if sufficient performance is unattainable, increased performance is counterproductive. There is evidence that high self-esteem subjects sometimes persist at tasks where they are unlikely to succeed. For example, McFarlin, Baumeister, and Blascovich (1985) found that high self-esteem subjects persisted longer in a truly unsolvable task than did low self-esteem subjects; this occurred even when subjects were instructed not to persist. Hence, because persistence was not a useful strategy, high self-esteem subjects performed more poorly than did low self-esteem subjects. McFarlin (1985) later demonstrated, however, that high self-esteem subjects did not persist if they were told that the task might be unsolvable, and they were also more prudent than low self-esteem subjects when they were aware of the contingency between outcome and effort. Similarly, Sandelands et al. (1988) found that high self-esteem subjects persisted longer than low self-esteem subjects only when they expected that persistence was a useful strategy (see also Janoff-Bulman & Brickman, 1982). If the situation has some degree of ambiguity, though, it seems that high self-esteem individuals may engage in nonproductive persistence.

In these studies, persistence was nonproductive rather than counterproductive. That is, subjects did not suffer any genuine negative consequences from persisting. Do high self-esteem subjects fail to self-regulate and continue to persist at tasks even when such behavior is counterproductive?

Baumeister, Heatherton and Tice (1993) recently demonstrated the counterproductive influence of high self-esteem in the face of ego threats on a complex self-regulatory task. Subjects in these experiments choose performance contingencies for themselves on a video game from among several options, with larger monetary rewards linked to greater chances of failure. In the absence of an ego threat, subjects with higher self-esteem showed a superior capacity for self-regulation than those with low self-esteem by setting appropriate goals and meeting them; thus, they left the experiment with more money than did low self-esteem subjects. However, under conditions of ego threat (the suggestion that subjects should set low goals because they might not be able to perform effectively under pressure), subjects with high self-esteem set inappropriate, risky goals and ended up with smaller monetary rewards than subjects with low self-esteem. Under threat, subjects with high self-esteem were also significantly more likely to choke under pressure (i.e., to show performance decrements under conditions when superior performance is important; see Baumeister, 1984) than subjects with low self-esteem. These results suggest that under some conditions, such as when their abilities are questioned or when their egos or self-esteem is threatened, high self-esteem individuals may fail to regulate appropriately. This study showed that the failure to make realistic goals in the face of ego threat had genuine monetary consequences for high self-esteem individuals.

Although people with high self-esteem are normally quite effective at complex self-regulation—they make accurate predictions that enable them to commit to reachable and appropriate goals, and they manage their performance so as to reach these goals successfully—under ego threat, high self-esteem persons become concerned with making a good, self-enhancing impression, fail to set realistic goals and do not perform optimally. Low self-esteem subjects make better use of external guides for performance (Brockner, 1983) and therefore, when the advice is useful (as it was in the Baumeister, Heatherton and Tice study), low self-esteem subjects outperform high self-esteem subjects. Thus, sensitivity to external demands might lead to positive consequences and therefore should not always be considered in the negative manner of yielding or submissive behavior (Brockner, 1983). Of course, a reliance on external guides and cues generally suggests poor self-regulatory capacities and therefore cannot always be considered an optimal strategy.

The influence of failure on subsequent self-regulatory performance as a function of self-esteem is largely unknown. Because high self-esteem individuals generally show better self-regulation than low self-esteem individuals, it is possible that they might learn from their failures. Conversely, it is possible that failures might lead to greater ego threat and therefore increase counterregulatory behavior. An example of such everyday self-regulatory behavior is the attempt to achieve weight loss.

DIETING, SELF-REGULATION, AND SELF-ESTEEM

One of the most common and interesting examples of making a commitment (which highlights the important role of self-regulation) is attempted weight reduction. Up to 80% of women and many men undertake dieting at some point in their lives (Heatherton & Polivy, 1992). Dieting obviously involves the need to make some form of cognitive commitment and to live up to that commitment. Studies have indicated that high self-esteem individuals might be better able to live up to a weight loss commitment (Mayo, 1978; Rodin, Elias, Silberstein, & Wagner, 1988); thus the low self-esteem dieter may underestimate the strength of her or his inhibitory powers and may be more likely to give in to temptation or to give up the weight loss effort. The greater persistence of those with high self-esteem may make them more likely to attempt repeated efforts at weight reduction, secure in the belief that their superior abilities will lead to ultimate victory.

The self-esteem difference in weight regulation is also illustrated by laboratory studies on the role of self-esteem in dietary disinhibition. Low self-esteem dieters are more likely than are high self-esteem dieters to engage in binge eating (Heatherton & Baumeister, 1991; Polivy, Heatherton, & Herman, 1988). When given a preload (such as a milkshake), most individuals show proper regulation, eating less after the preload than if they had not received one. A series of laboratory studies, however, have demonstrated that dieters eat more ice cream after a diet-breaking preload than if not preloaded (see Herman & Polivy, 1980). A recent study has shown that this counterregulatory response occurs only among low self-esteem dieters, although these are the majority of dieters; in contrast, high self-esteem dieters ate at an intermediate level and were unaffected by the preload manipulation (Polivy et al., 1988). Similarly, low self-esteem dieters are likely to overeat when their self-esteem is threatened, whereas high self-esteem dieters are less affected by such ego threats (Heatherton, Herman, & Polivy, 1991).

In these instances, the low self-esteem dieter shows extremely poor self-regulation. Note, however, that high self-esteem dieters do not necessarily show proper regulation. They fail to regulate their behavior at all, eating the same amount whether they are preloaded or not. Thus, dieters generally do not regulate their eating very well, and low self-esteem dieters are especially poor at regulation. It is possible that chronic dieters (whether high or low in self-esteem) may enter a spiral where each failure at dieting produces lower self-esteem, and lowered self-esteem in turn may lead to subsequent dietary failure (Heatherton & Polivy, 1992). Over time, these subsequent failures may be especially damaging for those with high self-esteem. After all, the low self-esteem dieter never expected to succeed, so failure has little attributional consequence. On the other hand, the high self-esteem dieter is used to success, and repeated failures may force the high self-esteem dieter to conclude that her or his self-regulatory skills are not as great as hoped. If high self-esteem individuals are indeed sensitive to performance capabilities, then they must find a way to reconcile their lofty self-views with the information that they have failed. Failure may humble high-esteem individuals, forcing them to downgrade their performance estimates; for some people, this humility may be coupled with decrements in self-esteem.

SELF-ESTEEM CHANGES

The possibility that self-regulation failures may have a negative and cumulative impact on trait self-esteem has not yet been examined. We speculate that repeated failures—in any domain—are likely to diminish feelings of self-worth. Research on this topic has been held back by conceptual ambiguity about self-esteem. Self-esteem is normally considered a stable trait, and therefore researchers have not often examined whether failure changes acute levels of self-esteem.

There is considerable evidence that situational factors can lead to temporary changes in self-evaluation (Baumgardner, Kaufman, & Levy, 1989; Jones, Rhodewalt, Berglas, & Skelton, 1981), and it appears that although self-esteem is a relatively enduring trait, there are fluctuations that can be measured (Heatherton & Polivy, 1991). Some aspects of the self may be more malleable than others, and individuals are generally able to offset a threat to one dimension of their self-esteem by affirming other, unrelated aspects of the self (Steele, 1988). This fluidity is probably more typical of individuals with high self-esteem; they seem more likely to make external attributions for their failures and to affirm other aspects of their selves. Those with low self-esteem may base their sense of self in only one domain, and therefore may be less able to affirm themselves in other areas. Because they tend to make internal attributions for failure, people with low self-esteem may generalize their negative feelings to other, unrelated domains (Kernis, Brockner, & Frankel, 1989). This may explain why low self-esteem has been implicated in the development of a variety of emotional problems, including chronic depression and severe anxiety (Brockner, 1983; Pyszczynski & Greenberg, 1987; Taylor & Brown, 1988; Tennen & Herzberger, 1987).

The recent development of a measurement scale for state self-esteem may facilitate research on the negative consequences of self-regulatory failure. Heatherton and Polivy (1991) developed the State Self-Esteem Scale (SSES) to measure temporary changes in self-esteem. The SSES is comprised of 20 items based on the Janis-Field Feelings of Inadequacy Scale (Janis & Field, 1959); it measures three different components of state self-esteem. The first component, performance self-esteem, is evaluated by items such as "I feel confident about my abilities" and "I feel like I'm not doing well." Social self-esteem is evaluated by items such as "I feel self-conscious" and "I am worried about what other people think of me." The third component, appearance-based self-esteem is evaluated by items such as "I feel satisfied with the way my body looks right now" and "I feel unattractive." A recent study using structural equation modeling and confirmatory factor analysis found that state self-esteem is distinct from mood (Bagozzi & Heatherton, 1991). Moreover, the SSES has been shown to be sensitive to real-world and laboratory manipulations and therefore may help determine the impact of failure on both high and low self-esteem subjects in order to understand the reciprocal interactions between self-esteem and performance (Heatherton & Polivy, 1991). That is, the SSES can be used to examine the negative consequences of failure on subsequent self-esteem, and the resultant effect that changes in self-esteem have on self-regulation.

SELF-ESTEEM: THE GOOD, THE BAD, AND THE UGLY

Our limited examination of the influence of self-esteem on commitments and self-regulation suggests that, just as there seems to be an optimal "margin of illusion" (Baumeister, 1989) for people not to become overly optimistic or pessimistic, there might be an optimal range of self-esteem for self-regulatory behavior. High self-esteem may lead to maladaptive consequences when the "positive illusions" that preserve self-esteem at normal levels become exaggerated and lead to out-of-control behavior. Taylor and Brown (1988) identified three major categories of positive illusions that are held by the majority of individuals and are beneficial for health and well-being: unrealistically positive views of the self, exaggerated perceptions of personal control, and unrealistic optimism. We are most concerned with the first illusion.

Extremely exaggerated views of the self (especially when unfounded) may be associated with poor self-regulation and poor reality testing, as seen in episodes of mania, grandiosity, and delusions of infallibility (Beck, 1967; Langer, 1975). (One could speculate that individuals who score extremely high on self-esteem inventories are posturing, but there is evidence that such positive self-evaluations are also held privately; Greenwald & Breckler, 1985). Such exaggerated views of the self are most likely to be seen in response to self-esteem threats (Greenwald, 1985; Raskin, Novacek, & Hogan, 1991). People with very high self-esteem may not be able to change maladaptive behavior, because all their effort and energy is directed toward preserving and enhancing their self-image. Thus, they may ignore information suggesting that their behavior is self-defeating. For instance, employees with very high self-esteem may not be able to accept criticism about their performance; they may attribute such criticism to prejudice or envy, and their subsequent performance will suffer. Similarly, academics with unrealistically high levels of self-esteem may keep trying unsuccessfully to publish a paper in a high-status journal when the better option in the long run would be to publish it in one of lower status. Extremely high levels of self-esteem might eventually be associated with feelings of paranoia when grandiose feelings are not supported by others (Raskin et al., 1991).

Conversely, people who are more realistic about the good and bad aspects of themselves (and thus score lower on self-esteem scales; Baumeister et al., 1989) are less vulnerable to illusions of control (Taylor & Brown, 1988). Such people are also likely to be depressed (Cohen et al., 1989; Tennen & Herzberger, 1987). Extremely low self-esteem is related to very poor self-regulation, such that a lack of effort and persistence at challenging tasks may lead to a variety of physical and mental symptoms, including chronic depression (Brockner, 1983), eating disorders (Heatherton & Baumeister, 1991), and many other self-defeating behaviors (Baumeister & Scher, 1988; Wahl, 1956). Thus, both extremely high self-esteem (i.e., far beyond the level warranted by one's abilities) and extremely low self-esteem (i.e., far below the level warranted by one's abilities) might be counterregulatory. The boundaries for very high and very low levels of self-esteem, still need to be identified.

The foregoing analysis suggests that there are negative consequences to holding either high or low self-esteem that contradicts one's actual level of competence. Thus, we can speculate about potential strategies to increase the functioning of those who are low and high in self-esteem. In order to optimize self-regulation, the confidence of low self-esteem individuals could be raised by identifying the dimensions of self-esteem most integral to that individual's sense of self and then bolstering that dimension. For example, individuals go on rigorous diets because they want to improve the physical-appearance aspect of their self-esteem. But very often dieting is unsuccessful, and repeated dietary experiences are likely to result in disinhibition, binge eating, and a loss of general self-esteem (Heatherton & Baumeister, 1991; Heatherton & Polivy, 1992). Therapeutic interventions aimed at increasing dieters' acceptance of their physical appearance increased both their state and trait self-esteem (Ciliska, 1990; Heatherton & Polivy, 1991). Once self-esteem was increased, these individuals were better able to deal with situations that promoted binge eating (Ciliska, 1990); that is, an increase in self-esteem led to increased self-regulatory capacities.

The self-regulation of individuals whose self-esteem is so high that they overestimate their capacities could be optimized by interventions aimed at preventing overconfidence in the face of ego threat. This could include teaching high self-esteem individuals to distance themselves from their performance, to become less ego-involved with tasks, and to help them learn from failure experiences. To our knowledge, no such interventions have been made. In fact, the notion that high self-esteem needs to be treated at all may seem radical. Examples of failure that are a direct result of overconfidence are commonplace, however, and individuals with high self-esteem are not immune to the effects of their failures.

CONCLUSIONS

High self-esteem individuals are often regarded to be better in setting and meeting their goals and commitments than are those with low self-esteem. Under certain circumstances, however, people with high self-esteem become overconfident, persevere at unsolvable tasks, or function poorly under pressure, suggesting that the approach of those with high self-esteem is not universally superior. This inferior response is most likely to occur when the abilities or capacities of high self-esteem persons are questioned or when other aspects of their self-esteem or ego are threatened. It appears that an optimal level of self-esteem for self-regulation is neither excessively high nor particularly low.

One aspect of this analysis that we believe deserves pursuing is that of the potentially negative consequences of high self-esteem. For instance, do high self-esteem individuals use information about failure to regulate future behavior? In instances when they fail to regulate their behavior on one trial and are given the chance to regulate on the next trial, will they do so, or will they continue the spiral of self-defeating behavior? What sorts of behaviors do they show when they are threatened? Are these behaviors always more risky? How can we identify extremely low and extremely high levels of self-esteem?

Researchers have long held the bias that high self-esteem is preferred to low self-esteem. Although occasional cautions have been voiced about defensive high self-esteem (Schneider & Turkat, 1975) and grandiosity (Raskin et al., 1991), there is a pervasive tendency for North American society to value and promote self-confidence. When this confidence is unfounded, however, or when it leads to self-regulatory failure because goals are set that are unattainable, then high self-esteem may be counterproductive and may interfere with the ability to make and live up to commitments.

REFERENCES

Bagozzi, R. P. & Heatherton, T. F. (1991). *Further evidence on the psychometric properties of the State Self-Esteem Scale*. Unpublished manuscript, University of Michigan.

Bandura, A. (1989). Human agency in social cognitive theory. *American Psychologist, 44,* 1175–1184.

Baumeister, R. F. (1982). Self-esteem, self-presentation, and future interaction: A dilemma of reputation. *Journal of Personality, 50,* 29–45.

Baumeister, R. F. (1984). Choking under pressure: Self-consciousness and paradoxical effects of incentives on skillful performance. *Journal of Personality and Social Psychology, 46,* 610–620.

Baumeister, R. F. (1989). The optimal margin of illusion. *Journal of Social and Clinical Psychology, 8,* 176–189.

Baumeister, R. F., Heatherton, T. F., & Tice, D. M. (1993). When ego threats lead to self-regulation failure: The negative consequences of high self-esteem. *Journal of Personality and Social Psychology, 64,* 141–156.

Baumeister, R. F., & Scher, S. J. (1988). Self-defeating behavior patterns among normal individuals: Review and analysis of common self-destructive tendencies. *Psychological Bulletin, 104,* 3–22.

Baumeister, R. F., & Tice, D. M. (1985). Self-esteem and responses to success and failure: Subsequent performance and intrinsic motivation. *Journal of Personality, 53,* 450–467.

Baumeister, R. F., Tice, D. M., & Hutton, D. G. (1989). Self-presentational motivations and personality differences in self-esteem. *Journal of Personality, 57,* 547–579.

Baumgardner, A. H. (1991). To know oneself is to like oneself: Self-certainty and self-affect. *Journal of Personality and Social Psychology, 58,* 1062–1072.

Baumgardner, A. H., Kaufman, C. M., & Levy, P. E. (1989). Regulating affect interpersonally: When low self-esteem leads to greater enhancement. *Journal of Personality and Social Psychology, 56,* 907–921.

Beck, A. T. (1967). *Depression: Clinical, experimental and theoretical aspects.* New York: Harper & Row.

Brockner, J. (1979). The effects of self-esteem, success-failure, and self-consciousness on task performance. *Journal of Personality and Social Psychology, 37,* 1732–1741.

Brockner, J. (1983). Low self-esteem and behavioral plasticity: Some implications. In L. Wheeler & P. Shaver (Eds.), *Review of personality and social psychology* (Vol. 4, pp.237–271). Beverly Hills, CA: Sage.

Campbell, J. D. (1990). Self-esteem and clarity of self-concept. *Journal of Personality and Social Psychology, 59,* 538–549.

Campbell, J. D. & Fairey, P. J. (1985). Effects of self-esteem, hypothetical explanations, and verbalizations on future performance. *Journal of Personality and Social Psychology, 48,* 1097–1111.

Carver, C. S., & Scheier, M. F. (1981). *Attention and self-regulation: A control theory approach to human behavior.* New York: Springer-Verlag.

Ciliska, D. (1990). *Beyond dieting—psychoeducational interventions for chronically obese women: A non-dieting approach.* New York: Brunner/Mazel.

Cohen, L., van den Bout, J., van Vliet, T., & Kramer, W. (1989). Attributional asymmetrics in relation to dysphoria and self-esteem. *Personality and Individual Differences, 10,* 1055–1061.

Coopersmith, S. (1967). *The antecedents of self-esteem.* San Francisco: Freeman.

Crocker, J., Thompson, L. L., McGraw, K. M., & Ingerman, C. (1987). Downward comparisons, prejudice, and evaluation of others: Effects of self-esteem and threat. *Journal of Personality and Social Psychology, 52,* 907–916.

Fitch, G. (1970). Effects of self-esteem, perceived performance, and choice on causal attributions. *Journal of Personality and Social Psychology, 16,* 311–315.

Greenwald, A. G. (1980). The totalitarian ego: Fabrication and revision of personal history. *American Psychologist, 35,* 603–618.

Greenwald, A. G., & Breckler, S. J. (1985). To whom is the self presented? In B. Schlenker (Ed.), *The self and social life* (pp. 126–145). New York: McGraw-Hill.

Heatherton, T. F., & Baumeister, R. F. (1991). Binge eating as escape from self-awareness. *Psychological Bulletin, 110,* 86–108.

Heatherton, T. F., Herman, C. P., & Polivy, J. (1991). Effects of physical threat and ego threat on eating behavior. *Journal of Personality and Social Psychology, 60,* 138–143.

Heatherton, T. F., & Polivy, J. (1991). Development and validation of a scale for measuring state self-esteem. *Journal of Personality and Social Psychology, 60,* 895–910.

Heatherton, T. F., & Polivy, J. (1992). Chronic dieting and eating disorders: A spiral model. In J. H. Crowther, S. E. Hobfall, M. A. P. Stevens, & D. L. Tennenbaum (Eds.), *The etiology of bulimia: The individual and familial context* (pp. 133–155). Washington, DC: Hemisphere.

Herman, C. P., & Polivy, J. (1980). Restrained eating. In A. Stunkard (Ed.), *Eating and its disorders* (pp. 141–156). Philadelphia: Saunders.

Ickes, W., & Layden, M. A. (1978). Attributional styles. In J. Harvey (Ed.), *New directions in attribution research* (Vol. 2, pp. 119–152). Hillsdale, NJ: Lawrence Erlbaum.

Janis, I. L., & Field, P. B. (1959). Sex differences and factors related to persuasibility. In C. I. Hovland & I. L. Janis (Eds.), *Personality and persuasibility* (pp. 55–68). New Haven, CT: Yale University Press.

Janoff-Bulman, R., & Brickman, R. (1982). Expectations and what people learn from failure. In N. T. Feather (Ed.), *Expectations and actions: Expectancy-value models in psychology* (pp. 207–237). Hillsdale, NJ: Lawrence Erlbaum.

Jones, E. E., Rhodewalt, F., Berglas, S., & Skelton, J. A. (1981). Effect of strategic self presentation in subsequent self-esteem. *Journal of Personality and Social Psychology, 41,* 407–421.

Josephs, R. A. (1990). *The threat of risky decision making to self-esteem.* Unpublished doctoral dissertation, University of Michigan.

Kernis, M. H., Brockner, J., & Frankel, B. S. (1989). Self-esteem and reactions to failure: The mediating role of overgeneralization. *Journal of Personality, 57,* 707–714.

Kirschenbaum, D. S., Tomarken, A. J., & Humphrey, L. L. (1985). Affect and adult self-regulation. *Journal of Personality and Social Psychology, 48,* 509–523.

Kuiper, N. (1978). Depression and causal attributions for success and failure. *Journal of Personality and Social Psychology, 36,* 236–246.

Langer, E. (1975). The illusion of control. *Journal of Personality and Social Psychology, 32,* 311–328.

Mayo, L. G. (1978). The correlates of success in a behavioral weight reduction program. *Dissertations Abstracts International, 38-8B,* 3897.

McFarlin, D. B. (1985). Persistence in the face of failure: The impact of self-esteem and contingency information. *Personality and Social Psychology Bulletin, 11,* 153–163.

McFarlin, D. B., & Blascovich, J. (1981). Effects of self-esteem and performance on future affective preferences and cognitive expectations. *Journal of Personality and Social Psychology, 40,* 521–531.

McFarlin, D. B., Baumeister, R. F., & Blascovich, J. (1984). On knowing when to quit: Task failure, self-esteem, advice, and nonproductive persistence. *Journal of Personality, 52,* 138–155.

Perez, R. C. (1973). The effect of experimentally-induced failure, self-esteem, and sex on cognitive differentiation. *Journal of Abnormal Psychology, 81,* 74–79.

Polivy, J., Heatherton, T. F., & Herman, C. P. (1988). Self-esteem, restraint, and eating behavior. *Journal of Abnormal Psychology, 97,* 354–356.

Pyszczynski, T., & Greenberg, J. (1983). Determinants of reduction in intended effort as a strategy for coping with anticipated failure. *Journal of Research in Personality, 17,* 412–422.

Raskin, R., Novacek, J., & Hogan, R. (1991). Narcissism, self-esteem, and defensive self-enhancement. *Journal of Personality, 59,* 19–38.

Rizley, R. (1978). Depression and distortion in the attribution of causality. *Journal of Personality and Abnormal Psychology, 87,* 32–48.

Rodin, J., Elias, M., Silberstein, L. R., & Wagner, A. (1988). Combined behavioral and pharmacologic treatment for obesity: Predictors of successful weight maintenance. *Journal of Consulting and Clinical Psychology, 56,* 399–404.

Sandelands, L. E., Brockner, J., & Glynn, M. A. (1988). If at first you don't succeed, try, try again: Effects of persistence-performance contingencies, ego involvement, and self-esteem on task persistence. *Journal of Applied Psychology, 73,* 208–216.

Scheier, M. F., & Carver, C. S. (1988). A model of behavioral self-regulation: Translating intention into action. *Advances in Experimental Social Psychology, 21,* 303–346.

Schlenker, B. R., Weigold, M. F., & Hallam, J. R. (1990). Self-serving attributions in social context: Effects of self-esteem and social pressure. *Journal of Personality and Social Psychology, 58,* 855–863.

Schneider, D. J., & Turkat, D. (1975). Self-presentation following success and failure: Defensive self-esteem models. *Journal of Personality, 43,* 127–135.

Shrauger, J., & Sorman, P. (1977). Self-evaluations, initial success and failure, and improvement as determinants of persistence. *Journal of Consulting and Clinical Psychology, 45,* 784–795.

Steele, C. M. (1988). The psychology of self-affirmation: Sustaining the integrity of the self. In L. Berkowitz (Ed.), *Advances in experimental social psychology* (Vol. 21, pp. 261–302) New York: Academic Press.

Taylor, S. E. (1989). *Positive illusions: Creative self-deception and the healthy mind.* New York: Basic Books.

Taylor, S. E., & Brown, J. D. (1988). Illusion and well-being: A social psychological perspective on mental health. *Psychological Bulletin, 103,* 193–210.

Tennen, H., & Herzberger, S. (1987). Depression, self-esteem, and the absence of self-protective attributional biases. *Journal of Personality and Social Psychology, 52,* 72–80.

Tice, D. M. (1991). Esteem protection or enhancement? Self-handicapping motives and attributions differ by trait self-esteem. *Journal of Personality and Social Psychology, 60,* 711–725.

Wahl, C. (1956). Some antecedent factors in the family histories of 109 alcoholics. *Journal of Studies on Alcohol, 17,* 643–654.

White, J. (1982). *Rejection.* Reading, MA: Addison-Wesley.

Zautra, A. J., Guenther, R. T., & Chartier, G. M. (1985). Attributions for real and hypothetical events: Their relation to self-esteem and depression. *Journal of Abnormal Psychology, 94,* 530–540.

Chapter 8

CAUGHT IN THE CROSSFIRE
POSITIVITY AND SELF-VERIFICATION STRIVINGS AMONG PEOPLE WITH LOW SELF-ESTEEM

Chris De La Ronde and William B. Swann, Jr.

Why do people with negative self-concepts consistently behave in ways that alienate their interaction partners? After all, such persons—that is, depressed persons and those with low self-esteem—typically suffer when they are rejected, and they seem motivated to bring others to like them. Yet, they persist in enacting precisely those behaviors that repel their interaction partners. It almost seems as if such persons have two individuals lurking within: one urging them to seek favorable reactions, the other demanding that they solicit unfavorable reactions.

The primary goal of this chapter is to explicate the ambivalence that characterizes people with negative self-views. We suggest that this ambivalence grows out of a tendency for such persons to be trapped in a crossfire between two competing motives. On the one hand, people with negative self-views desire favorable feedback; on the other, they desire feedback that confirms their self-views. We begin by examining the nature and consequences of their desire for favorable evaluations.

Chris De La Ronde and William B. Swann, Jr. • Dept. of Psychology, University of Texas at Austin, Austin, TX 78712.

Self-Esteem: The Puzzle of Low Self-Regard, edited by Roy F. Baumeister. Plenum Press, New York, 1993.

POSITIVITY STRIVINGS

Our cultural heritage, as well as a large body of theory and research, suggests that people preferentially seek favorable feedback about themselves regardless of whether their self-views happen to be positive or negative (e.g., S. C. Jones, 1973). In fact, there is abundant evidence that people employ a diverse and well-honed array of strategies for enhancing their appraisals of themselves, including their self-presentational activities (e.g., Baumeister, 1982; E. E. Jones, 1964; E. E. Jones & Pittman, 1982; Schlenker, 1980, 1985; Tedeschi & Lindskold, 1976), self-attributions (e.g., Bradley, 1978; Greenwald, 1980; Snyder & Higgins, 1988; Zuckerman, 1979), predictions of future success (e.g., Alloy & Abramson, 1988; Taylor & Brown, 1988; Weinstein, 1980), targets of social comparison (e.g., Taylor & Lobel, 1989; Tesser, 1986; Wills, 1981), and belief change (e.g., Steele, 1988).

A perusal of this evidence might lead one to conclude that positivity strivings can explain virtually all social behavior. Recent research on self-verification processes, however, suggests that this conclusion might be premature. In particular, several studies have shown that when people with negative self-views choose interaction partners, they display a relative preference for those who think poorly of them (for reviews, see Swann, 1990, 1992). Moreover, people with negative self-views prefer partners who appraise them unfavorably whether the self-view is relatively global (e.g., depression; Swann, Wenzlaff, Krull, & Pelham, 1992) or specific (e.g., sociability; Robinson & Smith-Lovin, 1992; Swann, Hixon, Stein-Seroussi, & Gilbert, 1990; Swann, Stein-Seroussi, & Giesler, 1992). People with negative self-views also prefer interacting with those who appraise them unfavorably over being in an unrelated experiment (Swann, Wenzlaff, & Tafarodi, 1992). Even when people with negative self-views happen to wind up in relationships in which they are appraised favorably by their partners, they tend to withdraw from the relationship (e.g., Swann, Hixon, & De La Ronde, 1992). In short, there is converging evidence that people will gravitate toward social relationships in which they anticipate self-confirmatory feedback and avoid relationships in which they expect self-discrepant feedback.

Although it might seem that positivity theories cannot handle evidence that people with negative self-views seek partners who appraise them negatively, recent permutations of the theories can accommodate such evidence, at least in principle (e.g,. Baumeister, 1982; Brown, Collins, & Schmidt, 1988; Epstein, 1973, 1983; Greenwald, 1980; E. E. Jones, 1990; E. E. Jones & Pittman, 1982; Schlenker, 1985; Steele, 1988; Tesser, 1986). Thus, for example, positivity theorists could argue that interaction partners who provide negative feedback may satisfy people's positivity strivings by allowing them to do the following:

- *Improve themselves.* Some (e.g., Trope, 1986) have argued that persons with negative self-concepts actively seek negative feedback to reduce uncertainty about themselves. Presumably, greater certainty will allow them to improve themselves and thus avoid negative feedback in the future.
- *Win converts.* People might choose interaction partners who appraise them unfavorably in the hope of "winning them over." Ultimately, converting an enemy into a friend could produce exceptionally strong feelings of positivity.
- *Interact with a similar other.* People with negative self-concepts might prefer partners with unfavorable appraisals because they believe that these partners are similar to themselves and find that interacting with such persons makes them feel better about themselves (e.g., Byrne, 1971).
- *Interact with a perceptive other.* To a person with a negative self-concept, an unfavorable appraisal might signal that the perceiver is perceptive and thus a desirable person to be around.

In principle, then, positivity strivings could explain why people with negative self-views prefer interaction partners who appraise them unfavorably. Nevertheless, research and theorizing on self-verification strivings suggest that people with negative self-views choose partners who appraise them unfavorably because, at some level, they actually *want* others to see them in a negative manner.

SELF-VERIFICATION THEORY

In the tradition of symbolic interaction theory (e.g., Cooley, 1902; Mead, 1934; Stryker, 1981) and self-consistency formulations (e.g., Aronson, 1968; Festinger, 1957; Lecky, 1945; Secord & Backman, 1965), self-verification theory assumes that as people mature, they learn that their relationships proceed most smoothly when others see them as they see themselves—even if they see themselves negatively. For example, people discover that those who develop overly positive appraisals may become disappointed and disgruntled with them. Through repeated exposure to this fact of social life, people come to associate self-verifying evaluations with feelings of authenticity and non-verifying evaluations with feelings of uneasiness or bemusement. Eventually, these epistemic concerns become functionally autonomous (Allport, 1961) of the interpersonal or pragmatic concerns that originally produced them and people self-verify for *either* epistemic or pragmatic reasons. Thus, for example, a man with low self-esteem may seek negative evaluations either because he fears the social consequences of being appraised in an overly positive fashion *or* because his past experiences have convinced him that he *should* expect to encounter such evaluations.

Thus, both epistemic and pragmatic considerations may motivate people to seek self-verifying appraisals, even if this means displaying a preference for unfavorable evaluations. Swann and Read (1981a) demonstrated that people do indeed prefer self-confirmatory feedback. In this research, participants first completed a series of questionnaires, including measures of self-perceived assertiveness and self-perceived emotionality. The experimenter then asked for the participants' consent to show their responses on the personality inventory to another person. Several minutes later, the experimenter returned and announced that the other person had read over the participant's responses on the personality inventory and answered some questions about the participant. Some questions probed for evidence of assertiveness (e.g., "What makes you think that this is the type of person who will complain in a restaurant if the service is bad?"); other questions probed for evidence of unassertiveness (e.g., "Why would this person not be likely to complain if someone cut into line in front of him or her at a movie?"). The experimenter told the participant to read the questions and select the five questions for which he or she was most interested in seeing the answers.

The results indicated that participants sought information that would confirm their self-conceptions. Just as those who viewed themselves as assertive asked to examine more questions that probed for evidence of assertiveness, those who viewed themselves as unassertive asked to examine more questions that probed for evidence of unassertiveness.

Swann and Read (1981a) conducted two follow-up investigations to assess the generality of this preference for self-confirmatory feedback. One study showed that males and females were equally likely to manifest a desire for self-confirmatory feedback, and that participants were even willing to relinquish their private funds to acquire such feedback. Another study indicated that people with negative self-views preferentially solicited unfavorable feedback even though they had just acknowledged that such feedback made them feel depressed (Swann, Wenzlaff, Krull, & Pelham, 1992).

The message emerging from this research is clear: Not only do people prefer information that confirms their self-conceptions, they also will engage in active efforts to acquire such information. Subsequent research has shown that in their quest for self-verifying feedback, people may enact any of at least three distinct strategies. They may gravitate toward self-verifying relationship partners (e.g., Robinson & Smith-Lovin, 1992; Swann, Hixon, & De La Ronde, 1992; Swann, Hixon, Stein-Seroussi, & Gilbert, 1990; Swann, Pelham, & Krull, 1989; Swann, Stein-Seroussi, & Giesler, 1992; Swann, Wenzlaff, Krull, & Pelham, 1992; Swann, Wenzlaff, & Tafarodi, 1992), they may display signs and symbols of who they are (e.g., Englander, 1960; Goffman, 1959; Stern & Scanlon, 1958), or they may enact behaviors that cause their interaction partners to appraise them in a self-consistent manner (e.g., Swann & Ely, 1984; Swann & Hill, 1982; Swann, Pelham, & Chidester, 1988; Swann & Read, 1981b).

Why People Self-Verify: Prediction and Control, or Positivity?

In short, research on self-verification processes suggests that people enact a wide range of behavioral strategies in an effort to bring others to see them as they see themselves. Why? Both self-verification and positivity theorists agree that people with negative self-views prefer interaction partners who are apt to provide them with unfavorable feedback because doing so is reinforcing. There is some debate, however, about why they find negative evaluations reinforcing. On the one hand, self-verification theorists believe that self-confirmatory stimuli is reinforcing because it bolsters perceptions of predictability and control. As noted above, however, advocates of positivity strivings have argued that self-verifying feedback makes people feel good by enabling them to improve themselves, interact with similar or perceptive others, or win converts.

Three independent investigations offer converging evidence that self-verification strivings are motivated by a desire for prediction and control rather than positivity strivings. In the research of Swann, Hixon, and De La Ronde (1992), married persons with positive self-views were most committed to spouses who appraised them favorably, and married persons with negative self-views were more committed to partners who appraised them unfavorably. Ancillary measures suggested that this pattern of commitment was best explained by self-verification theory. That is, participants were more committed to the extent that they felt that their spouses' appraisals "made them feel that they really knew themselves," rather than "confused them." In contrast, commitment was *not* associated with the extent to which participants believed that their spouse was perceptive or would help them improve themselves. In addition, there was evidence that people did *not* commit themselves to spouses who appraised them unfavorably in the hopes of winning them over; in fact, people with negative self-views were more committed to spouses to the extent that they expected their spouses' appraisals would *worsen*.

Swann, Stein-Seroussi, and Giesler (1992) provided further evidence that the epistemic and pragmatic concerns specified by self-verification theory cause people with negative self-views to choose interaction partners who appraise them unfavorably. Specifically, they asked participants to think aloud as they chose between interacting with someone who had appraised them favorably or someone who appraised them unfavorably. These protocols were then tape-recorded, transcribed, and rated by judges who were trained to recognize positivity concerns (e.g., self-improvement, winning converts, a desire for a similar or perceptive partner), epistemic concerns (i.e., putting the person at ease by confirming his or her self-view) and pragmatic concerns (i.e., fostering the perception that the interaction would proceed smoothly). The results indicated that epistemic considerations best explained why people with negative self-views chose partners who appraised them unfavorably.

Finally, Swann, Wenzlaff, and Tafarodi (1992) showed that participants sought self-verifying information in a setting in which epistemic factors only appeared to be operating. After receiving criticism or praise regarding one set of abilities, participants chose feedback from a different evaluator concerning an unrelated ability. Just as participants with positive self-views responded to criticism by intensifying their efforts to obtain favorable feedback, participants with negative self-views responded to praise by intensifying their search for unfavorable feedback. Such findings fit well with self-verification theory but seem difficult to interpret in terms of positivity strivings.

THE INTERPLAY OF POSITIVITY AND SELF-VERIFICATION STRIVINGS

In arguing that positivity strivings cannot explain why people with negative self-views choose interaction partners who appraise them unfavorably, we are not questioning their importance. To the contrary, we believe that a primary source of tension among people with negative self-views is that they are trapped in a crossfire between desires for positivity and self-verification, a crossfire that demands compromises that are never entirely satisfying. To understand the nature of this crossfire better, we begin by considering how it develops.

DEVELOPMENTAL ANTECEDENTS OF POSITIVITY AND SELF-VERIFICATION STRIVINGS

Children are probably born with a desire for favorable evaluations; if not, they develop it soon afterward. For example, 5-month-old children attend more to smiling faces than nonsmiling ones shortly after developing the ability to discriminate facial characteristics (Shapiro, Eppler, Haith, & Reis, 1987). Similarly, as early as 4½ months, children tend to orient to voices that have the melodic contours of acceptance rather than nonacceptance (Fernald, 1989). Furthermore, young children endorse positive descriptions of themselves much earlier than they accept negative ones (e.g., Benenson & Dweck, 1986; Eshel & Klein, 1981; Nicholls, 1978, 1979; Stipek, 1981; Stipek & Daniels, 1988; Stipek & Tannatt, 1984). The research literature therefore suggests that even very young children display a propensity to approach superficially accepting persons and to avoid threatening ones (see also Taylor & Brown, 1988).

The cognitive prerequisites for self-verification do not emerge until much later in development. Not until 18 months does the sense of self as object, an integral component of the self-verification process, emerge (e.g., Lewis, 1987). Even after children develop rudimentary self-conceptions, they will not self-verify until they accumulate sufficient evidence to warrant a modicum of self-concept certainty. In the case of such relatively concrete characteristics as gender, certainty may emerge fairly early; witness the consternation of 4-year-olds when their gender identity is mistaken. Relatively certain self-conceptions regarding abstract personality traits and dispositions presumably emerge somewhat later (e.g., Damon, 1983).

The fact that positivity strivings emerge earlier in development than self-verification strivings suggest that they may be triggered by a relatively simple process (i.e., one requiring relatively few mental computations). This also stands to reason from a strictly logical perspective. Whereas both self-verification and positivity strivings require this initial characterization of self-relevant stimuli, positivity strivings should require no more than a relatively simple characterization. That is, merely identifying a stimulus as favorable or unfavorable should enable people to approach the former and avoid the latter. In contrast, self-verification should require more cognitive effort. If people are to approach a stimulus only when it confirms their self-view, then (a) the stimulus must be characterized as favorable or unfavorable, (b) the relevant self-view must be accessed, and (c) the two must be compared. Therefore, although both positivity and self-verification strivings require the initial characterization of self-relevant stimuli, only self-verification strivings requires accessing the self and a comparison between the stimulus and the relevant conception of self.

Because self-verification strivings are logically predicated on a relatively complex set of sequential operations, they should require more cognitive resources than should positivity strivings. Depleting people's cognitive resources may therefore disrupt the additional steps that underlie self-verification, but not the earlier characterization stage. In other words, resource-deprived people should have difficulty comparing self-relevant feedback to their self-concepts to assess its accuracy and therefore may be guided solely by the earlier assessment of the positivity of the feedback. People who are not deprived of cognitive resources, however, should be guided by the later comparison of the feedback with a relevant self-conception.

Swann, Hixon, Stein-Seroussi, and Gilbert (1990) tested this reasoning by depriving people of cognitive resources while they chose between interaction partners who evaluated them in a relatively favorable or unfavorable manner. The first study set the stage for testing this hypothesis by demonstrating that depriving people of cognitive resources did, in fact, interfere with their ability to access their self-conceptions. A second study tested the primary hypothesis by having participants choose an interaction partner while their cognitive resources were or were not depleted. Specifically, people were deprived of cognitive resources by choosing a partner hurriedly, whereas control participants were allowed to take their time. In the rushed condition, all participants (i.e., those with positive and negative self-views) tended to choose the favorable evaluator over the unfavorable evaluator, presumably because they lacked the cognitive resources to perform the additional mental operations underlying self-verification. In the unrushed condition, however, participants self-verified, presumably because they possessed the cognitive resources required for self-verification. Thus, given sufficient time, participants with negative self-views chose the negative evaluator over the favorable evaluator.

A follow-up study provided further support for the hypothesis that depriving people of cognitive resources diminishes their tendency to self-verify. In this study, the researchers deprived participants of cognitive resources by having them rehearse a phone number while they were choosing an interaction partner. Resource-deprived participants were particularly likely to choose an interaction partner who appraised them favorably. In addition, when participants were liberated from the cognitive load manipulation, they tended to choose a self-verifying partner. The latter finding shows that cognitively loaded participants tended to choose the favorable evaluator because they lacked the cognitive resources needed to self-verify, rather than because the load manipulation somehow prevented them from picking up the information needed.

Taken together, this research provides converging evidence that positivity strivings grow out of a computationally simple tendency to approach friendly stimuli and avoid menacing stimuli. Further, it appears that positivity strivings may be triggered by the mere categorization of feedback. In contrast, self-verification seems to be a relatively complex process that grows out of the comparison of social feedback with representations of the self that are stored in memory. The distinction between positivity and self-verification strivings therefore seems somewhat analogous to the distinction between affective and cognitive responses (e.g., Shrauger, 1975; Zajonc, 1980).

Given the relative complexity of self-verification and the fact that social interaction is cognitively demanding, one implication of this analysis is that people display positivity strivings more often than self-verification strivings. Nevertheless, when people make *important* decisions (e.g., choosing a spouse or a career), they are apt to take their time and muster all the mental resources they have at their disposal. The upshot may be that positivity strivings are relatively common, but that self-verification strivings have more impact on relatively important decisions.

Such generalizations about the pervasiveness of positivity and self-verification strivings, however, must be treated cautiously. Thus far, we have said nothing about what happens when people are motivated and able to continue information processing beyond both the categorization phase (which produces positivity strivings) and the comparison phase (which produces self-verification). In such instances, there occurs a cost-benefit analysis or strategic phase that utilizes the outputs of the two earlier phases (probably in the form of affect or emotional readout; see Buck, 1985; Pittman & Heller, 1987). This strategic analysis presumably uses information about the self, the feedback, and social-contextual factors to generate hypothetical if-then scenarios that are designed to construct an optimal set of behavioral choices (see also Hoffman, 1986).

If such strategic analyses always follow the categorization and comparison phases, it may be easier to understand why *compensatory* positivity strivings (in which people with negative self-views are more inclined to seek positive feedback than people with positive self-views) have been so difficult to produce reliably (e.g., Brown, 1986; Brown,

Collins & Schmidt, 1988; Campbell, 1986; Shrauger, 1975; Swann, 1990; Taylor & Brown, 1988).* To display compensatory positivity strivings, not only must people with negative self-views be able and willing to access their self-concept, their strategic analyses must also favor positivity over self-verification strivings. The joint probability of all of these events occurring, of course, is smaller than the probability associated with the occurrence of either positivity or self-verification strivings.

Some Moderators of Self-Verification and Positivity Strivings: Self-Conception, Response, and Social Context

Mental resources are a necessary, but not sufficient, condition for self-verification. The availability of mental resources means only that people will be *able* to access a self-view relevant to the behavior at hand; self-verification strivings will override positivity strivings only insofar as the self-conception and response have epistemic and pragmatic consequences. The characteristics of self-conceptions, responses, and social context that influence such consequences are considered below.

Characteristics of the Self-Conception

People should be particularly apt to verify self-views of which they are certain; there are at least two reasons why this is so. Because people perceive that they have especially consistent and plentiful evidence supporting firmly held self-views (e.g., Pelham, 1991), they should rely heavily on such self-views epistemically (i.e., in organizing their perceptions of the world) and pragmatically (i.e., in orchestrating their social relationships). As a result, relatively certain self-views should be accessed more quickly than relatively uncertain ones. Heightened accessibility of a self-view should, in turn, increase the likelihood that people will translate the self-view into behavior. There is evidence that raising the accessibility of beliefs by asking people to think about them (e.g., Snyder & Swann, 1976) or by challenging them (e.g., Sherman & Gorkin, 1980; Swann & Read, 1981b) increases the likelihood that people will later act on those beliefs (see also Fazio, 1986; Tesser, 1989).

---

*In principle, people with negative self-views might develop a chronically elevated appetite for self-enhancement (because of the infrequency with which they receive favorable feedback) that might motivate compensatory self-enhancement processes. Although this form of compensatory self-enhancement would not require people to access their self-conceptions, the research literature suggests that it rarely operates. Several studies show that the self-enhancement strivings of people with low self-esteem are no greater than those of people with high self-esteem (e.g., Swann et al., 1989).

Increments in self-certainty should also raise the probability of self-verification because, as people become more certain of their self-views, the range of behaviors they regard as being compatible with their self-views shrinks [Pelham, 1991; see also Sherif, Sherif, & Nebergall's analysis (1961) of latitude of acceptance]. This means, for example, that a man who is highly certain of his self-conceived dominance may define dominance quite narrowly and thus demand highly dominant (i.e., self-verifying) behavior of himself.

Consistent with this reasoning, several studies have shown that people are particularly inclined to verify their firmly held self-views. Some investigators have shown that people tend to verify self-views of which they are relatively certain (e.g., Maracek & Mettee, 1972; Pelham, 1991; Swann & Ely, 1984; Swann, Pelham, & Chidester, 1988). Others, noting that belief certainty is related to extremity, have shown that people who have extreme self-views are particularly inclined to self-verify (e.g., Swann, Wenzlaff, Krull, & Pelham, 1992; Swann et al., 1989).

Of course, the foregoing analysis could be used as a basis for predicting a curvilinear relation between self-certainty and self-verification. Although moderate (as compared to low) levels of certainty might motivate people to self-verify, high levels of certainty might engender so much confidence in self-views that people perceive little reason to enact active self-verification strategies. Although this seems plausible in principle, the indeterminate character of most personality attributes and the fickleness of social feedback probably prevents most people from ever becoming excessively certain of most of their self-views.

The evidence that people verify only their firmly held self-views may help explain why attraction researchers have encountered little evidence of self-verification strivings. Past researchers have often *manipulated* rather than measured self-concepts (e.g., Aronson & Carlsmith, 1962; Dittes, 1959; Jacobs, Berscheid, & Walster, 1971; S. C. Jones & Pines, 1968; S. C. Jones & Ratner, 1967; S. C. Jones & Schneider, 1968; Skolnik, 1971; Walster, 1970). Given that most people in our society possess chronic self-views that are quite positive (e.g., Swann, 1987; Taylor & Brown, 1988), attempting to produce negative self-concepts by confronting people with several doses of unfavorable feedback may actually prompt them to work to verify their positive self-views; it is very unlikely that such feedback will suddenly convince them that they are deficient.* Quite possibly, researchers would have uncovered more evi-

---

*Some investigators (e.g., Aronson & Carlsmith, 1962) attempted to induce participants to form *new* self-views (unfettered by chronic self-conceptions) by providing them with feedback on a novel task (e.g., diagnosing schizophrenia). We believe that although this

dence of self-verification had they identified people who possessed chronically negative self-views.

Characteristics of the Response

Some responses are more relevant to the epistemic and pragmatic considerations underlying self-verification than are others. At one end of this continuum are cognitive responses, such as perceptions of the accuracy of feedback (e.g., Shrauger, 1975). To make such judgments, people must engage in the comparison process that underlies self-verification processes, which is to say that these responses explicitly demand that people access their self-conceptions. Not surprisingly, then, the research literature shows that cognitive responses conform closely to self-verification theory (e.g., Swann, Griffin, Predmore, & Gaines, 1987). At the other end of this continuum are affective responses, such as mood states following feedback. These types of responses are logically independent of people's representations of self. As a result, when asked to report their moods, people feel under no obligation to access their self-views and consequently refrain from doing so (see Simon's discussion, 1957, of "satisficing strategies" and Langer's discussion, 1989, of mindless behavior). By default, the only processes left to influence affective responses are those that underlie positivity strivings (e.g., Tesser, 1989).

This suggests that the cognitive or affective character of a response (e.g., Shrauger, 1975; Swann et al., 1987) is significant, because only *"cognitive" responses* encourage people to access relevant self-conceptions and contemplate the epistemic/pragmatic consequences of various courses of action. In support of this, Swann et al. (1989) found that people displayed positivity or self-verification strivings on behaviors that fell in the *same* response class (and were therefore similarly cognitive versus affective). Specifically, participants completed two measures of feedback seeking: a within-attribute and a between-attribute measure. To complete the within-attribute measure, participants specified whether they wanted favorable or unfavorable feedback regarding their specific (positive or negative) self-views. This meant that people could seek favorable feedback only if they were willing to solicit self-discrepant feedback and confront the aversive epistemic/pragmatic consequences associated with having done so. Not surprisingly, then, people solicited self-verifying feedback (see also Swann & Read, 1981b; Swann,

---

strategy is feasible in principle, it is problematic in practice because of a tendency for people to assimilate new experiences to past ones. For example, although college student participants may rarely diagnose schizophenics, they routinely estimate the psychological health of the people they encounter (particularly if they live in large urban areas).

Wenzlaff, Krull, & Pelham, 1992) on this measure. Participants completed the between-attribute measure by indicating whether they preferred to sample feedback pertaining to their strengths or weaknesses. Participants chose feedback pertaining to their positive self-views, presumably because receiving praise regarding a strength is more pleasant—and no less self-verifying—than receiving criticism regarding a weakness.

We suggest the within- and between-attribute distinction of Swann et al. (1989) is representative of a larger dichotomy. Many responses are akin to the within-attribute measure in that they are highly sensitive to and constrained by the epistemic and pragmatic considerations underlying self-verification strivings. Such responses include (a) ratings of the diagnosticity and accuracy of feedback, attributions regarding feedback, and perceptions of the evaluator's credibility (e.g., Swann et al., 1987); (b) overt interaction strategies (e.g., Curtis & Miller, 1986; Swann & Ely, 1984; Swann & Hill, 1982; Swann, Pelham, & Chidester, 1988; Swann & Read, 1981a); and (c) choice of partners with whom to interact (e.g., Swann et al., 1990; Swann et al., 1989; Swann, Stein-Seroussi, & Giesler, 1992; Swann, Wenzlaff, Krull, & Pelham, 1992; Swann, Wenzlaff, & Tafarodi, 1992).

At the same time, many responses are, like the between-attribute measure, logically unrelated to the considerations underlying self-verification strivings. Social comparison processes offer a good example. The desire for prediction and control should not compel people who are certain of their negative self-views to make themselves feel worse by comparing themselves to their superiors. For this reason, people who lack talent may enjoy the fruits of downward comparison without suffering the epistemic and pragmatic consequences associated with failing to self-verify (e.g., Taylor & Lobel, 1989; Tesser, 1986; Tesser & Campbell, 1983; Wills, 1981). Other responses are similarly immune to the considerations underlying self-verification strivings. Brown, Collins, and Schmidt (1988), for example, have shown that persons with low self-esteem promote their own group when they are indirectly, but not directly, responsible for the group's performance (see Cialdini & Richardson, 1980). Baumgardner, Kaufman, and Levy (1989) similarly have shown that by publicly derogating others, victims of chronic negative feedback can make themselves feel good without claiming to be persons that they are not.

Characteristics of the Social Context

One final factor may be the social psychological context in which the response occurs. Thus, for example, the type of relationship that people with negative self-views are involved in may play an important role in determining whether they will seek positive or relatively negative appraisals. People who are dating, for example, know that they must recruit the affections of their partner if the relationship is to survive. When courtship culminates in marriage, however, such goals are replaced by a desire to be known. In short, it seems that the goals associated with dating relationships foster a desire for positive feedback, whereas the goals associated with marriage foster a desire for self-verifying feedback. Swann, De La Ronde, and Hixon (1993) tested this hypothesis by assessing the self-views and partner appraisals of people involved in dating and marital relationships. Couples completed identical questionnaires assessing specific self-conceptions and their appraisals of their partner on a complementary measure. A measure of intimacy (e.g., relationship satisfaction, time spent together, self-disclosure) served as the primary criterion variable. The results suggested that people do indeed approach courtship and marital relationship differently. Specifically, dating persons were more intimate with partners who viewed them favorably, and married persons were more intimate with partners who saw them as they saw themselves.

We should add two general comments regarding factors that contribute to the epistemic/pragmatic consequences of responses. First, these consequences should be an additive function of characteristics of the self-concept, the response, and the context, which means that high levels of epistemic/pragmatic consequences on the part of one may compensate for deficits in the other. That is, just as people may strive to verify self-conceptions that are only moderately high in certainty when the response occurs in a social context that is exceptionally high in epistemic/pragmatic relevance (e.g., a marriage relationship), only self-views of which they are highly certain may foster self-verification if the context entails few epistemic/pragmatic consequences.

Second, our model does not require that people must "compute" the epistemic/pragmatic consequences of a potential response every time they contemplate it. Presumably, such computations may sometimes become automatized so that people can instantaneously discriminate responses that entail many versus few epistemic/pragmatic consequences.

CONCLUSIONS AND IMPLICATIONS

We believe that people are motivated by desires for both positivity and self-verification, and that both of these motives are influential determinants of human behavior. For people with negative self-views, these forces place them in a crossfire: Just as their positivity strivings cause them to seek favorable feedback, their self-verification strivings cause them to seek unfavorable feedback.

Is there a way out of this crossfire? Perhaps. The desire to be adored and the desire to be known can be satisfied simultaneously among persons with positive self-views. This suggests that changing the self-views of people with negative self-concepts is the most effective, as well as most permanent, means for them to escape the crossfire. To change self-conceptions effectively, however, therapists must first foster people's perceptions of predictability and control by providing them with relatively accurate, self-verifying feedback. Once having reassured people that their self-conceptions are veridical, the therapist can venture into the psychologically threatening arena of proposing strategies for altering their lives that will eventually lead to improvements in those self-conceptions (e.g., Andrews, 1991; Finn & Tonsager, 1991).

Our formulation also suggests that a second, equally critical step toward permanent self-concept change involves changing the social environments of persons with negative self-concepts. The research reviewed in this chapter suggests that the roots of self-concept stability are not "all in the head"; rather, people stabilize their self-conceptions by creating around themselves social environments that offer support for those conceptions. The stability inherent in these environments, in turn, stabilizes their behavior and their self-views. For this reason, for negative self-views to be vanquished, it is not enough to alter the self-concepts themselves; the social environments that feed into and sustain those self-views must also be changed.

ACKNOWLEDGMENTS

The preparation of this chapter was supported by research funds (MH 37598) and a research-scientist development award (MH 00498) from the National Institute of Mental Health to the second author.

REFERENCES

Alloy, L. B., & Abramson, L. Y. (1988). Depressive realism: Four theoretical perspectives. In L. B. Alloy (Ed.), *Cognitive processes in depression* (pp. 223–265). New York: Guilford.
Andrews, J. D. W. (1991). *The active self in psychotherapy: An integration of therapeutic styles.* Boston: Allyn & Bacon.
Aronson, E. (1968). A theory of cognitive dissonance: A current perspective. In L. Berkowitz (Ed.), *Advances in experimental social psychology, Vol. 4* (pp. 1–34). New York: Academic Press.

Aronson, E., & Carlsmith, J. M. (1962). Performance expectancy as a determinant of actual performance. *Journal of Abnormal and Social Psychology, 65*, 178–182.

Baumeister, R. F. (1982). A self-presentational view of social phenomena. *Psychological Bulletin, 91*, 3–26.

Baumgardner, A. H., Kaufman, C. M., & Levy, P. E. (1989). Regulating affect interpersonally: When low self-esteem leads to greater enhancement. *Journal of Personality and Social Psychology, 56*, 907–921.

Benenson, J., & Dweck, C. (1986). The development of trait explanations and self-evaluations in the academic and social domains. *Child Development, 57*, 1179–1187.

Bradley, G. W. (1978). Self-serving biases in the attribution processes: A recrimination of the fact or fiction question. *Journal of Personality and Social Psychology, 36*, 56–71.

Brown, J. D. (1986). Evaluations of self and others: Self-enhancement biases in social judgments. *Social Cognition, 4*, 353–376.

Brown, J. D., Collins, R. L., & Schmidt, G. W. (1988). Self-esteem and direct versus indirect forms of self-enhancement. *Journal of Personality and Social Psychology, 55*, 445–453.

Buck, R. (1985). Prime theory: An integrated view of motivation and emotion. *Psychological Review, 92*, 111–135.

Byrne, D. (1971). *The attraction paradigm*. New York: Academic Press.

Campbell, J. D. (1986). Similarity and uniqueness: The effects of attribute type, relevance, and individual differences in self-esteem and depression. *Journal of Personality and Social Psychology, 50*, 281–294.

Cialdini, R. B., & Richardson, K. D. (1980). Two indirect tactics of image management: Basking and blasting. *Journal of Personality and Social Psychology, 39*, 406–415.

Cooley, C. H. (1902). *Human nature and the social order*. New York: Scribner's.

Curtis, R. C., & Miller, K. (1986). Believing another likes or dislikes you: Behavior making the beliefs come true. *Journal of Personality and Social Psychology, 51*, 284–290.

Damon, W. (1983). *Social and personality development*. New York: W. W. Norton.

Dittes, J. E. (1959). Attractiveness of group as a function of self-esteem and acceptance by group. *Journal of Abnormal and Social Psychology, 59*, 77–82.

Englander, M. A. (1960). A psychological analysis of vocational choice: Teaching. *Journal of Counseling Psychology, 7*, 257–264.

Epstein, S. (1973). The self-concept revisited: Or a theory of a theory. *American Psychologist, 28*, 404–416.

Epstein, S. (1983). The unconscious, the precocious, and the self-concept. In J. Suls & A. G. Greenwald (Eds.), *Psychological perspectives on the self* (Vol. 2, pp. 219–247). Hillsdale, NJ: Erlbaum.

Eshel, Y., & Klein, Z. (1981). Development of academic self-concept of lower-class and middle-class primary school children. *Journal of Educational Psychology, 73*, 287–293.

Fazio, R. H. (1986). How do attitudes guide behavior? In R. M. Sorrentino & E. Tory Higgins (Eds.), *Motivation and cognition: Foundations of social behavior*. New York: Guilford.

Fernald, A. (1989). *Emotion and meaning in mothers' speech to infants*. Paper presented at annual meetings of Society for Research in Child Development, Kansas City, KS.

Festinger, L. (1957). *A theory of cognitive dissonance*. Evanston, IL: Row & Peterson.

Finn, S. E., & Tonsager, M. E. (1991). *The therapeutic effects of providing MMPI-2 feedback to college students awaiting psychotherapy*. Manuscript submitted for publication.

Goffman, E. (1959). *The presentation of self in everyday life*. New York: Anchor.

Greenwald, A. G. (1980). The totalitarian ego: Fabrication and revision of personal history. *American Psychologist, 35*, 603–618.

Hoffman, M. L. (1986). Affect, cognition and motivation. In R. M. Sorrentino & E. T. Higgins (Eds.), *Handbook of motivation and cognition* (pp. 244–280). New York: Guilford.

Jacobs, L. E., Berscheid, E., & Walster, E. (1971). Self-esteem and attraction. *Journal of Personality and Social Psychology, 17,* 84–91.

Jones, E. E. (1964). *Ingratiation.* New York: Appleton-Century-Crofts.

Jones, E. E. (1990). *Interpersonal perception.* New York: W. H. Freeman.

Jones, E. E., & Pittman, T. S. (1982). Toward a general theory of strategic self-presentation. In J. Suls (Ed.), *Psychological perspectives on the self* (pp. 231–262). Hillsdale, NJ: Lawrence Erlbaum.

Jones, S. C. (1973). Self and interpersonal evaluations: Esteem theories versus consistency theories. *Psychological Bulletin, 79,* 185–199.

Jones, S. C., & Pines, H. A. (1968). Self-revealing event and interpersonal evaluation. *Journal of Personality and Social Psychology, 8,* 277–281.

Jones, S. C., & Ratner, C. (1967). Commitment to self-appraisal and interpersonal evaluations. *Journal of Personality and Social Psychology, 6,* 442–447.

Jones, S. C., & Schneider, D. J. (1968). Certainty of self-appraisal and reactions to evaluations from others. *Sociometry, 31,* 395–403.

Langer, E. J. (1989). *Mindfulness.* Reading, MA: Addison-Wesley.

Lecky, P. (1945). *Self-consistency: A theory of personality.* New York: Island.

Lewis, M. (1987). Social development in infancy and early childhood. In J. D. Osofsky (Ed.), *Handbook of infant development.* New York: John Wiley.

Maracek, J., & Mettee, D. R. (1972). Avoidance of continued success as a function of self-esteem, level of esteem certainty, and responsibility for success. *Journal of Personality and Social Psychology, 22,* 90–107.

Mead, G. H. (1934). *Mind, self and society.* Chicago: University of Chicago Press.

Nicholls, J. (1978). The development of the concepts of effort and ability, perceptions of academic attainment and the understanding that difficult tasks require more ability. *Child Development, 49,* 800–814.

Nicholls, J. (1979). The development of the perception of own attainment and causal attributions for success and failure in reading. *Journal of Educational Psychology, 71,* 94–99.

Pelham, B. W. (1991). On confidence and consequence: The certainty and importance of self-knowledge. *Journal of Personality and Social Psychology, 60,* 518–530.

Pittman, T. S., & Heller, J. F. (1987). Social motivation. In M. R. Rosenzweig & L. W. Porter (Eds.), *Annual Review of Psychology, 38,* 461–489.

Robinson, D. T., & Smith-Lovin, L. (1992). Selective interaction as a strategy for identity negotiation: A case of irrational choice. *Social Psychology Quarterly, 55,* 12–28.

Schlenker, B. R. (1980). *Impression management.* Belmont, CA: Wadsworth.

Schlenker, B. R. (1985). Identities and self-identification. In B. R. Schlenker (Ed.), *The self and social life.* New York: McGraw-Hill.

Secord, P. F., & Backman, C. W. (1965). An interpersonal approach to personality. In B. Maher (Ed.), *Progress in experimental personality research, vol. 2* (pp. 91–125). New York: Academic Press.

Shapiro, B., Eppler, M., Haith, M., & Reis, H. (1987). *An event analysis of facial attractiveness and expressiveness.* Paper presented at the Society for Research in Child Development, Baltimore, MD.

Sherif, C. W., Sherif, M., & Nebergall, R. E. (1961). *Attitude and attitude change: The social judgment-involvement approach.* Philadelphia: Saunders.

Sherman, S. J., & Gorkin, L. (1980). Attitude bolstering when behavior is inconsistent with central attitudes. *Journal of Experimental Social Psychology, 16,* 388–403.

Shrauger, J. S. (1975). Responses to evaluation as a function of initial self-perceptions. *Psychological Bulletin, 82,* 581–596.

Simon, H. A. (1957). *Models of man.* New York: John Wiley.

Skolnik, P. (1971). Reactions to personal evaluations: A failure to replicate. *Journal of Personality and Social Psychology, 18*, 656–666.

Snyder, C. R., & Higgins, R. L. (1988). Excuses: Their effective role in the negotiation of social reality. *Psychological Bulletin, 104*, 25–35.

Snyder, M., & Swann, W. B., Jr. (1976). When actions reflect attitudes: The politics of impression management. *Journal of Personality and Social Psychology, 34*, 1034–1042.

Steele, C. M. (1988). The psychology of self-affirmation: Sustaining the integrity of the self. In L. Berkowitz (Ed.), *Advances in experimental social psychology, vol. 21* (pp. 261–302). New York: Academic Press.

Stern, C. C., & Scanlon, J. C. (1958). Pediatric lions and gynecological lambs. *Journal of Medical Education, 33*, 12–18.

Stipek, D. (1981). Children's perceptions of their own and their classmates' ability. *Journal of Educational Psychology, 73*, 404–410.

Stipek, D. J., & Daniels, D. H. (1988). Declining perceptions of competence: A consequence of changes in the child or in the educational environment? *Journal of Educational Psychology, 80*, 352–356.

Stipek, D., & Tannatt, L. (1984). Children's judgments of their own and their peers' academic competence. *Journal of Educational Psychology, 76*, 75–84.

Stryker, S. (1981). *Symbolic interactionism.* Menlo Park, CA: Benjamin/Cummings.

Swann, W. B., Jr. (1987). Identity negotiation: Where two roads meet. *Journal of Personality and Social Psychology, 53*, 1038–1051.

Swann, W. B., Jr. (1990). To be adored or to be known: The interplay of self-enhancement and self-verification. In R. M. Sorrentino & E. T. Higgins (Eds.), *Motivation and cognition, Vol. 2* (pp. 408–448). New York: Guilford.

Swann, W. B., Jr. (1992). Seeking truth, finding despair: Some unhappy consequences of a negative self-concept. *Current Directions in Psychological Science, 1*, 15–18.

Swann, W. B., Jr., & Ely, R. J. (1984). A battle of wills: Self-verification versus behavioral confirmation. *Journal of Personality and Social Psychology, 46*, 1287–1302.

Swann, W. B., Jr., Griffin, J. J., Predmore, S., & Gaines, B. (1987). The cognitive-affective crossfire: When self-consistency confronts self-enhancement. *Journal of Personality and Social Psychology, 52*, 881–889.

Swann, W. B., Jr., & Hill, C. A. (1982). When our identities are mistaken: Reaffirming self-conceptions through social interaction. *Journal of Personality and Social Psychology, 43*, 59–66.

Swann, W. B., Jr., De La Ronde, C., & Hixon, J. G. (1993). Authenticity strivings in courtship and marriage. Manuscript submitted for publication.

Swann, W. B., Jr., Hixon, J. G., & De La Ronde, C. (in press). Embracing the bitter truth: Negative self-concepts and marital commitment. *Psychological Science, 3*, 118–121.

Swann, W. B., Jr., Hixon, J. G., Stein-Seroussi, A., & Gilbert, D. T. (1990). The fleeting gleam of praise: Behavioral reactions to self-relevant feedback. *Journal of Personality and Social Psychology, 59*, 17–26.

Swann, W. B., Jr., Pelham, B. W., & Chidester, T. (1988). Change through paradox: Using self-verification to alter beliefs. *Journal of Personality and Social Psychology, 54*, 268–273.

Swann, W. B., Jr., Pelham, B. W., & Krull, D. S. (1989). Agreeable fancy or disagreeable truth? How people reconcile their self-enhancement and self-verification needs. *Journal of Personality and Social Psychology, 57*, 782–791.

Swann, W. B., Jr., & Read, S. J. (1981a). Acquiring self-knowledge: The search for feedback that fits. *Journal of Personality and Social Psychology, 41*, 1119–1128.

Swann, W. B., Jr., & Read, S. J. (1981b). Self-verification processes: How we sustain our self-conceptions. *Journal of Experimental Social Psychology, 17*, 351–372.

Swann, W. B., Jr., Stein-Seroussi, A., & Giesler, R. B. (1992). Why people self-verify. *Journal of Personality and Social Psychology, 62,* 392–401.

Swann, W. B., Jr., Wenzlaff, R. M., Krull, D. S., & Pelham, B. W. (1992). The allure of negative feedback: Self-verification strivings among depressed persons. *Journal of Abnormal Psychology, 101,* 293–306.

Swann, W. B., Jr., Wenzlaff, R. M., & Tafarodi, R. W. (1992). Depression and the search for negative evaluations: More evidence of the role of self-verification strivings. *Journal of Abnormal Psychology, 101,* 314–317.

Taylor, S. E., & Brown, J. D. (1988). Illusion and well being: Some social psychological contributions to a theory of mental health. *Psychological Bulletin, 103,* 193–210.

Taylor, S. E., & Lobel, M. (1989). Social comparison activity under threat: Downward evaluation and upward contacts. *Psychological Review, 96,* 569–575.

Tedeschi, J. T., & Lindskold, S. (1976). *Social psychology: Interdependence, interaction, and influence.* New York: John Wiley.

Tesser, A. (1986). Some effects of self-evaluation maintenance on cognition and action. In R. M. Sorrentino & E. T. Higgins (Eds.), *Handbook of motivation and cognition* (pp. 435–464). New York: Guilford.

Tesser, A. (1989). Self-generated attitude change. In L. Berkowitz (Ed.), *Advances in experimental social psychology, vol. 8* (pp. 193–232). New York: Academic Press.

Tesser, A., & Campbell, J. (1983). Self-definition and self-evaluation maintenance. In J. Suls & A. G. Greenwald (Eds.), *Social psychological perspectives on the self, vol. 2* Hillsdale, NJ: Lawrence Erlbaum.

Trope, Y. (1986). Self-enhancement and self-assessment in achievement behavior. In R. M. Sorrentino & E. T. Higgins (Eds.), *Handbook of motivation and cognition, vol. 1* (pp. 350–378). New York: Guilford.

Walster, E. (1970). The effect of self-esteem on liking for dates of various social desirability. *Journal of Experimental Social Psychology, 6,* 248–253.

Weinstein, N. D. (1980). Unrealistic optimism about future life events. *Journal of Personality and Social Psychology, 39,* 806–820.

Wills, T. A. (1981). Downward comparison principles in social psychology. *Psychological Bulletin, 90,* 245–271.

Zajonc, R. B. (1980). Feeling and thinking: Preferences need no inferences. *American Psychologist, 35,* 151–175.

Zuckerman, M. (1979). Attribution of success and failure revisited, or the motivational bias is alive and well in attribution theory. *Journal of Personality, 47,* 245–287.

CHAPTER 9

THE ROLES OF STABILITY AND LEVEL OF SELF-ESTEEM IN PSYCHOLOGICAL FUNCTIONING

MICHAEL H. KERNIS

During the past 30 years, a considerable amount of research has been conducted to examine the role of self-esteem in individuals' thoughts, feelings, and actions. For the most part, this research has been directed toward the examination of *level* of self-esteem as the critical aspect of self-esteem. Some researchers, however, have begun to focus on such other aspects as *certainty* and *stability* of self-esteem (e.g., Baumgardner, 1990; Harris & Snyder, 1985; Maracek & Mettee, 1972; Rosenberg, 1986; Savin-Williams & Demo, 1983). In this chapter, I summarize the recent efforts of myself and colleagues to understand the role of stability of self-esteem (in combination with its level) in psychological functioning. I will begin by describing briefly the nature of stability of self-esteem and its assessment. Then I present a theoretical framework for understanding the joint influences of stability and level of self-esteem on people's reactions to evaluative events. Following this, research that bears on this framework will be described. As will be shown, important individual

MICHAEL H. KERNIS • Department of Psychology and Institute for Behavioral Research, University of Georgia, Athens, GA 30602.

Self-Esteem: The Puzzle of Low Self-Regard, edited by Roy F. Baumeister. Plenum Press, New York, 1993.

differences would have been obscured if both stability and level of self-esteem had not been taken into consideration. I conclude by focusing on some issues of validity related to the assessment and conceptualization of stability of self-esteem.

CONCEPTUALIZATION AND ASSESSMENT OF STABILITY OF SELF-ESTEEM

Stability of self-esteem has been conceptualized in terms of either long-term or short-term fluctuations. Viewed as long-term fluctuations, stability of self-esteem reflects change in an individual's baseline level of self-esteem that occurs "slowly and over an extended period of time" (Rosenberg, 1986, p. 126). For example, gradual change in self-esteem may occur over several years in response to academic or career success. Viewed as short-term fluctuations, stability of self-esteem reflects the magnitude of change in immediate, contextually based self-esteem (Kernis, Grannemann, & Barclay, 1989; Rosenberg, 1986; Savin-Williams & Demo, 1983). Examples of short-term fluctuations are the temporary increases or decreases in self-esteem that people may experience in response to specific evaluative events. It is crucial to distinguish between these two conceptualizations of self-esteem stability, because individuals may exhibit substantial short-term fluctuations while manifesting little or no long-term change in baseline self-esteem (see Rosenberg, 1986). Although both types of stability are likely to have important implications for psychological functioning, our research has focused on stability of self-esteem as manifested in short-term fluctuations.

To measure the magnitude of these short-term fluctuations, my colleagues and I obtain multiple assessments, on a daily or more frequent basis, of individuals' self-esteem as they are going about their everyday activities. Specifically, participants complete Rosenberg's Self-Esteem Scale (1965) under instructions to base their responses on how they feel *at that particular moment* (i. e., current or contextually based self-esteem). An index of self-esteem stability is then formed by computing the standard deviation of total self-esteem scores across these repeated assessments; the greater the standard deviation, the greater the degree of self-esteem instability. Issues related to the validity of this assessment technique will be discussed in a later section.

A THEORETICAL FRAMEWORK

Theoretically, self-esteem (or self-concept) instability has been associated with enhanced sensitivity to evaluative events, increased concern about one's self-view, and an overreliance on social sources of evaluation (Kernis, Grannemann, & Barclay, 1989; Kugle, Clements, & Powell, 1983; Rosenberg, 1986; Turner, 1968). Note that these characteristics can *promote* unstable self-esteem as well as be products of it. Rosenberg (1986), for example, suggests that overreliance on social sources of evaluation can promote unstable self-esteem as a result of the ambiguous and potentially contradictory nature of others' sentiments. Likewise, heightened sensitivity to specific evaluative events can promote unstable self-esteem. Viewed as products, on the other hand, these characteristics suggest that individuals with unstable self-esteem may react more strongly to a wide range of evaluative events than do individuals with stable self-esteem. The nature of the reactions, however—as well as the types of events reacted to—may also depend on individuals' level of self-esteem (Kernis, Grannemann, & Barclay, 1992). I turn now to a discussion of these issues.

I assume, as have others, (e. g., Rogers, 1961), that people typically strive to feel as positively about themselves as they can. For unstable high self-esteem individuals, the goal would seem to be more stable and secure positive self-feelings.* For unstable low self-esteem individuals, though, a variety of environmental and personal constraints are likely to place stable positive self-feelings beyond their immediate grasp (Brown, Collins, & Schmidt, 1988). Instead, a more likely goal for these individuals is the avoidance of continuously (i.e., stable) negative self-feelings.

I believe that as a consequence of the desire to achieve more stable and secure positive self-feelings, individuals with unstable high self-esteem will be especially sensitive to both positive and negative evaluative events. In response to positive events, they are expected to react especially favorably, perhaps even embellishing the events' positive self-relevant implications. In so doing, they are at least able to maintain their positive, yet tenuous self-feelings. In fact, if this can be done often enough, they may be able to create artificially a semblance of secure positive self-feelings for themselves (see Kernis, Grannemann, & Barclay, 1992). The precarious nature of their positive self-feelings, however, can be easily uncovered by their strong, adverse reactions to negative evaluative events. In contrast, individuals with stable high self-esteem are thought to possess very secure positive self-feelings and, as a consequence, to be not very reactive to either positive or negative self-relevant events.

---

*For ease of presentation, throughout the chapter I refer to stable and unstable low and high self-esteem individuals. It is important to note, however, that stability of self-esteem is conceptualized and operationalized as a continuous dimension along which people vary.

Among individuals with low self-esteem, the psychological qualities thought to be associated with unstable self-esteem are somewhat
more complex. In my view, individuals with unstable self-esteem
"work" at avoiding a continuously negative self-view, in part by using
strategies that reduce the adverse impact of potentially threatening
events. Stated differently, individuals with unstable low self-esteem are
thought to be more resilient and have less adverse reactions to threatening self-relevant events, compared to individuals with stable low self-
esteem. I do not believe, however, that individuals with unstable low
self-esteem will react substantially more favorably to positive events
than their stable low self-esteem counterparts, because of concerns as to
whether a positive identity can be successfully defended (Brown et al.,
1988). Table 1 summarizes the hypothesized psychological qualities and
manifestations of stable and unstable low and high self-esteem.

In the following sections, I describe a series of studies in which my
colleagues and I have examined the roles of stability and level of self-
esteem in anger and hostility proneness, excuse making following success and failure, reactions to interpersonal feedback, and depression.
These particular phenomena were examined because of their central
relevance to self-esteem-related processes and psychological functioning.

INDIVIDUAL DIFFERENCES IN ANGER AROUSAL AND HOSTILITY

Numerous arguments have been made linking either low or high
self-esteem to heightened tendencies to experience anger and hostility.
For example, it has been suggested that high self-esteem individuals may
be quick to respond to threats with anger and hostility in order to protect
their positive self-feelings (Crocker, Thompson, McGraw, & Ingerman,
1987). In addition, it has been argued that self-esteem threats are more
likely to be perceived as unjustified if one's self-esteem is high than if it is
low, and that unjustified threats are more likely to prompt anger (Averill,
1982). On the other hand, it has been suggested that low self-esteem may
be associated with greater proneness to experience anger and hostility,
because threats to an already low self-view are likely to be particularly
aversive (Averill, 1982).

Interestingly, investigations of the relationship between level of self-
esteem and aggression have yielded conflicting findings. Sometimes high
self-esteem appears to be related to greater aggression, yet at other times,
low self-esteem appears to be related to greater aggression (Licht, 1966;
Olweus, 1978; Rosenbaum & DeCharms, 1960; Toch, 1969; Worchel, 1958).

TABLE 1. Self-Esteem Status Descriptions

Self-esteem Status	Psychological Qualities and Manifestations
Stable high	Secure in positive self-feelings, not easily threatened Manifestations: not very reactive to specific instances of positive or negative evaluative events
Unstable high	Fragile self-feelings, easily threatened Manifestations: strong adverse reactions to negative evaluative events; embellish favorable implications of positive evaluative events
Unstable low	More resilient than individuals with stable low self-esteem, attempt to avoid continuous negative self-feelings Manifestations: less adverse reactions to negative evaluative events; increased use of strategies to counteract adverse impact of threatening events; do not react especially favorably to positive self-relevant events
Stable low	Continuous negative self-feelings Manifestations: little attempt to counteract adverse impact of negative self-relevant events or to assimilate positive self-relevant events

Prior to our research (Kernis, Grannemann, & Barclay, 1989), however, the relation between level of self-esteem (let alone stability of self-esteem) and anger/hostility proneness had yet to be examined.

Our sample consisted of 45 male and female undergraduate students who completed, in addition to measures of stability and level of self-esteem, a number of anger and hostility inventories, including the Novaco Anger Inventory (Novaco, 1975), the Trait Anger Scale (Spielberger, Jacobs, Russell, & Crane, 1983), and the Buss-Durkee Hostility Inventory (Buss & Durkee, 1957). Several important findings emerged. First, self-esteem instability, especially among individuals with high self-esteem, was related to greater anger and hostility proneness. In fact, unstable high self-esteem individuals reported the highest tendencies to experience anger and hostility, whereas stable high self-esteem individuals reported the lowest. Anger and hostility are often instigated by self-esteem threats of an interpersonal nature, such as insults or criticism (e. g., Averill, 1982; da Gloria, 1984; Feshbach, 1970; Maslow, 1941). In these instances, becoming angry and hostile may serve a variety of functions, including defending against negative self-feelings (Novaco, 1975) and restoring one's damaged self-esteem (Feshbach, 1970) or public self-image (Felson, 1984).

The fact that individuals with unstable high self-esteem reported especially high tendencies to experience anger and hostility is consistent with the assertion that they possess fragile self-feelings that are highly vulnerable to challenge from various kinds of provocations. For these individuals, it appears, anger and hostility serve a self-protective function. At the other extreme, the especially low tendencies of individuals with stable high self-esteem to experience anger and hostility supports the assertion that these individuals have little reason to feel threatened by provocations. Instead, given their secure positive self-feelings, provocations are likely to "roll off" them without arousing much ire.

A second finding was that stable and unstable low self-esteem individuals reported moderate tendencies, greater than stable high self-esteem individuals but less than unstable high self-esteem individuals. This pattern is especially illuminating in light of the inconsistent findings reported in the literature concerning the relation between level of self-esteem and aggression. Low self-esteem individuals may be more likely to experience anger and hostility than stable high self-esteem individuals because of the sheer aversiveness of various provocations to an already low self-view (Averill, 1982). Furthermore, for many low self-esteem individuals, anger and hostility may be relatively primitive and automatic reactions to this heightened aversiveness (see Berkowitz & Heimer, 1989), rather than reactions that serve a self-protective function. The possibility that anger and hostility serve different functions for high and low self-esteem individuals is speculative at this point; nonetheless, it seems intriguing enough to warrant direct examination.

Third, among low self-esteem individuals, stability of self-esteem had virtually no impact on anger/hostility proneness. As will be described in a later section, however, unstable low self-esteem individuals do react less defensively than stable low self-esteem individuals to explicit interpersonally-based self-esteem threats. Finally, no overall differences in anger and hostility proneness emerged as a function of level of self-esteem per se. This last finding is very important because it indicates that heightened tendencies to experience anger and hostility are not simply a function of either low or high self-esteem.

EXCUSE MAKING

Excuse making can serve both self-protective and self-enhancement functions. Following poor performance, excuse making can be considered self-protective because it reduces the negative diagnostic value of the outcome. Most theoretical and empirical treatments of excuse making emphasize its self-protective function (Darley & Goethals, 1980; Kernis & Grannemann, 1990; Schlenker, 1980; Snyder & Higgins, 1988). In addition, however, excuse making following success can be considered self-enhancing because it implies that success occurred in spite of the operation of inhibitory factors (Kelley, 1972).

The question we (Kernis, Grannemann, & Barclay, 1992) addressed was whether stability and level of self-esteem predict differential tendencies to make excuses in either a self-protective or self-enhancing manner. Our participants were students in a large introductory psychology class who agreed to take part in the project in exchange for extra credit. Stability and level of self-esteem were measured several weeks prior to their first exam. For purposes of the study, participants were placed into the success category if the letter grade they received on the exam was equal to or better than what they had previously stated was their minimally satisfying grade; conversely, they were placed into the failure category if their grade fell below their minimally satisfying grade. Immediately following receipt of performance feedback, they completed a measure of excuse making derived from the attributional model of Darley and Goethals (1980). Specifically, participants rated the extent to which a variety of inhibiting *power* (e.g., "I didn't get enough sleep the night before the exam"), *motivational* (e.g., "I didn't care enough to study hard for this exam"), and *task difficulty* (e.g., "The amount of material covered on this exam was too much") factors affected their performance (for a full description of this measure, see Kernis & Grannemann, 1990; Kernis et al., 1992).

Several findings emerged that are of particular importance in the present context. Among individuals with high self-esteem, self-esteem instability was related to greater excuse making in a self-enhancing manner following success, but not in a self-protective manner following failure. Thus, individuals with unstable high self-esteem engaged in excuse making primarily to embellish the positive implications of successful performance. The fact that they did not engage in enhanced excuse making following failure suggests that (a) they were not very threatened by the failure, or (b) even though they were threatened, they were not well versed in the use of strategies that could reduce the negative diagnostic implications of failure. Unfortunately, the data do not allow us to distinguish between these two alternatives, so resolution of this issue awaits further research.

In contrast, among individuals with low self-esteem, self-esteem instability was related to greater excuse making following failure, but not following success. Thus, individuals with unstable low self-esteem appear to engage in excuse making primarily as a way of diminishing the negative implications of a poor performance. In other research (Kernis, Brockner, & Frankel, 1989), we have shown that low self-esteem is associated with a greater tendency to overgeneralize the implications of specific instances of failure (Carver & Ganellen, 1983). Most importantly, other data that we have collected indicate that this seems to be more true for stable than for unstable low self-esteem individuals. Thus, not only are unstable low self-esteem individuals less likely to overgeneralize the impact of failure than stable low self-esteem individuals, they are also more likely to offer excuses that can help to reduce the adverse impact of failure. The fact that individuals with unstable low self-esteem did not engage in enhanced excuse making following success indicates that, as anticipated, they do not attempt to embellish the positive implications of their own performances.

The asymmetrical effects of unstable self-esteem among high versus low self-esteem individuals are striking. They suggest that whereas unstable high self-esteem individuals attempt to embellish the positive implications of a successful performance, unstable low self-esteem individuals attempt to diminish the negative implications of a poor performance. As was the case for anger/hostility proneness, no differences in excuse making emerged as a function of level of self-esteem per se. Thus, once again, a full explanation of the results necessitated considering both stability and level of self-esteem.

REACTIONS TO INTERPERSONAL FEEDBACK

In a recent study (Swann, Griffin, Predmore, & Gaines, 1987), socially confident and socially insecure individuals received either positive or negative feedback regarding their social skills. A variety of cognitive and affective reactions to the feedback then were assessed. Cognitive reactions included judgments of the accuracy of the feedback, the validity of the evaluation technique, and the competence of the evaluator. Affective reactions and liking for the evaluator (considered to be a hybrid cognitive-affective measure) were also assessed. On all of the cognitive measures (and the hybrid measure), socially confident individuals responded more favorably to positive feedback and less favorably to negative feedback than did socially insecure individuals. Overall, emotional reactions were more favorable following positive than negative feedback; no self-confidence differences emerged.

The procedures that my colleagues and I (Kernis, Cornell, Sun, Berry, & Harlow, 1993, Study 1) employed were very similar to those of Swann et al. (1987), except that we (a) assessed participants' global self-esteem (both with regard to level and stability) rather than their social confidence, (b) used a different measure of emotional reactions, and (c) included a measure of excuse making.

Although there were several notable exceptions, the findings that emerged for level of self-esteem per se were generally consistent with those that emerged in the Swann et al. (1987) study (for a description of these data, see Kernis et al., 1993, Study 1). Most importantly for the present purposes, differences among both high and low self-esteem individuals emerged in our study as a function of self-esteem stability. Among high self-esteem individuals who received positive feedback, self-esteem instability was related to viewing the feedback as somewhat more accurate, to regarding the evaluator as being especially competent and likable, and to experiencing more positive affect. Thus, among high self-esteem individuals, unstable self-esteem was related to more favorable reactions to positive feedback.

In contrast, among high self-esteem individuals who received negative feedback, self-esteem instability was associated with greater derogation of the evaluation technique and the evaluator, and with somewhat greater excuse-making. Minimizing the relevance of negative evaluations and attacking the credibility of the source are important to achieving a more secure positive self-view. In essence, individuals with unstable high self-esteem appeared to be attempting to locate the cause of the negative feedback within the evaluator and the evaluation technique. This tendency to externalize the cause of interpersonal threats may be one reason why individuals with unstable high self-esteem are especially prone to experience anger and hostility (Kernis et al., 1989; Kulik & Brown, 1979).

Among individuals with low self-esteem who received negative feedback, self-esteem instability was associated with less rejection of the evaluator (i.e., viewing her as more competent and likable). Interestingly, these reactions occurred even though self-esteem instability was related to greater perceived accuracy of the feedback and perceived validity of the evaluative technique. Thus, even though unstable low self-esteem individuals viewed negative feedback as more accurate and valid than did stable low self-esteem individuals, they nevertheless were less likely to "take it out" on the evaluator. Finally, as anticipated, among individuals with low self-esteem, self-esteem stability did not relate to more favorable reactions to positive feedback.

In sum, among high self-esteem individuals, self-esteem instability is related to more favorable reactions to positive feedback and more defensive reactions to negative feedback. Among low self-esteem individuals, self-esteem instability is related to less defensive reactions to negative feedback. These findings indicate that both level and stability of self-esteem are related to individual differences in reactions to interpersonal feedback.

DEPRESSION

There are strong theoretical and empirical justifications for linking low self-esteem with depression. Beck's theory of depression (1967), for example, holds that negative self-evaluations are an important component (perhaps even a causal determinant) of depressive episodes. Also, negative self-evaluations are one of the diagnostic criteria for clinical depression (American Psychiatric Association, 1987). In support of this proposed linkage, the results of numerous studies document the strong inverse relation between self-esteem and depression (e.g., Tennen & Herzberger, 1987). Recently, my colleagues and I (Kernis, Grannemann, & Mathis, 1991) examined the extent to which stability of self-esteem moderates the predictive relationship between level of self-esteem and depression.

Recall that individuals with stable self-esteem experience less extreme day-to-day self-esteem fluctuations than do individuals with unstable self-esteem. Thus, for individuals with stable self-esteem, the esteem with which they view themselves at any point in time is likely to be highly congruent with their level of self-esteem. It follows that any predictive relationship that exists between self-esteem level and depression should be especially strong for these individuals. For individuals with unstable self-esteem, however, the esteem in which they hold themselves at any point in time may be very different from their self-esteem level. Consequently, for these individuals, the predictive relation between level of self-esteem and depression should be much weaker.

Participants in this study completed the Center for Epidemiological Studies Depression Scale (CES-D; Weissman, Sholomskas, Pottenger, Prusoff, & Locke, 1977) approximately 5 weeks after they completed measures of stability and level of self-esteem. Consistent with much prior research, a strong inverse relation emerged between self-esteem level and depression. Most important, stability of self-esteem significantly moderated this relation. Predicted values indicated that, as anticipated, self-esteem level was a much stronger predictor of subsequent depression for stable than for unstable self-esteem individuals. In fact, among individuals with unstable self-esteem, there was little relationship between level of self-esteem and depression. Subsequent analyses indicated that the greater predictability of depression for stable than for unstable self-esteem individuals was not attributable to the former individuals possessing more extreme levels of self-esteem (see Paunonen, 1988; Tellegen, 1988).

Examination of predicted values also indicated that unstable self-esteem was associated with less depression among individuals with low self-esteem, but to greater depression among individuals with high self-esteem. Thus, to the extent that low self-esteem promotes depression (Wilson & Krane, 1980), it appears that stable low self-esteem individuals are most vulnerable. The decrease in depression associated with unstable low self-esteem may reflect the fact that these individuals are more resilient and react less adversely to negative evaluative events (e.g., Kernis et al., 1992). At the other extreme, it appears that stable high self-esteem individuals are least vulnerable to experiencing depression. The increase in depression associated with unstable high self-esteem may reflect the fact that these individuals possess fragile self-feelings that are highly vulnerable to challenge. Further research is needed, however, to document the validity of these speculations and to examine more directly the factors that link stability and level of self-esteem to depression.

ISSUES OF ASSESSMENT AND VALIDITY

Is There an Easier Way to Assess Stability of Self-Esteem?

The assessment of self-esteem stability through repeated assessments necessitates a substantial level of involvement on the part of both participants and researchers. It would be much easier to conduct research if stability of self-esteem could be assessed with a single administration of a self-report measure. In our research, we have included a variety of self-report measures to see if they relate strongly enough to our measure of self-esteem stability to serve as an adequate substitute. Specifically, my colleagues and I have examined the utility of (a) Rosenberg's Stability of Self Scale (1965), (b) an index of certainty of self-esteem, (c) responses to the Crowne and Marlowe (1960) Social Desirability Scale (which is thought to tap defensive self-esteem), (d) a self-report measure of the extent to which individuals' self-views are affected by transient evaluative events (Kernis & Grannemann, 1987), and (e) simply asking people how much they think that they would change their self-esteem responses on a day-to-day basis. None of these measures, however, correlated highly enough ($rs < \pm.28$) with our stability of self-esteem measure to be considered a viable substitute. Moreover, when we have substituted these alternative measures for stability of self-esteem in analyses predicting various outcomes, they do not yield similar (nor readily interpretable) patterns. Consequently, we are increasingly convinced that to measure stability of self-esteem, repeated assessments of contextually-based (i.e., current) self-esteem are needed.

Is Stability of Self-Esteem the Same Thing as Mood Variability?

Because fluctuations in self-esteem may be accompanied by fluctuations in mood, the extent to which the two overlap is an important issue. Fortunately, we have collected some relevant data. Kernis et al. (1989) obtained repeated assessments of both mood (via the self-feelings coding sheet; see Savin-Williams & Demo, 1983; Demo, 1985) and self-esteem; stability of self-esteem was not significantly correlated with mood variability ($r[43] = .26$). Furthermore, mood variability related to anger and hostility proneness in a very different manner than did stability of self-esteem. In other research, we (Cornell, Kernis, & Berry, 1991) have administered the Affective Intensity Measure (AIM; Larsen, 1984) to participants whose stability of self-esteem was also assessed. The AIM is designed to assess individual differences in the frequency and intensity of experiencing positive and negative emotions. High scores are reflective, therefore, of greater mood variability. Although (in)stability of self-esteem correlated significantly with scores on the Affective Intensity Measure (AIM; Larsen, 1984), this correlation was not very large ($r[98] = .28$). Taken together, these data indicate that although there is some relationship between stability of self-esteem and mood variability, they are distinct constructs.

Is Stability of Self-Esteem Merely a Statistical Issue of Reliability?

Can we consider individuals with unstable self-esteem simply to be more unreliable in their responses than individuals with stable self-esteem? For several reasons, I believe that it would be wrong to do so. First, it would mean ignoring the psychological significance of stability of self-esteem. As my colleagues and I have shown repeatedly, theoretically meaningful differences within (and between) self-esteem levels have emerged as a function of stability of self-esteem. Second, when assessing stability of self-esteem, we explicitly direct people to respond on the basis of how they feel at a particular moment in time. These current, contextually based responses can be thought of as reflecting the unstable component of self-esteem. Moreover, because people can legitimately change how they feel about themselves from day to day, there is ample justification for viewing such changes as reflecting the true-score component of responses rather than the error component (for a related discussion, see Tellegen, 1988). In contrast, when assessing *level* of self-esteem, we now explicitly direct people to respond on the basis of how they typically, or generally, feel about themselves. In my view, such responses are more akin to the stable or baseline component of self-esteem. Evidence supporting the distinction between current and typical self-evaluations is reported in Kernis and Johnson (1990).

SUMMARY AND CONCLUSIONS

The research discussed in this chapter suggests that it may not be enough to ask how individuals with low self-esteem differ from individuals with high self-esteem. Specifically, it suggests that a full understanding of the role of self-esteem in psychological functioning will necessitate taking into consideration both stability and level of self-esteem.

This chapter has provided a framework for understanding the joint effects of these two aspects of self-esteem. The framework holds that unstable self-esteem has different implications for individuals with high versus low self-esteem. Among high self-esteem individuals, unstable self-esteem appears to reflect more fragile and vulnerable self-feelings, and greater reactivity to both positive and negative self-relevant events. In contrast, among low self-esteem individuals, unstable self-esteem appears to reflect more resilient self-feelings, and less adverse reactions to negative self-relevant events.

Initial evidence bearing on the viability of these assertions was presented. Among high self-esteem individuals, unstable self-esteem was shown to relate to greater tendencies to experience anger, hostility, and depression, greater excuse making following success, and more (or less) favorable reactions to positive (or negative) feedback. Among low self-esteem individuals, unstable self-esteem was shown to relate to lower tendencies to experience depression, greater excuse making following failure, and less defensive reactions to negative feedback. These findings are encouraging. Much more work is needed, however, to assess fully the adequacy of the framework presented in this chapter.

In closing, it may be worthwhile to note that self-esteem instability also represents the possibility of change. Among individuals with high self-esteem, this should be relatively threatening, because it implies that they may lose esteem. Among individuals with low self-esteem, though, this should be relatively encouraging, as it implies that they may gain esteem. The extent to which such changes actually occur, as well as the factors that facilitate or inhibit them, also constitute important research agendas for the future.

ACKNOWLEDGMENTS

The author would like to thank Roy Baumeister and Sid Rosen for their valuable comments on a previous version of this chapter.

REFERENCES

American Psychiatric Association. (1987). *Diagnostic and statistical manual of mental disorders* (3rd ed., rev.). Washington, DC: Author.

Averill, J. R. (1982). *Anger and aggression: An essay on emotion.* New York: Springer-Verlag.

Baumgardner, A. H. (1990). To know oneself is to like oneself: Self-certainty and self-affect. *Journal of Personality and Social Psychology, 58,* 1062–1072.

Beck, A. T. (1967). *Depression: Clinical, experimental and theoretical aspects.* New York: Harper & Row.

Berkowitz, L., & Heimer, K. (1989). On the construction of the anger experience: Aversive events and negative priming in the formation of feelings. In L. Berkowitz (Ed.), *Advances in experimental social psychology, vol. 22.* New York: Academic Press.

Brown, J. D., Collins, R. L., & Schmidt, G. W. (1988). Self-esteem and direct versus indirect forms of self-enhancement. *Journal of Personality and Social Psychology, 55,* 445–453.

Buss, A. H., & Durkee, A. (1957). An inventory for assessing different kinds of hostility. *Journal of Abnormal and Social Psychology, 21,* 343–349.

Carver, C. S., & Ganellen, R. J. (1983). Depression and components of self-punitiveness: High standards, self-criticism, and overgeneralization. *Journal of Abnormal Psychology, 92,* 330–337.

Cornell, D., Kernis, M. H., & Berry, A. (1991). Stability of global and specific aspects of self-esteem. Unpublished manuscript.

Crocker, J., Thompson, L. L., McGraw, K. M., & Ingerman, C. (1987). Downward comparison, prejudice, and evaluations of others: Effects of self-esteem and threat. *Journal of Personality and Social Psychology, 52,* 907–916.

Crowne, D. P., & Marlowe, D. (1960). A new scale of social desirability independent of psychopathology. *Journal of Consulting Psychology, 24,* 349–354.

da Gloria, J. (1984). Frustration, aggression, and the sense of justice. In A. Mummendey (Ed.), *Social psychology of aggression: From individual behavior to social interaction*(pp. 127–142). Berlin: Springer-Verlag.

Darley, J. M., & Goethals, G. R. (1980). People's analyses of ability-linked performances. In L. Berkowitz (Ed.), *Advances in experimental social psychology, vol. 13.* New York: Academic Press.

Demo, D. H. (1985). The measurement of self-esteem: Refining our methods. *Journal of Personality and Social Psychology, 48,* 1490–1502.

Felson, R. B. (1984). Patterns of aggressive social interaction. In A. Mummendey (Ed.), *Social psychology of aggression: From individual behavior to social interaction* (pp. 107–126). Berlin: Springer-Verlag.

Feshbach, S. (1970). Aggression. In P. H. Mussen (Ed.), *Carmichael's manual of child psychology, vol. 2* (pp. 159–259). New York: John Wiley.

Harris, R. N., & Snyder, C. R. (1986). The role of uncertain self-esteem in self-handicapping. *Journal of Personality and Social Psychology, 51,* 451–458.

Kelley, H. H. (1972). Causal schemata and the attribution process. In E. E. Jones, D. E.

Kanouse, H. H. Kelley, R. E. Nisbett, S. Valins, & B. Weiner (Eds.), *Attribution: Perceiving the causes of behavior*. Morristown, NJ: General Learning Press.

Kernis, M. H., Brockner, J., & Frankel, B. S. (1989). Self-esteem and reactions to failure: The mediating role of overgeneralization. *Journal of Personality and Social Psychology, 57,* 707–714.

Kernis, M. H., & Grannemann, B. D. (1987). *Development of the Self-Validation Scale*. Unpublished manuscript, University of Texas at Arlington.

Kernis, M. H., & Grannemann, B. D. (1990). Excuses in the making: A test and extension of Darley and Goethals' attributional model. *Journal of Experimental Social Psychology, 26,* 337–349.

Kernis, M. H., Grannemann, B. D., & Barclay, L. C. (1989). Stability and level of self-esteem as predictors of anger arousal and hostility. *Journal of Personality and Social Psychology, 56,* 1013–1023.

Kernis, M. H., Grannemann, B. D., & Mathis, L. C. (1991). Stability of self-esteem as a moderator of the relation between level of self-esteem and depression. *Journal of Personality and Social Psychology, 61,* 80–84.

Kernis, M. H., Grannemann, B. D., & Barclay, L. C. (1992). Stability of self-esteem: Assessment, correlates, and excuse making. *Journal of Personality, 60,* 621–644.

Kernis, M. H., & Johnson, E. K. (1990). Current and typical self-appraisals: Differential responsiveness to evaluative feedback and implications for emotions. *Journal of Research in Personality, 24,* 241–257.

Kernis, M. H., Cornell, D. P., Sun, C. R., Berry, A., & Harlow, T. (1993). There's more to self-esteem than whether it's high or low: The importance of self-esteem stability. Manuscript submitted for publication.

Kernis, M. H., Cornell, D. P., Sun, C. R., Berry, A., & Harlow, T. (in press). There's more to self-esteem than whether it's high or low: The importance of self-esteem stability. *Journal of Personality and Social Psychology.*

Kugle, C. L., Clements, R. O., & Powell, P. M. (1983). Level and stability of self-esteem in relation to academic behavior of second graders. *Journal of Personality and Social Psychology, 44,* 201–207.

Kulik, J. A., & Brown, R. (1979). Frustration, attribution of blame, and aggression. *Journal of Experimental Social Psychology, 15,* 183–194.

Larsen, R. J. (1984). Theory and measurement of affect intensity as an individual difference characteristic. *Dissertation Abstracts International, 85,* 2297B (University Microfilms, No. 84-22112).

Licht, L. A. (1966). *Direct and displaced physical aggression as a function of level of self-esteem and method of anger arousal*. Unpublished doctoral dissertation, University of California at Los Angeles.

Maracek, J., & Mettee, D. (1972). Avoidance of continued success as a function of self-esteem, level of esteem certainty, and responsibility for success. *Journal of Personality and Social Psychology, 22,* 98–107.

Maslow, A. H. (1941). Deprivation, threat, and frustration. *Psychological Review, 48,* 364–366.

Novaco, R. W. (1975). *Anger control: The development and evaluation of an experimental treatment*. Lexington, MA: D. C. Heath.

Olweus, D. (1978). *Aggression in the schools: Bullies and whipping boys*. Washington, DC: Hemisphere.

Paunonen, S. V. (1988). Trait relevance and the differential predictability of behavior. *Journal of Personality, 56,* 599–620.

Rogers, C. R. (1961). *On becoming a person: A therapist's view of psychotherapy.* Boston: Houghton Mifflin.

Rosenbaum, M. E., & DeCharms, R. (1960). Direct and vicarious reduction of hostility. *Journal of Abnormal and Social Psychology, 60,* 105–111.

Rosenberg, M. (1965). *Society and the adolescent self-image.* Princeton, NJ: Princeton University Press.

Rosenberg, M. (1986). Self-concept from middle childhood through adolescence. In J. Suls & A. G. Greenwald (Eds.), *Psychological perspectives on the self* (Vol.3). Hillsdale, NJ: Lawrence Erlbaum.

Savin-Williams, R. C., & Demo, D. H. (1983). Situational and transituational determinants of adolescent self-feelings. *Journal of Personality and Social Psychology, 44,* 824–833.

Schlenker, B. R. (1980). *Impression management: The self-concept, social identity, and interpersonal relations.* Monterey, CA: Brooks/Cole.

Snyder, C. R., & Higgins, R. L. (1988). Excuses: Their effective role in the negotiation of reality. *Psychological Bulletin, 104,* 23–35.

Spielberger, C. D., Jacobs, G., Russell, S., & Crane, R. (1983). Assessment of anger: The State-Trait Anger Scale. In J. N. Butcher & C. D. Spielberger (Eds.), *Advances in personality assessment*(Vol.2,pp.159–187). Hillsdale, NJ: Lawrence Erlbaum.

Swann, W. B., Jr., Griffin, J. J., Predmore, S., & Gaines, B. (1987). The cognitive-affective crossfire. When self-consistency confronts self-enhancement. *Journal of Personality and Social Psychology, 52,* 881–889.

Tellegen, A. (1988). The analysis of consistency in personality assessment. *Journal of Personality, 56,* 621–663.

Tennen, H., & Herzberger, S. (1987). Depression, self-esteem, and the absence of self-protective attributional biases. *Journal of Personality and Social Psychology, 52,* 72–80.

Toch, H. (1969). *Violent men.* Chicago: Aldine.

Turner, R. H. (1968). The self-conception in social interaction. In C. Gordon & K. J. Gergen (Eds.), *The self in social interaction.* New York: John Wiley.

Weissman, M. M., Sholomskas, D., Pottenger, M., Prusoff, B. A., & Locke, B. Z. (1977). Assessing depressive symptoms in five psychiatric populations: A validation study. *American Journal of Epidemiology, 106,* 203–214.

Wilson, A. R., & Krane, R. V. (1980). Change in self-esteem and its effects on symptoms of depression. *Cognitive Therapy and Research, 4,* 419–421.

Worchel, P. (1958). Personality factors in the readiness to express aggression. *Journal of Consulting and Clinical Psychology, 14,* 355–359.

CHAPTER 10

ON THE HIGHLY POSITIVE THOUGHTS OF THE HIGHLY DEPRESSED

BRETT W. PELHAM

Most contemporary theories of the self-concept emphasize the self-defeating nature of low self-regard. Along these lines, most researchers would probably agree that one of the most serious drawbacks of low self-esteem is its close connection to clinical disorders such as depression. Consider the story of Ron, a typical student suffering from low self-esteem. After receiving a low score on an exam, Ron became mildly depressed. As suggested by research on the specific beliefs of people low in self-esteem (e.g., see Pelham & Swann, 1989), Ron had always harbored doubts about his abilities. Under the influence of his negative mood, these doubts were transformed into highly negative beliefs, and these negative beliefs eventually increased Ron's emotional distress, which contributed still further to his negative beliefs (see Beck, 1967, 1976, for a relevant discussion). Consistent with work on depression and attributional style, Ron then began to make self-blaming attributions for his growing list of failures, and these self-blaming attributions further intensified his misery (e.g., see Metalsky, Seligman, Semmel, & Peterson, 1982).

BRETT W. PELHAM • Department of Psychology—UCLA, 1285 Franz Hall—405 Hilgard Avenue Los Angeles, CA 90024-1563 Phone: (310) 206-4050, (310) 826-7148.

Self-Esteem: The Puzzle of Low Self-Regard, edited by Roy F. Baumeister. Plenum Press, New York, 1993.

By now, Ron had become severely depressed, and his growing depression, combined with his plummeting self-esteem, increased his tendency to engage in self-focus after failure. This excessive self-focus, however, only contributed to additional failures, which further increased his depression (see, for example, Pyszczynski & Greenberg, 1987). As he spiraled downward into deep despair, Ron began to court rejection in his interpersonal relationships by working to verify his firmly held negative self-views (see Andrews, 1989; Swann, Wenzlaff, Krull, & Pelham, 1992). This rejection, of course, only magnified his agony. Finally, all of his positive illusions about himself were completely shattered, and for the rest of his life, Ron became more excruciatingly miserable with each passing day. His poor health grew poorer, his troubled relationships became increasingly troubling, and his miserable failures became steadily more miserable (see Taylor & Brown, 1988). Perhaps Ron's one consolation was that, in keeping with work on explanatory style and well-being, his pessimistic attributional style drove him to an early grave (see Peterson, Seligman, & Vaillant, 1988; Scheier & Carver, 1987).

Although this hypothetical story is theoretically plausible, all but the most forgiving reader would probably consider it difficult to believe. Surely, even Ron could have found *some* way to cope with his problems. Casual observation and common sense suggest that even those who are low in self-esteem do not suffer from chronic depression. Moreover, even those who do become depressed do not experience increasing misery every moment of their lives. Instead, most people who are low in self-esteem find ways to make their lives meaningful, and most depressed people eventually recover from their distress. In fact, most appear to do so without the benefit of chemical or therapeutic intervention (Lewinsohn, Hoberman, Teri, & Hautzinger, 1988; Vernon & Roberts, 1982). The fact that depressed people recover, however, highlights a limitation of many contemporary theories of depression (and related theories of low self-esteem), for many of these theories suggest that depression begets something (e.g., negative beliefs, self-focus, self-verification) that systematically begets further depression. Because no cyclical theory of depression identifies a mechanism for reversing the vicious cycle of depression, no cyclical theory can account for the fact that people frequently recover from depression. In other words, if one takes most theories of depression and low self-esteem seriously, then it is unclear why Ron's story is the exception rather than the rule.

The purpose of this chapter is to complement existing accounts of depression and low self-esteem by suggesting that, in addition to its many negative consequences, depression may also have positive consequences. More specifically, it is argued that the typical depressed person not only possesses at least one extremely positive specific self-view but also considers this highly positive belief a highly meaningful aspect of his or her identity. Furthermore, it is argued that in the service of developing and maintaining their most favorable self-views, depressed persons (a) engage in self-serving downward social comparisons, (b) solicit highly positive feedback from others, and (c) make self-serving attributions (e.g., they take special credit for success and deny special responsibility for failure in the area of their most favorable self-evaluation). Next, some preliminary evidence is presented suggesting that depressed persons' self-serving investments in their positive self-views may play a role in the process of recovery from depression. Finally, the limitations and implications of depressed persons' positive beliefs are discussed, with special emphasis on their relation to theoretical accounts of low self-esteem.

DEPRESSED PERSONS POSSESS NEGATIVE BELIEFS

It is well established that depressed persons possess an abundance of negative beliefs (Beck, 1967; Lewinsohn, Mischel, Chaplin, & Barton, 1980; Pietromonaco & Markus, 1985). To provide only a partial list, negative thoughts among depressed persons have been documented in such diverse forms as self-blaming attributions, pessimistic probability judgments, perceptions of incompetence, self-disserving social comparisons, self-ideal discrepancies, suicidal ideation, attraction to rejecting relationship partners, selective memory for negative events, excessive self-awareness, and negative self-definition (e.g., see Beck, 1967; Higgins, 1987; Nelson & Craighead, 1977; Peterson et al., 1982; Swallow & Kuiper, 1988; Swann et al., in press). To make matters worse, recent evidence also suggests that the negative thoughts and judgments of depressed persons (a) are applied to the self but not to others (Garber & Hollon, 1980; Pietromonaco & Markus, 1985), and (b) are both automatic and highly accessible and thus difficult to control (Bargh & Tota, 1988). In view of such evidence, is there any reason to expect that depressed people possess positive beliefs? It appears so.

DEPRESSED PERSONS POSSESS POSITIVE BELIEFS

To begin with, research in the self-enhancement tradition suggests that all people are born with a basic desire for approval and positive feedback. In fact, some have suggested that distressed persons or those who view themselves negatively should be *especially* interested in developing positive self-views (see Jones, 1973; Shrauger, 1975; Wills, 1981; but compare Swann, 1990). Although researchers are still debating this theoretical issue, there is ample evidence that people react to threats to their self-worth by striving to restore their positive self-evaluations (Greenberg & Pyszczynski, 1985; Taylor, 1983; Tesser, 1986).

Thus, there is plenty of theoretical reason to believe that depressed persons should be interested in developing especially positive self-views. This idea might appear to contradict the evidence that depressed persons possess negative self-views, but if one adopts a multifaceted (i.e., an idiographic) view of the self-concept, it quickly becomes clear that negative and positive self-views may co-occur in the same person (Markus & Wurf, 1987; Pelham, 1991a; Swann, Pelham, & Krull, 1989; Taylor & Brown, 1988). Consistent with this idea, there is growing evidence that positive and negative beliefs and feelings are relatively independent of one another (Peterson, 1991; Watson, Clark, & Tellegen, 1988), and that depression and low self-esteem are more strongly related to negative than to positive beliefs and judgments (Bargh & Tota, 1988; Gotlib & Olson, 1983; see Miller & Moretti, 1988, for a review). In fact, even those who have emphasized the negative, self-defeating nature of depression have often found that depressed and nondepressed persons differ primarily in the degree to which they possess negative beliefs or respond to negative information. When it comes to positive beliefs or their reactions to positive events, depressed and nondepressed persons are frequently indistinguishable (Bargh & Tota, 1988; Pietromonaco & Markus, 1985).

Depressed Persons Possess Highly Positive Beliefs

Building on the assumption that depressed persons possess positive beliefs, my colleagues and I have recently begun to address the simple question that is the primary focus of this chapter: How positive? For example, in an initial examination of depressed people's positive self-views (Pelham, 1991b, Study 1), participants were given both a traditional measure of depression (the Beck Depression Inventory; Beck, Ward, Mendelson, Mock, & Erbaugh, 1961) and a traditional set of self-concept measures, including both Rosenberg's unitary measure (1965) of self-esteem and Pelham and Swann's multifaceted measure (1989) of people's specific self-views (e.g., intelligence, social skills, athletic ability). To examine the possibility that depressed persons might possess at least one form of highly positive belief, an idiographic analysis of depressed persons' specific self-views was conducted in this study. More specifically, both the typical (i.e., composite) beliefs of depressed and nondepressed persons and the best (i.e., most favorable) specific self-views of the same depressed and nondepressed persons were compared. To examine the possibility that increasing levels of depression might increase people's efforts to enhance their best self-views, participants were placed in four distinct categories based on their depression scores (nondepressed and mildly, moderately, and severely depressed).

Consistent with past research, it was expected that where most of their beliefs were concerned, depressed persons would possess especially negative self-views, and this was true. As illustrated in the right-hand column of Table 1, the composite self-views (i.e., most of the self-views) of severely depressed persons were extremely negative relative to those of the nondepressed (although they were not extremely negative in an absolute sense). Consistent with a compensatory model of depression, however, it was also expected that severely depressed persons' best self-views might compare quite favorably with those of the nondepressed; this was true as well. As suggested in the left-hand column of Table 1, the best self-views of severely depressed persons were nearly identical to the best self-views of the nondepressed. Because the participants in this study reported their self-views on a percentile scale (relative to other college students), it is also possible to see that the best self-views of severely depressed students were quite favorable in an absolute sense. In particular, as a group, severely depressed participants subjectively rated themselves at the 86th percentile on their best self-views.

Depressed Persons Possess Extremely Positive Beliefs

It is possible, however, that depressed persons' positive self-views are not exactly what they appear to be. Because measures of depression are highly correlated with measures of global self-esteem, it is possible that the effects reported in Table 1 have more to do with low self-esteem than with depression. To address this issue, an auxiliary analysis (an analysis of covariance) was conducted, controlling for self-esteem differences between participants in the four depressive categories. This analysis proved highly informative. First, as shown in Table 2, when global self-esteem was controlled in the four groups, the advantage for the nondepressed group evaporated for the composite measure (suggesting that low self-esteem, rather than depression, was responsible for depressed persons' negative composite self-views; see Tennen & Herzberger, 1987; Tennen, Herzberger, & Nelson, 1987). More to the point,

TABLE 1. Relation Between Depression
and People's Specific Self-views

| Level of Depression | Self-View | |
	Best	Composite
Nondepressed ($n = 161$)	88	65
Mild ($n = 94$)	85	56
Moderate (n = 49)	80	46
Severe ($n = 18$)	86	41

NOTE: The theoretical range for all self-views was 2.5 to 97.5 on a percentile scale (i.e., a rating of 50 indicates that a participant believes that she or he is neither better nor worse than the average college student). Adapted from Pelham (1991b).

an analysis of participants' best self-views revealed that severely depressed persons possessed *especially* positive self-views.

This has proven to be a replicable effect. A follow-up study (Pelham, 1991b, Study 2) revealed the same advantage for the severely depressed group, and subsequent studies have produced the same findings for people's self-ratings on valenced personality traits (e.g., extraversion, agreeableness, conscientiousness) rather than dimensions of self-perceived ability. Finally, auxiliary analyses of these effects have revealed that they are not readily explained as a statistical artifact. For example, the same results have appeared consistently in simultaneous regression analyses, and conceptually similar results have also been observed at a purely descriptive level (i.e., without using covariance analyses; see Pelham, 1991b).

DEPRESSED PERSONS APPRECIATE THEIR POSITIVE BELIEFS

The findings reviewed thus far suggest quite clearly that the typical severely depressed person possesses at least one exceptionally positive

TABLE 2. Relation Between Depression
and People's Specific Self-Views Controlling
for Self-Esteem (Covariate-Adjusted Means)

| Level of Depression | Self-View | |
	Best	Composite
Nondepressed	86	60
Mild	86	59
Moderate	85	55
Severe	93	60

NOTE: The theoretical range for all self-views was 2.5 to 97.5. Adapted from Pelham (1991b).

self-evaluation. It is possible, however, that depressed persons attach very little significance to their unusually favorable self-evaluations. More specifically, previous analyses of both depression and low self-esteem suggest that depressed persons might place little confidence in their positive self-views and might consider their exceptional self-views exceptionally unimportant (Beck, 1967; Pelham & Swann, 1989; Warren & McEachren, 1983).

In the studies reviewed in this chapter, however, this possibility was addressed by assessing both the certainty and the importance of participants' best specific self-views. These studies have revealed little evidence that depressed persons lack confidence in their most favorable self-evaluations. Instead, they have revealed that precisely the opposite is true. In fact, when considered together, all of the studies conducted to date have revealed that, relative to the nondepressed, severely depressed persons are *especially* confident of their most favorable self-views. The same studies have also shown that, like the nondepressed, severely depressed persons consider their best self-views much more personally important than their other self-views (see Pelham, 1991b, for more detail). Thus it appears that depressed persons' especially positive self-views are especially meaningful aspects of their identities.

HOW DO THEY DO IT?

If depressed persons possess at least one category of meaningful, highly positive self-views, then it is possible that, in at least one area of their lives, severely depressed persons behave much like their nondepressed counterparts. In other words, it is possible that in the interest of developing positive self-views in one specific area, depressed people engage in many of the same self-serving strategies that characterize most of the thoughts of the nondepressed. If it is true that depressed persons engage in self-serving biases in the area of their best self-views, this could represent a potential route through which depressed persons could recover from their depression. It has been shown, for example, that self-enhancing downward comparisons have short-term emotional benefits (e.g., Gibbons, 1986; Gibbons & Gerrard, 1989). Similarly, it has also been shown that depressed persons who are trained to make self-serving attributions experience long-term psychological benefits (Layden, 1982). With findings such as these in mind, my colleagues and I have recently begun to explore the origins and consequences of depressed persons' positive self-views. Although our preliminary studies have not allowed us to disentangle fully the causes and consequences of depressed persons' positive self-views, they have shown that depressed persons engage in a number of self-serving biases that are specific to their best self-views. These include (a) the tendency to make self-serving downward social comparisons, (b) attempts to obtain positive feedback from others, and (c) the tendency to make self-serving attributions.

DEPRESSED PERSONS MAKE SELF-SERVING SOCIAL COMPARISONS

In his theory of downward social comparison processes, Wills (1981) argues that, in order to restore their sense of subjective well-being, distressed persons sometimes make self-serving downward social comparisons (e.g., comparisons with less fortunate others). In fact, Wills has argued that, to reduce their suffering, distressed persons will sometimes derogate others to generate favorable social comparisons where none actually exist. Instead of suffering by comparison, for instance, a distressed shot-putter may convince herself that her opponent's record toss was produced by a heavy dose of steroids instead of a heavy dose of ability. In short, Wills has suggested that among distressed persons the derogation of others is a common form of self-serving social comparison. If this is true, it is possible that such self-serving derogations might play a role in the development of depressed persons' highly positive beliefs.

In support of this idea, preliminary evidence suggests that depressed persons do indeed derogate others in the area of their best self-views (Pelham, 1991b, Study 2). In particular, a study of recent acquaintances focused on depressed and nondepressed participants' views of their partners on the dimension of ability that target participants identified as their most favorable. This study revealed that whereas nondepressed persons viewed their partners in much the same way that their partners viewed themselves, depressed persons clearly derogated their partners. These effects were dramatic: Whereas severely depressed persons rated their partners quite negatively (at the 44th percentile on the dimension of the depressed person's best self-view), their partners rated themselves quite favorably (at the 83rd percentile on the same dimension). Moreover, the more depressed persons derogated their partners, the more positively they viewed themselves. In addition, these effects were specific to depressed persons' best self-views. On a composite measure of self-views, neither depressed nor nondepressed participants derogated their partners at all.

In a related study (Pelham & Swinkels, 1992) depressed persons were asked to rate people with whom they had had no previous contact (film personalities in one study, and a nondescript student in another study). In addition, participants reported their current mood both before and after they rated these strangers. Both of these studies revealed that although depressed and nondepressed persons were equally likely to derogate a stranger on the dimension of their best self-view, only depressed persons experienced emotional benefits from doing so. In the study involving ratings of celebrities, these effects were especially clear. An examination of the change in participants' mood over the course of the study revealed that among the nondepressed, derogations (i.e., negative evaluations of the targets) were weakly but reliably associated with *decreases* in mood. In contrast, among severely depressed participants, those who rated the targets most negatively reported the greatest *increases* in mood. As in the study cited above, these effects were confined to depressed participants' best self-views; there were no effects on the composite measure. Thus, there is tentative evidence that depressed participants sometimes engage in self-serving downward comparisons. Moreover, when they do engage in such comparisons, depressed participants appear to experience emotional benefits not shared by the nondepressed.

DEPRESSED PERSONS SOLICIT POSITIVE FEEDBACK FROM OTHERS

Although preliminary evidence suggests that self-serving social comparisons may play a role in the development of depressed persons' positive self-views, there is little reason to believe that depressed persons develop their positive beliefs by means of downward comparisons alone. In fact, it is possible that most of the self-serving strategies that permeate the thinking of the nondepressed may be shared, in at least one circumscribed area, by those who are severely depressed.

Consider, for instance, the recent finding (Swann et al., 1992) that depressed people are especially likely to solicit negative feedback from their relationship partners (e.g., "Why do you think I'm unlikely to do well in school?" or "Why am I likely to make a bad impression in social settings?"). Although these findings appear to describe depressed persons' overall pattern of information seeking, depressed persons might be much more likely to solicit positive interpersonal feedback when it comes to their best self-views (e.g., "But before we discuss my intellectual and social incompetence, why don't you tell me what you like best about my latest sculpture?").

A recent study provided empirical support for this line of reasoning. In that study (Pelham, Swinkels, & Karney, 1992), participants were given the opportunity to solicit positive versus negative interpersonal feedback from their friends and roommates in five different areas. Consistent with the findings of Swann et al. (1992), severely depressed participants sought relatively negative self-relevant feedback from their partners in most areas. In fact, when given a choice between asking their relationship partners positive leading questions (i.e., that fished for compliments) and negative leading questions (i.e., that fished for criticisms), severely depressed persons chose negative leading questions slightly more often than they chose positive ones. (In contrast, nondepressed participants showed a clear preference for favorable feedback.) When it came to the one belief that severely depressed persons considered their most favorable, however, their pattern of feedback seeking was virtually indistinguishable from that of the nondepressed (i.e., they showed a dramatic preference for positive feedback). Finally, like the nondepressed, severely depressed persons not only indicated that they wished to receive positive feedback about their best self-views, they also reported that they were more *interested* in hearing about this area than they were in hearing about their less positive self-views.

Depressed Persons Make Self-Serving Causal Attributions

Both conventional wisdom and empirical research suggest that self-blame is one of the hallmarks of depression. Dozens of studies have supported this idea by demonstrating that depressed people characteristically make more self-blaming causal attributions than the nondepressed (e.g., see Peterson, Schwartz, & Seligman, 1981; Peterson et al., 1982). In comparison with the nondepressed, that is, depressed persons make more internal, stable, and global attributions for their personal failures and misfortunes ("It happened because of me, it'll probably continue to happen forever, and it affects all areas of my life.") In fact, this self-disserving brand of explanations has even been dubbed the "depressive attributional style" (e.g., see Abramson, Seligman, & Teasedale, 1978; Tennen et al., 1987). The model outlined in this chapter suggests, however, that the depressive attributional style might not permeate all of the attributions made by depressed persons.

To test this possibility, we (Pelham et al., 1992) recently conducted a study in which we measured the attributions that depressed persons made for positive and negative life events in five different areas (including the area that participants had earlier identified as the area of their best self-view). Thus, for example, for a participant who had identified intellectual ability as her best self-view, we could compare her attributions for academic events with her typical attributions in four other areas. When we examined a composite measure of participants' attributions across most areas, we replicated the findings of previous studies.

Thus, in most areas, severely depressed persons evenhandedly took slightly more credit for failure than for success, and nondepressed persons heavy-handedly took more credit for success than for failure. In the area of their best self-views, however, severely depressed persons made attributions that were slightly *more* self-serving than those made by the nondepressed. Similar findings were observed when we examined attributions of controllability and globality. The dreary attributions that depressed persons made in most areas became much sunnier when we examined events in the area of their best self-views.

Like the findings on social comparison and information seeking, these findings are correlational, and thus it is not clear whether these self-serving attributions produce or are produced by depressed persons' positive self-views. Independent of where these self-serving biases come from, however, one thing is clear: Depressed people are quite capable of entertaining self-serving thoughts. They simply appear to be very selective about when they do so.

DOES IT DO THEM ANY GOOD?

If depressed persons possess highly positive self-views and engage in self-serving biases when it comes to their positive self-views, this may help explain why depression does not always beget further depression. As people become increasingly depressed, they may react to their miseries by becoming especially invested in their most positive beliefs. To the degree that they do so, they should facilitate their own recovery from depression. We have gathered preliminary evidence that this is the case. In particular, we (Pelham & Karney, 1992) recently completed a prospective study of mildly depressed persons. In that study, we found that the importance depressed persons attributed to their best self-views predicted their recovery from depression. More specifically, those who attributed the greatest importance to their best self-views showed the greatest evidence of recovery 8 weeks later (see Needles & Abramson, 1990, for related findings).

In future studies, my colleagues and I will attempt to gain clearer insights on the precise mechanisms through which this process operates. For example, research on the self-investment model (Pelham, 1991a) suggests that belief importance should energize almost all forms of self-enhancing behavior, any of which could facilitate recovery from depression. On the other hand, there is also reason to believe that investing oneself heavily in a single belief can have costs as well as benefits (Linville, 1987), and in future studies we intend to pay special attention to both the costs and benefits of positive beliefs among the depressed. All in all, it seems reasonable to assume at this point that the benefits of depressed persons' positive self-views outweigh their costs. Thus, for instance, depressed persons' self-serving attributions probably have relatively few drawbacks. Even if they contribute little to long-term recovery from depression, they almost certainly provide temporary relief from distress. Just as we feel better about our important achievements when we believe that we are personally responsible for them, we may become less distraught over our failures when we attribute them to external causes (Weiner, 1986).

CONCLUSIONS

Although it is becoming increasingly clear that depressed persons possess at least one highly positive belief, the work reviewed in this chapter clearly leaves many questions unanswered. To select only a few examples, very little is known about the precise mechanisms that allow the typical depressed person to recover. It is even possible that depressed persons' highly positive beliefs are the cause rather than the consequence of their distressed states. Finally, there is no guarantee that depressed persons' positive beliefs loom large in their daily lives. In fact, a recent pilot study suggested that although depressed persons privately report possessing highly positive beliefs, they are not very likely to mention them in their spontaneous self-descriptions.

On the whole, however, preliminary studies have suggested that depressed persons emphasize, enjoy, and enhance their positive beliefs in ways that belie their acute distress. It is also important to remember that the findings highlighted in this chapter have included replications of previous findings for composite measures of depressed persons' beliefs. Thus, if depressed persons' most positive self-views had not been singled out in these investigations, they would have merely reinforced the well-established idea that depressed persons possess negative self-views. In the final analysis, these findings are meant to complement rather than challenge the traditional wisdom on depression. Although it is clear that depression is associated with numerous forms of negative thinking, it may be instructive to remember that, like other painful experiences (e.g., divorce, dieting, dental work), depression may occasionally have positive consequences.

Because many theoretical treatments of low self-esteem bear a strong resemblance to theories of depression, it is tempting to conclude that the compensatory model of depression presented here may be translated directly into a compensatory analysis of low self-esteem. Although this model does have some obvious implications for theories of low self-esteem (e.g., persons low in self-esteem appear to be especially susceptible to depression), our initial findings have suggested that it is primarily *acute distress* rather than the perception that one is unworthy that drives the self-enhancing compensations reported in this chapter. For instance, covariance analyses assessing the unique contributions of depression and global self-esteem to people's best self-views have consistently shown that both high levels of self-esteem and high levels of depression are associated with especially positive best self-views. In other words, most of the compensations reported in this chapter appear to be uniquely associated with depression rather than with low self-esteem.

Does this mean, then, that persons low in self-esteem are doomed to experience the kind of self-perpetuating vicious cycles from which depressed persons eventually manage to escape? The answer may depend on which particular cycles (or potential escape routes) one examines. First of all, the implicit assumptions researchers typically make about depression and self-esteem suggest that low self-esteem is more of a self-perpetuating problem than depression. Even our use of the terms in everyday language suggests that whereas depression is usually temporary, low self-esteem is usually permanent. Thus, it makes perfect sense for Willie to say that he was depressed yesterday but is feeling fine today. If Willie claims that he was a low self-esteem *person* yesterday but has since become a high self-esteem person, however, we may begin to suspect that his psychological problems extend well beyond depression or low self-esteem.

On the other hand, the critique of cyclical theories put forth in this chapter suggests that even low self-esteem cannot have exclusively negative consequences. Thus, it seems likely that those who are low in self-esteem may develop their own unique ways of coping with their perceptions of unworthiness. For example, Brown (in Chapter 6 of this volume) has suggested that persons low in self-esteem may engage in indirect rather than direct forms of self-enhancement, presumably with the goal of safely enhancing their self-worth (see also Baumgardner, Kauffman, & Levy, 1989; Brockner & Hulton, 1979).

And just as depression and low self-esteem may sometimes have their advantages, optimism and high self-esteem may occasionally have their disadvantages. Heatherton and Ambadi (in Chapter 7 of this volume) have suggested that, when their sense of self-worth is challenged in an achievement setting, people high in self-esteem may unwittingly engage in self-defeating behaviors by biting off more than they can chew. Similarly, Pelham and Taylor (1992) have recently shown that persons high in self-esteem are especially likely to engage in highly enjoyable but highly risky behaviors such as riding a motorcycle. The same study also revealed that, relative to their less esteemed counterparts, people high in global self-esteem (a) reported higher rates of driving while under the influence of alcohol and (b) reported receiving more citations for speeding during a 1-year interval. Thus, in at least one area of their lives, high self-esteem persons may typically place themselves at risk for both physical injury and emotional hardship. Although the costs of high self-esteem may be somewhat circumscribed, as in the studies cited above, it seems unlikely that high self-esteem could have exclusively positive consequences. Just as there must be mechanisms for keeping depression and low self-esteem from spiraling into abject misery, there must also be mechanisms for keeping high self-esteem from skyrocketing upward into unabashed self-adoration.

In summary, at both a practical and a theoretical level, the analysis offered in this chapter is intended to stand as a reminder that neither depression nor low self-esteem can have exclusively negative consequences. Whether investment in positive self-views represents a primary or a trivial route to recovery from depression, it is clear that most depressed people do typically recover. If we wish to understand how they manage to do so, we must expand our focus beyond the ways in which the distressed and devaluated reinforce their miseries and pay greater attention to the ways in which they attempt to relieve them.

ACKNOWLEDGMENTS

This research and the preparation of this manuscript were supported by a seed grant and a university research grant to Brett W. Pelham from the University of California, Los Angeles. I thank Laura Myaskovsky and Shelley Taylor for their insightful comments on this chapter.

REFERENCES

Abramson, L. Y., Seligman, M. E. P., & Teasedale, J. F. (1978). Learned helplessness in humans: Critique and reformulation. *Journal of Abnormal Psychology, 87,* 49–74.

Andrews, J. D. W. (1989). Psychotherapy of depression: A self-confirmation model. *Psychological Review, 96,* 576–607.

Bargh, J. A., & Tota, M. E. (1988). Context-dependent automatic processing in depression: Accessibility of negative constructs with regard to self but not others. *Journal of Personality and Social Psychology, 54,* 925–939.

Baumgardner, A. H., Kauffman, C. M., & Levy, P. E. (1989). Regulating affect interpersonally: When low esteem leads to greater enhancement. *Journal of Personality and Social Psychology, 56,* 907–921.

Beck, A. T. (1967). *Depression: Clinical, experimental and theoretical aspects.* New York: Harper & Row.

Beck, A. T. (1976). *Cognitive therapy and the emotional disorders.* New York: International Universities Press.

Beck, A. T., Ward, C. H., Mendelson, M., Mock, J., & Erbaugh, J. (1961). An inventory for measuring depression. *Archives of General Psychiatry, 4,* 561–571.

Brockner, J., & Hulton, A. J. (1979). How to reverse the vicious cycle of low self-esteem: The importance of attentional focus. *Journal of Experimental Social Psychology, 14,* 564–578.

Garber, J., & Hollon, S. D. (1980). Universal versus personal helplessness in depression: Belief in uncontrollability or incompetence? *Journal of Abnormal Psychology, 89,* 56–66.

Gibbons, F. X. (1986). Social comparison and depression: Company's effect on misery. *Journal of Personality and Social Psychology, 51,* 140–148.

Gibbons, F. X., & Gerrard, M. (1989). Effects of upward and downward social comparisons on mood states. *Journal of Social and Clinical Psychology, 8,* 14–31.

Gotlib, I. H., & Olson, J. M. (1983). Depression, psychopathology, and self-serving attributions. *British Journal of Clinical Psychology, 22,* 309–310.

Greenberg, J., & Pyszczynski, T. (1985). Compensatory self-inflation: A response to the threat to self-regard of public failure. *Journal of Personality and Social Psychology, 49,* 273–280.

Higgins, E. T. (1987). Self-discrepancy: A theory relating self and affect. *Psychological Review, 94,* 319–340.

Jones, S. C. (1973). Self- and interpersonal evaluations: Esteem theories versus consistency theories. *Psychological Bulletin, 79,* 185–199.

Layden, M. A. (1982). Attributional therapy. In C. Antaki & C. Brewin (Eds.), *Attributions and psychological change: Applications of attributional theories to clinical and educational practice.* London: Academic Press.

Lewinsohn, P. M., Hoberman, H., Teri, L., & Hautzinger, M. (1988). An integrative theory of depression. In S. Reiss & R. R. Bootzin (Eds.), *Theoretical issues in behavior therapy.* Orlando, FL: Academic Press.

Lewinsohn, P. M., Mischel, W., Chaplin, W., & Barton, R. (1980). Social competence and depression: The role of illusory self-perceptions. *Journal of Abnormal Psychology, 89,* 203–212.

Linville, P. (1987). Self-complexity as a cognitive buffer against stress-related illness and depression. *Journal of Personality and Social Psychology, 52,* 663–676.

Markus, H., & Wurf, E. (1987). The dynamic self-concept: A social psychological perspective. *Annual Review of Psychology, 38,* 299–337.

Metalsky, G. I., Seligman, M. E. P., Semmel, A., & Peterson, C. (1982). Attributional styles and life events in the classroom: Vulnerability and invulnerability to depressive mood reactions. *Journal of Personality and Social Psychology, 43,* 612–617.

Miller, D. T., & Moretti, M. M. (1988). The causal attributes of depressives: Self-serving or self-disserving. In L. Alloy (Ed.), *Cognitive processes in depression.* New York: Guilford.

Needles, D. J., & Abramson, L. Y. (1990). Positive life events, attributional style, and hopelessness: Testing a model of recovery from depression. *Journal of Abnormal Psychology, 99,* 156–165.

Nelson, R. E., & Craighead, W. E. (1977). Selective recall of positive and negative feedback, self-control behaviors, and depression. *Journal of Abnormal Psychology, 86,* 379–388.

Pelham, B. W. (1991a). On confidence and consequence: The certainty and importance of self-knowledge. *Journal of Personality and Social Psychology, 60,* 518–530.

Pelham, B. W. (1991b). On the benefits of misery: Self-serving biases in the depressive self-concept. *Journal of Personality and Social Psychology, 61,* 670–681.

Pelham, B. W., & Karney, B. (1993). [Self-investment and recovery from depression.] Unpublished raw data, University of California, Los Angeles.

Pelham, B. W., & Swann, W. B., Jr. (1989). From self-conceptions to self-worth: On the sources and structure of global self-esteem. *Journal of Personality and Social Psychology, 57,* 672–680.

Pelham, B. W., & Swinkels, A. H. (1993). [Depression and social comparison: A self-investment perspective.] Unpublished raw data. University of California, Los Angeles.

Pelham, B. W., Swinkels, A. H., & Karney, B. (1992). *Self-defeated but self-inflating: Interpersonal and intrapersonal self-enhancement among the depressed.* Manuscript in preparation.

Pelham, B. W., & Taylor, S. E. (1992). *On the limits of illusions: Exploring the costs and hazards of high self-regard.* Manuscript in preparation.

Peterson, C. (1991). The meaning and measurement of explanatory style. *Psychological Inquiry, 2,* 1–10.

Peterson, C., Schwartz, S. M., & Seligman, M. E. P. (1981). Self-blame and depressive symptoms. *Journal of Personality and Social Psychology, 49,* 253–259.

Peterson, C., Seligman, M. E. P., & Vaillant, G. E. (1988). Pessimistic explanatory style is a risk factor for physical illness: A thirty-five-year longitudinal study. *Journal of Personality and Social Psychology, 55,* 23–27.

Peterson, C., Semmel, A., von Baeyer, C., Abramson, L. Y., Metalsky, G. I., & Seligman, M. E. P. (1982). The attributional style questionnaire. *Cognitive Therapy and Research, 6,* 287–300.

Pietromonaco, P. R., & Markus, H. (1985). The nature of negative thoughts in depression. *Journal of Personality and Social Psychology, 48,* 799–807.

Pyszczynski, T., & Greenberg, J. (1987). Self-regulatory perseveration and the depressive self-focusing style: A self-awareness theory of reactive depression. *Psychological Bulletin, 102,* 122–138.

Rosenberg, M. (1965). *Society and the adolescent self-image.* Princeton, NJ: Princeton University Press.

Scheier, M. F., & Carver, C. S. (1987). Dispositional optimism and physical well-being: The influence of generalized outcome expectancies on health. *Journal of Personality, 55,* 169–210.

Shrauger, J. S. (1975). Responses to evaluation as a function of initial self-perceptions. *Psychological Bulletin, 82,* 581–596.

Swallow, S. R., & Kuiper, N. A. (1988). Social comparison and negative self-evaluations: An application to depression. *Clinical Psychology Review, 8,* 55–76.

Swann, W. B., Jr. (1990). To be known or to be adored?: The interplay of self-enhancement and self-verification. In R. M. Sorrentino & E. T. Higgins (Eds.), *Handbook of motivation and cognition, vol. 2* (pp. 408–448). New York: Guilford.

Swann, W. B., Pelham, B. W., & Krull, D. S. (1989). Agreeable fancy or disagreeable truth?: Reconciling self-enhancement and self-verification. *Journal of Personality and Social Psychology, 57,* 782–791.

Swann, W. B., Wenzlaff, S., Krull, D. S., & Pelham, B. W. (1992). Allure of negative feedback: Self-verification strivings among depressed persons. *Journal of Abnormal Psychology, 101,* 293–306.

Taylor, S. E. (1983). Adjustment to threatening events: A theory of cognitive adaptation. *American Psychologist, 38,* 1161–1173.

Taylor, S. E., & Brown, J. D. (1988). Illusion and well-being: A social psychological perspective on mental health. *Psychological Bulletin, 103,* 193–210.

Tennen, H., & Herzberger, S. (1987). Depression, self-esteem, and the absence of self-protective attributional biases. *Journal of Personality and Social Psychology, 52,* 72–80.

Tennen, H., Herzberger, S., & Nelson, H. F. (1987). Depressive attributional style: The role of self-esteem. *Journal of Personality, 55,* 631–660.

Tesser, A. (1986). Some effects of self-evaluation maintenance on cognition and action. In R. M. Sorrentino & E. T. Higgins (Eds.), *Handbook of motivation and cognition* (pp. 435–464). New York: Guilford.

Vernon, S. W., & Roberts, S. E. (1982). Prevalence of treated and untreated psychiatric disorders in three ethnic groups. *Social Science and Medicine, 16,* 1575–1582.

Warren, L. W., & McEachren, L. (1983). Psychological correlates of depressive symptomatology in adult women. *Journal of Abnormal Psychology, 92,* 151–160.

Watson, D., Clark, A. L., & Tellegen, A. (1988). Development and validation of brief measures of positive and negative affect: The PANAS scales. *Journal of Personality and Social Psychology, 54,* 1063–1070.

Wills, T. A. (1981). Downward comparison principles in social psychology. *Psychological Bulletin, 90,* 245–271.

Weiner, B. (1986). *An attributional theory of motivation and emotion.* New York: Springer-Verlag.

CHAPTER 11

UNDERSTANDING THE INNER NATURE OF LOW SELF-ESTEEM
UNCERTAIN, FRAGILE, PROTECTIVE, AND CONFLICTED

ROY F. BAUMEISTER

In recent decades, psychologists have offered many speculations and hypotheses about people with low self-esteem. Perhaps they hate themselves. Perhaps they seek to distort things in a negative, pessimistic direction. Perhaps they are indifferent to praise and popularity. Perhaps they lack some key drive to succeed or to think well of themselves. Perhaps they are irrational and self-destructive. In the last two decades, however, a growing body of enlightening data on low self-esteem has allowed psychologists to move beyond the earlier, more speculative theories. One can begin to sort the welter of competing theories into a coherent set of empirically grounded conclusions.

It is clear that there is no one key, no single answer to the puzzle of low self-esteem. But taken together, the various contributions covered in this book may finally allow us to understand the person with low self-esteem better. Let me summarize some main themes emerging from the previous chapters.

ROY F. BAUMEISTER • Department of Psychology, Case Western Reserve University, Cleveland OH 44106.

Self-Esteem: The Puzzle of Low Self-Regard, edited by Roy F. Baumeister. Plenum Press, New York, 1993.

THE NEED FOR SELF-WORTH

It is apparent that the vast majority of people generally want to think well of themselves. Intuitively, this is easy to accept; favorable views of self are associated with happiness, pleasant emotional states, and other positive subjective results. People with low self-esteem do not lack the desire for self-worth. Thus, to understand low self-esteem, one should not think in terms of the absence of needs, but rather in terms of unfulfilled needs and possibly conflicting, competing needs.

The need for self-worth is indicated in many of the chapters. Spencer, Josephs, and Steele (Chapter 2) make self-affirmation the cornerstone of their argument (following Steele, 1988) and contend that this need for self-worth, which they label *self-integrity*, is fundamental and widespread. They note that self-affirming gestures are particularly relevant to coping with threats. Blaine and Crocker (Chapter 4) explore the variety of strategies people use to nurture a positive sense of self, both before and after threatening events. Tice (Chapter 3) argues that people desire to protect their self-esteem against loss and to enhance their positive views of themselves when possible. Pelham (Chapter 10) points out convincingly that even depressed people manage to find something about themselves to be proud of, and they are quite jealously protective of that basis for self-worth.

What distinguishes people with low self-esteem is not the size of their desire to think well of themselves, but rather some interference with fulfilling that desire. Their basis for thinking well of themselves may be smaller than other people's, in the sense that they have fewer reasons to regard themselves as superior beings. This shortage makes them more vulnerable to threats insofar as when events impugn their self-worth, they are less able to point to alternative positive qualities they have (Spencer et al., Chapter 2). Because of this fragility, they need to emphasize protection rather than enhancement of self-worth (Tice, Chapter 3). This weakness, which Spencer et al. portray as a deficiency in resources, may be an important reason that people with very low self-esteem will become jealously defensive of their few positive attributes: They cannot afford to have these undermined, because they depend heavily on these for their sense of self-worth.

The only view that even begins to suggest any exceptions to the basic, universal need for self-worth is the one advanced by De La Ronde and Swann (Chapter 8), who contend that the need to confirm one's view of oneself is a powerful motive, especially for cognitive functioning. Still, even their position does not suggest that people with low self-esteem desire to change for the worse. Their data suggest that people are more likely to believe criticism than praise where their faults are concerned, even though they may have initial reactions that emotionally prefer the praise. Ultimately, according to De La Ronde and Swann, people with low self-esteem therefore desire neither highly positive nor strongly negative feedback. They do not want to change their self-conceptions in either a positive or a negative direction.

Combining these various views, it seems safe to conclude that people with low self-esteem hate to experience anything that threatens to lower their self-esteem further. They want to think well of themselves, and most seem to find some basis for doing so, although this basis tends to be more fragile and limited than what someone with high self-esteem might have. Events that threaten to undermine self-worth may therefore bring out defensive and protective reactions among people with low self-esteem. The view of low self-esteem as a weakly or inadequately satisfied desire for self-worth is an important part of the key to understanding such people.

SELF-CONCEPTIONS ACCOMPANYING LOW SELF-ESTEEM

The essence of self-esteem is how a person regards himself or herself, and it is therefore extremely valuable to understand the self-conceptions of people with low self-esteem. Two key insights into the nature of these self-conceptions have been articulated and elaborated in this book. They complement each other and form a vital foundation for understanding the person with low self-esteem.

The first insight is articulated in detail by Campbell and Lavallee (Chapter 1; based on Campbell, 1990; see also Baumgardner, 1990): People with low self-esteem seem to know less about themselves than people with high self-esteem. Campbell and Lavallee have labeled this as *self-concept confusion*, which takes a variety of forms. People with low self-esteem have self-conceptions that change and fluctuate from day to day. Their views about themselves may contain contradictions and inconsistencies, and they simply have fewer definite beliefs about what they are like than other people have. In short, what they know about themselves tends to be uncertain, incoherent, and in flux.

This deficient self-knowledge is a powerful key to understanding a great deal about people with low self-esteem. Even seemingly paradoxical patterns, such as the occasional apparent preference for failure or criticism (as described by De La Ronde and Swann in Chapter 8), may be linked to self-knowledge. De La Ronde and Swann contend that people mainly seek to confirm their most firmly held self-conceptions (see also

Swann, 1987), and that many people with low self-esteem will have relatively few such firm self-conceptions. A motive to maintain consistency with one's firmly held self-conceptions would therefore be largely irrelevant to people with low self-esteem, although in a few well-selected domains such consistency effects may be quite powerful and may extend to a rejection of praise or other overly positive feedback.

The self-knowledge deficiency is also relevant to understanding how people with low self-esteem fare in the large and small events that fill everyday life. Heatherton and Ambady (Chapter 7) analyze how people manage their lives: People must make appropriate commitments and then live up to them. Making appropriate commitments and undertaking the most promising projects depends, however, on self-knowledge. People with high self-esteem can draw on their extensive self-knowledge to manage their lives effectively. Lacking such firm and clear self-knowledge, people with low self-esteem may fall into various problems of setting inappropriate goals, starting things that are too difficult to achieve or too easy to be worth achieving, and so forth.

The second insight into low self-esteem is spelled out by Tice (Chapter 3; see also Baumeister, Tice, & Hutton, 1989). By and large, low self-esteem is low only in a *relative* sense; in an absolute sense, it is medium. To be sure, there may be occasional people who hate themselves or think they are utterly worthless (although Pelham in Chapter 10 questions even that), but if so these are probably a small minority marked by pathological extremes. The vast majority of people who end up classified as low in self-esteem do not regard themselves as hopeless, worthless individuals, as contemptible rejects, as wicked, morally despicable villains, or as chronic losers. They describe themselves instead in neutral, intermediate, noncommittal terms.

Low self-esteem can thus be understood more as the absence of positive views of self rather than as the presence of negative views. Consistent with this, Blaine and Crocker (Chapter 4) have discussed the relative lack of self-aggrandizing patterns or biases exhibited by people with low self-esteem. Whereas many people systematically interpret events in ways that favor themselves, people with low self-esteem show an absence of such self-serving biases. It would be wrong to suggest that people with low self-esteem twist things in the opposite direction or bias their thoughts to give themselves less credit or more blame than they deserve. Rather, what distinguishes them is the absence of positive, self-serving patterns.

Pelham (Chapter 10) indicates that even the self-views of severely depressed people are not low or negative in an absolute sense. Ironically, depressed people hold "best" views of themselves as being superior to 86% of other people on selected dimensions. These people clearly do not despise themselves. It is the lack of more positive views about the self, rather than the definite assertion of negative views, that characterizes people with low self-esteem.

These two key insights are, of course, highly compatible, as Campbell and Lavallee suggest. A confused, incoherent pattern of self-knowledge could easily lead to a globally intermediate, neutral self-evaluation.

ROADBLOCKS TO SELF-LOVE

The central dilemma of low self-esteem, then, is what prevents these people from holding the positive views of themselves that others have. The key factor that needs explaining is not the presence of self-hate (for self-hate is not generally there), but rather the absence of self-love. As Tice indicates, people with low self-esteem generally evaluate themselves in neutral, intermediate ways. Or, as articulated in the chapters by Campbell and Lavallee and by Spencer et al., what afflicts people with low self-esteem is a relative lack of positive things to assert and believe about themselves, rather than a firm belief in one's own bad qualities. Understanding what keeps low self-esteem low is not, therefore, a matter of explaining how they became convinced that they are bad, but rather of analyzing what keeps them from adopting a broadly positive view of self.

Harter in Chapter 5 points out some important factors that restrain people from coming to regard themselves in more favorable terms. By and large, nobody is good at everything, and so each person has good points and bad points. Many people maintain high self-esteem by convincing themselves that the things they are good at are important, widely valued ones, whereas their weaknesses are confined to relatively trivial domains. But there are substantial limits on what one can come to regard as trivial, because society places considerable value on certain attributes. People get stuck at a low level of self-esteem when they are unable to minimize the importance of their weaknesses. Physical attractiveness, charm and sex appeal, charisma, and intelligence are generally recognized as important traits, and people who lack these qualities may not be able to dismiss them as unimportant, unlike people who may be tone-deaf or poor at swimming or inept at video games. Although many researchers have emphasized intellectual and social aspects of self-esteem, Harter points out that physical attractiveness is a strong and stable predictor of self-esteem, partly because the culture emphasizes

the importance of physical attractiveness (perhaps especially for females). If you are ugly, it will be harder to think very highly of yourself.

Social forces operate in another way to keep self-esteem low in
some people, according to Harter: People compare themselves with others, and these comparisons inevitably reveal many of one's shortcomings. Thus, in principle one might be able to discount one's shortcomings as long as one is improving, but at certain stages in life (especially
childhood) everyone else is improving, too, and so improving in an
absolute sense may still leave one at the bottom of the heap. Because so
many abilities are evaluated solely in comparison with others, people
may find it hard to persuade themselves that they are better than they
are. Too often, it will be obvious that others are superior to oneself.

Blaine and Crocker (Chapter 4) offer a broad context for this inability to dismiss one's weaknesses. Normally, people support favorable
views of themselves by using a variety of biases and defenses. Taylor
and Brown (1988) proposed that these *positive illusions* are an integral
part of mental health and adjustment. People with low self-esteem seem
to lack these biases and distortions to some extent.

Inevitably, circular relationships develop. If one's view of self is not
all that favorable, then one may shy away from forming large positive
illusions about oneself, because these are vulnerable to being disconfirmed (Blaine & Crocker, Chapter 4). To convince oneself erroneously
that one will accomplish great things is to invite disappointment. People
with low self-esteem prefer to see themselves in a fairly accurate and
unbiased fashion, which deters them from distorting daily feedback so
as to form great, exaggerated expectations about the future. In this way,
they can protect themselves against loss and disappointment, but they
sacrifice the chance to inflate self-esteem through such biases and distortions.

Another circular pattern was suggested by Harter in Chapter 5. Low
self-esteem is often based on an accurate appraisal of one's abilities (or
lack thereof). If one can see one's own shortcomings, others may see
them, too, and in many cases social rejection may ensue. As Harter has
persuasively explained, self-esteem is based mainly on those two pillars,
namely, competence and social acceptance. If you see yourself as lacking
competence and as rejected by others, the combination is likely to be a
very persuasive basis for keeping self-esteem low.

As these people gradually become convinced of their own shortcomings and weaknesses, these firm self-conceptions generate their
own consistency pressures. De La Ronde and Swann (Chapter 8) review
evidence that people resist changing their views of themselves after
these are firmly in place, and this applies even to unflattering views.

Once low self-esteem is established, people will tend to be skeptical of highly flattering messages, will distrust others who may hold excessively favorable opinions of them, and will tend to fit new information into these firm and stable self-conceptions. Low self-esteem can thus become self-perpetuating.

Further self-perpetuating patterns were suggested by Heatherton and Ambady (Chapter 7). Poor self-regulation strategies deprive one of chances for successful experiences that might have raised self-esteem. Because of their poor self-knowledge and resultant inability to make appropriate commitments, and perhaps because of their broadly self-protective orientation, people with low self-esteem may skip some undertakings that might have brought them important success experiences. Meanwhile, the commitments they do make will sometimes be excessive and unrealistic, leading to the vicious spiraling effect described by Heatherton and Ambady in terms of dieting. They set goals that are too high, and so they fail, and so their self-esteem remains low or becomes even lower.

EMOTIONAL PATTERNS

Thus far I have focused on beliefs about the self, interpretations of the world, and other cognitive patterns associated with low self-esteem, but a number of chapters have shed light on emotional patterns as well. Self-esteem goes beyond cognition to involve motivation and emotion. Campbell and Lavallee (Chapter 1) reviewed evidence linking low self-esteem to a high frequency of mood swings. The deficit in self-knowledge results in a surplus of emotion. The reason, presumably, is that people with low self-esteem are more at the mercy of situations and events because they lack a firm sense of who they are. When situations and events go against what might be expected or desired, emotional responses are intensified. A firm and positive sense of self enables one to navigate life on an even keel. People with low self-esteem, who lack this firm and positive self-knowledge, experience more of an emotional roller coaster in their daily lives.

Harter's data in Chapter 5 are consistent with the picture of emotionality among people with low self-esteem. In particular, Harter says that low self-esteem is typically accompanied by a relatively high frequency of emotional distress and negative affect. Moreover, emotion is not merely linked to one's stable, ongoing level of self-esteem. Kernis's ground-breaking work on stability of self-esteem, as reviewed by him in Chapter 9, makes clear that emotion is strongly linked to temporary changes and fluctuations in self-esteem (see also Harris & Snyder, 1986). He has shown convincingly that some people have stable levels of self-esteem, whereas others show fluctuations. For the latter, emotions follow; when self-esteem rises, people experience good moods and pleasant emotions. Losing self-esteem is linked to anger, hostility, and probably a host of other bad emotions.

If low self-esteem is marked by a surplus of bad emotions, it may also bring some special ways of experiencing positive emotion. An especially interesting one is discussed by Pelham in Chapter 10. As already noted, Pelham points out that depressed people (who have low self-esteem) also have a few strongly positive views about themselves, about which they are very protective. One form this protectiveness takes is that they derogate others on these dimensions. Derogating others on things about which one cherishes special images of one's own competence is something that everyone does, but only these depressed, low self-esteem individuals appear to derive strong emotional benefits from doing so. It makes them feel good to describe others in unflattering terms, at least on dimensions where they pride themselves on being superior.

INTERPERSONAL PATTERNS

Low self-esteem is also marked by some distinctive patterns of interpersonal behavior. To a substantial extent, these can be understood on the basis of the cognitive and emotional patterns already covered, but they are of considerable interest in their own right and can lead to social consequences that in turn affect self-esteem.

Tice in Chapter 3 articulates one broad and fundamental pattern. In contrast to people with high self-esteem, who are generally trying to make a good impression on others and to boost their reputations, people with low self-esteem are cautious and tentative in their self-presentations. Their first goal is to avoid any loss of self-esteem. This self-protective orientation can be understood in the context of the analysis by Spencer et al. (Chapter 2) of self-esteem as a personal resource. When resources are scarce, people want to preserve them and avoid taking any chances with them. Campbell and Lavallee's exposition of self-concept confusion (Chapter 1) is also relevant. When people are not sure about themselves, it is prudent to be cautious in one's self-presentational claims and interpersonal acts.

Thus, people with low self-esteem do desire social approval and acceptance, and they want to think well of themselves, but they are reluctant to approach social interactions with an aggressive, self-aggrandizing attitude. Bold, confident claims about one's own fine qualities generate pressures and anxieties to live up to inflated images of oneself, along with risks of disconfirmation, failure, and disappointment. People with low self-esteem eschew such claims because these might lead ultimately to further losses in esteem.

The reluctance to seek self-enhancement in an open, direct manner does not mean, however, that people with low self-esteem entirely abandon the project of boosting their self-worth through interpersonal contacts. They are merely forced to use safer, more roundabout means. Brown in Chapter 6 highlights some of the *indirect* methods of self-enhancement that people with low self-esteem prefer. Instead of claiming to be personally superior to others, they claim that the group to which they belong is superior. (In fact, they are careful to boost their group's esteem in ways that will not obviously implicate themselves or put pressure on themselves to maintain this superiority.) Superiority, after all, does not have to be achieved individually; through most of history, people have derived the better part of their self-worth from belonging to esteemed groups (Baumeister, 1991a). Brown's research indicates that the collective path to self-worth is still preferred by some people, particularly those with low self-esteem.

Pelham's research with depressed people suggests another indirect approach. Rather than exaggerating one's own good qualities, the depressed person demeans and derogates other people on selected dimensions. One can thus achieve superiority relative to others without making excessive claims about oneself. Rather than saying, "I'm wonderful," people say "I'm so-so, but you and he and she are terrible." Baumgardner, Kaufman, and Levy (1989) have likewise suggested that people with low self-esteem use derogation of others to shore up their sense of self-worth, rather than using directly self-enhancing strategies. Spencer et al. (Chapter 2) have also provided useful evidence of the downward comparison patterns favored by people with low self-esteem. In these studies, subjects who were low in self-esteem sought out others who were performing poorly or making a poor impression, because comparing oneself with such people is reassuring.

Confidence is, of course, an asset in social situations, and people with low self-esteem may suffer from a lack of confidence in approaching others or initiating social interactions. I have already touched on Harter's discussion in Chapter 5 of the social problems that accompany and reinforce low self-esteem. Physical attractiveness and general competence in life are important foundations of self-esteem, and many children and adults have low self-esteem partly because they know, correctly, that they are deficient in these areas. These deficiencies—that is, unattractiveness and incompetence—increase the likelihood of social rejection. Because social rejection is extremely painful, causing acute anxiety, people with low self-esteem may gravitate toward shyness and reticence. After all, a few painful or embarrassing rejections may make one reluctant to continue approaching others or initiating conversations. But because good interpersonal relationships are important foundations for high self-esteem (as well as for emotional health and adjustment), these people therefore may remain low in self-esteem.

CHANGING LEVELS OF SELF-ESTEEM

Researchers have generally found self-esteem to be relatively stable. If one measures self-esteem on two separate occasions, correlations are quite high; in my own research, for example, I found a test-retest correlation of .904 on self-esteem as measured by Fleming and Courtney's version (1984) of the Janis and Field (1959) scale (Baumeister, 1991c). Still, this general stability should not be overestimated. Self-esteem levels do fluctuate from day to day, and there is significant evidence of long-term change in level of self-esteem, particularly at certain periods in life.

Heatherton and Ambady, in Chapter 7, summarize some of their work measuring state self-esteem. It appears that there is a substantial correlation between state and trait self-esteem. The implication is that each person's self-esteem fluctuates around a baseline level, and it returns to that baseline after the short-term effects of daily events wear off. Receiving a compliment, an unexpected exam grade, or a romantic rejection will alter one's view of oneself temporarily, but after a while it returns to where it was initially. Yet the temporary states of self-esteem are of interest in their own right, and one may expect research on them to build, especially now that a reliable measure of state self-esteem has been furnished (Heatherton & Polivy, 1991).

Another approach to examining fluctuations in self-esteem has been taken by Kernis and his colleagues, and this approach has yielded interesting and exciting findings (see Chapter 9). Kernis's approach begins with the insight that certain people fluctuate more than others, and so his work compares people with stable self-esteem against people whose self-esteem is prone to fluctuating. Depression, for example, has been linked to low self-esteem in many studies, but Kernis finds that only people with *stable* low self-esteem exhibit depression. Low but fluctuating self-esteem is not associated with depression. By the same token,

only people with stable low self-esteem tend to overgeneralize the implications of failure. A setback or disappointment leads them to believe
they are helpless and incompetent, and that the future will be full of
more such failures. In contrast, people with unstable low self-esteem
respond to failure by making excuses and attempting to minimize the
implications.

The core of the distinction between stable and unstable low self-
esteem is the chance to feel very positively about oneself. Unstable low
self-esteem contains grounds for hope and for struggle, because one
does occasionally enjoy a very positive view of oneself. In contrast,
stable low self-esteem means that the person rarely or never experiences
moments of high self-esteem.

Of course, high self-esteem can also be either stable or unstable,
and Kernis shows that there are important differences at that level, too.
The essence, again, is that people who are high and stable simply do not
feel vulnerable to losing self-esteem, whereas the person with unstable
high self-esteem knows what it is like to feel very badly about oneself.
The threat of a severe drop into low self-esteem is familiar and palpable
to the people with unstable high self-esteem, whereas such a threat does
not touch the individual with stable high self-esteem.

Thus, the individual with unstable high self-esteem is of particular
interest, even to the study of low self-esteem, because this individual
sees low self-esteem as a familiar and threatening—but still basically
uncharacteristic—state. The responses of these people confirm the un-
desirable nature of low self-esteem, for they seem driven to defend
themselves against these low moments and against anything that might
provoke a loss of esteem. According to Kernis, their defenses go well
beyond the interpretive biases and other patterns described by Blaine
and Crocker in Chapter 4. Indeed, unstable high self-esteem is associated with unusually high levels of aggression and hostility. Kernis's
work thus furnishes an essential insight into the psychology of the bully.
Most likely, the bully is someone with an insecure but inflated view of
self. Feeling that he or she may lose esteem at any moment, the bully
responds zealously, even violently, to potential threats. Bullies may
seem egotistical, but they are very different from the secure person with
high self-esteem, who does not feel vulnerable to threat or loss. Entering
a state of low self-esteem is thus apparently an extremely aversive experience, and people who are familiar with that threat show all manner of
defensive reactions designed to avoid the experience.

Not all changes in self-esteem, however, involve temporary states.
In principle, it should be possible for self-esteem to show a permanent
change in either direction. Harter (Chapter 5) provides important evi-

dence that substantial, long-term self-esteem change does occur, at least among young people. She finds, though, that these changes are far more likely to occur around major transition points in life than during periods of external stability. Major changes in social roles, statuses, relationships, and identities are crucial points for self-esteem: People reassess who they are when they begin or leave a job, graduate from school, enter or leave a marriage, and so forth.

Still, it is reassuring that self-esteem can change substantially, regardless of what circumstances bring it about. This important part of personality is not fixed in concrete for one's whole life. Significant changes in one's life structure may often be accompanied by significant changes in how one regards oneself.

RESPONDING TO IMAGE THREATS

Many of the themes covered in this work converge in the issue of how people respond to threats to self-esteem. It is undeniably true that daily life contains many events that have the potential to deflate self-esteem, to prove that we are not as good as we like to think we are, to embarrass and humiliate us. Dealing with these threats is an important key to adjustment and happiness. People with low self-esteem do not deal with these threats in the same ways that people with high self-esteem do; indeed, their ways of dealing with these threats almost certainly contribute to making their self-esteem low.

Several perspectives agree that people with low self-esteem are more vulnerable to these threats than people with high self-esteem. For one thing, people with low self-esteem do not have firm, strongly held views about themselves, and this uncertainty of self-knolwedge leaves them at the mercy of external sources of feedback and information (Campbell & Lavallee, Chapter 1). (Kernis in Chapter 9 adds that instability of self-esteem, in which one fluctuates among high and low levels of self-esteem, also involves a lack of firm self-knowledge and a vulnerability to external evaluation.) People with secure, high self-esteem can dismiss or ignore criticism because they feel certain that it does not describe them correctly. But a person with low self-esteem, lacking these firm convictions about the self, may pause to think that the criticism might be correct and accurate.

Thus, a lack of secure certainty in one's good qualities increases one's fragility, that is, one's vulnerability to threat. Spencer et al. (Chapter 2) elaborate another aspect of this vulnerability. When events threaten self-esteem in one realm, some people can simply turn their attention to arenas where they excel. A person with high self-esteem presumably has plenty of strengths, capabilities, and virtues (at least in his or her own opinion), and so a threat to any one of them will not seriously damage the overall positivity of self-regard. But a person with low self-esteem does not have all these alternative supports for self-worth. There are fewer alternative strengths or virtues to ruminate about when consoling oneself for a particular failure or setback. Threats are therefore more devastating to the person with low self-esteem.

This may well be why, as Pelham explains in Chapter 10, people with low self-esteem are particularly jealous and defensive about their good points. These people certainly do think they have some exceptionally positive qualities, but they cannot afford to have these jeopardized or undermined, because they do not have others to fall back on. More generally, it seems likely that the fragility and vulnerability associated with low self-esteem persons may be an important reason for the defensive, cautious, self-protective orientation that they show.

If people with low self-esteem are more defensive, however, then what is the basis for the "breakdown in motivation to enhance the self" discussed by Blaine and Crocker in Chapter 4? Why do these people seem to lack various interpretive and self-serving biases? On the face of it, this conclusion seems to run contrary to the findings of an important body of research. Blaine and Crocker provide a valuable insight into this seeming contradiction by stressing the importance of distinguishing between how people act before versus after the threat. The lack of defensive reactions by people with low self-esteem is more apparent than real. In truth, people with low self-esteem seem quite aware of their vulnerability, and so they begin dealing with threats before these arise. (In Tice's terms, they develop a self-protective approach to events in general.)

People with high self-esteem may exhibit dramatic defensive responses after a failure, but these are exaggerated because such individuals normally do not expect to fail and normally manage their lives to cultivate and maximize success. To them, failure is a rare, unforeseen, and even shocking outcome, and so they exhibit drastic responses. To persons with low self-esteem, in contrast, failure is a familiar, ongoing concern, neither rare nor unforeseen. Blaine and Crocker emphasize that these individuals start preparing for possible failure (and other threats) long in advance, and so when these threats do arise, they can be taken more in stride. The blow has been softened in advance.

Another factor pointed out by Blaine and Crocker is that identical failures may provoke more defensive after-the-fact responses from high than low self-esteem persons because the responses are more discrepant with how the people regard themselves. Simply put, a C on an exam is less discrepant to an acknowledged mediocre student than to someone who fancies himself or herself to be a genius. People with high self-esteem may show drastic responses to such a setback because they need to rebuild their views of themselves back to an extremely high level. But people with low self-esteem may not even want to rebuild their self-images to that extreme, because they anticipate further problems or disappointments in the future.

Still, it is apparent that people with low self-esteem do use some defenses and strategies to boost their self-regard. One of these is downward social comparison, discussed in Chapters 2 and 10. When events imply that you are less than excellent, it may be easier to convince yourself that other people also fall short than to convince yourself that you are excellent after all. And if other people also fall short, then it is not so bad for you to fall short, too. For this reason, downward social comparisons seem to have a strong appeal to people with low self-esteem.

Thus, people with low self-esteem do not seem to respond to threats by trying to bounce back to a highly favorable opinion of themselves. Rather, they seem to stay where they are and seek out company. Or, better yet, they like to find others who have done even worse than they have.

But why don't people with low self-esteem want to build themselves up to a high level after some threatening event? As Blaine and Crocker suggest, they are well aware that an overly favorable view of self is vulnerable to future disconfirmations. This danger is not merely an abstract exercise, as revealed in some of the fascinating findings covered by Brown in Chapter 6. When unexpectedly favorable things happen, people with low self-esteem feel bad and actually begin to get sick. In a sense, strongly favorable feedback and positive life events constitute a different sort of "threat" to people with low self-esteem, because these events undermine their views about themselves. People resist change in either direction, especially if an upward change may bring an increased burden of expectations.

GOALS AND MOTIVATIONS

These various insights make it possible to return to one of this book's fundamental questions, namely, the issue of what goals and motivations guide people with low self-esteem. As we have seen, in many respects their goals and motives are not very different from those of people with high self-esteem; however, they do have some distinctive features.

It is clear, first of all, that people with low self-esteem want to avoid losing esteem. Whether this is described as a general self-protective orientation (Tice, Chapter 3) or a wish to conserve a scarce resource (Spencer et al., Chapter 4), people with low self-esteem are strongly motivated to prevent any further losses. Even the apparent preference for negative feedback that De La Ronde and Swann (Chapter 8) discuss is only a desire for confirmation of their current level of self-esteem, and certainly not any desire to fall even lower.

There are several aspects to the interest shown by people low in self-esteem in hearing about their faults or shortcomings. Both Tice and Spencer et al. have emphasized the desire to remedy deficiencies and shortcomings; these persons want to learn about their faults and flaws so that they can fix them. Spencer et al. report evidence that people with low self-esteem only want to hear about their shortcomings if these can be remedied, and that they avoid hearing about unchangeable faults or inadequacies. By the same token, Kernis (Chapter 9) finds that people with unstable low self-esteem—that is, people who know they can occasionally escape from low self-esteem—defend themselves aggressively against failure and its threatening implications. Taken together, these findings show that people with low self-esteem are oriented toward finding some positive self-worth. They want to avoid threatening events, remedy their shortcomings, and reach a level of adequacy that will enable them to think well of themselves.

There are other signs of an interest in positive self-worth among people low in self-esteem. Pelham (Chapter 10) shows that these people seek out negative feedback about their weaknesses but prefer favorable feedback in connection with the few things they think they are good at. The indirect ego-boosting strategies elucidated by Brown (Chapter 6), Blaine and Crocker (Chapter 4), and others provide further testimony to a general wish for positive self-worth.

Still, low self-esteem individuals find it difficult to think well of themselves, and the risks associated with an overly inflated egotism seem to deter them from pursuing ego-boosting strategies with too much zeal. Blaine and Crocker note that a too-favorable image of self is highly vulnerable to disconfirmation and disappointment, and so a broad tendency toward modest humility is a strategic adaptation designed to avoid such painful letdowns. Brown has detailed how overly positive outcomes can undermine the stable security of the self-concept.

De La Ronde and Swann explain how overly positive feedback can jeopardize one's sense of knowing oneself and can disrupt one's social life and interaction patterns.

Elsewhere, I have analyzed some of the dangers and stresses that attend the maintenance of a highly positive image of self (see Baumeister, 1991b; also 1989). These risks include an increased chance of disconfirmation, vulnerability to attack, a demand for successes to live up to inflated images of oneself, a tendency toward overconfidence and overcommitment, and various interpersonal difficulties. People with low self-esteem seem to have an acute grasp of the risks that accompany such a surfeit of egotism.

Perhaps the best integration of these views is Brown's suggestion in Chapter 6 that low self-esteem is often marked by a motivational conflict. Low self-esteem individuals would like to gain in esteem and develop highly positive views of themselves, but they also may fear and distrust such an inflation of self-regard. For people with high self-esteem, consistency motives and favorability motives agree in furnishing a wish for positive feedback, but for people with low self-esteem, the two sets of motives are in conflict.

Shrauger (1975) concluded that people with low self-esteem favor positive feedback on emotional measures but favor negative feedback on measures of cognition. In other words, they feel better after success or flattery than after failure or criticism, but they are also more skeptical. As several chapters have noted, his hypothesis has continued to receive empirical support (e.g., McFarlin & Blascovich, 1981; Swann, Griffin, Predmore, & Gaines, 1987) and still appears to be valid today. As they go through life, people with low self-esteem are frequently caught in the crossfire between thought and feeling.

An analogy to financial investments is useful in understanding the psychology of low self-esteem. As Tice and Spencer et al. suggest, low self-esteem persons resemble investors with limited financial resources. Such individuals want to avoid risk and preserve their capital. Only after this initial objective is met do they begin to look for gains. Like stocks that offers safe returns, the projects undertaken by people with low self-esteem are likely to be cautious, conservative enterprises with small yields but minimal risks. These people cannot afford to enter a situation that holds a significant possibility of some esteem-threatening outcome, even if there is also a large possibility of some significantly esteem-enhancing outcome. As Heatherton and Ambady (Chapter 7) suggest, this caution will result in substantial differences in the way people with low as opposed to high self-esteem go about managing their affairs. It is important to recognize, however, that both strategies have a rational, comprehensible core. Both make sense in terms of the resources, prospects, and expectations of the individual.

CONCLUSION

The work covered in this book furnishes, at last, a powerful and multifaceted basis for understanding people with low self-esteem. For decades researchers have been puzzled over what inner states and drives lie behind people who seemingly say bad things about themselves (the operational definition of low self-esteem). Various self-destructive, irrational, and maladaptive mechanisms have been suggested. Many of those speculations can now be laid to rest, as a viable picture has emerged.

Low self-esteem can be understood in terms of confusion or uncertainty in self-knowledge, a cautious and self-protective approach to life, a shortage of positive resources in the self, and a chronic internal conflict. To elaborate: People with low self-esteem lack a clear, consistent, unified understanding of who they are, which leaves them at the mercy of events and changing situations and which makes it difficult for them to manage their affairs optimally. They favor self-protection over self-enhancement, inclining toward low-risk situations and preferring to expose themselves mainly to safe, neutral, noncommittal circumstances, even if this strategy means giving up some opportunities for success and prestige. Having fewer positive beliefs about themselves to fall back on in times of stress or pressure, they feel vulnerable to threatening events and sometimes have difficulty coping with adversity. Positive, flattering events, however, elicit an inner conflict between (a) an emotional desire to gain esteem and (b) a skeptical distrust mixed with a reluctance to accept the risks and pressures of a highly positive image.

Generalizing about large numbers of people is always hazardous, of course, and certainly there may be isolated individuals who combine low self-esteem with irrational, self-destructive, or other pathological signs. Sampling techniques that aggressively seek out extremes of self-regard may indeed find enough pathological individuals to yield unusual results and confirm some of the more unsavory impressions and hypotheses about low self-esteem. For the most part, however, low self-esteem is not marked by those patterns. People with low self-esteem can be well understood as ordinary people who are trying in a fairly sensible, rational fashion to adapt effectively to their circumstances and to make their way through life with a minimum of suffering, distress, and humiliation. In that, of course, they are no different from people with high self-esteem. They do differ, however, in how present and familiar these risks seem, and hence in how necessary it seems to take these risks into account in making the choices and decisions that mark the course of human life.

REFERENCES

Baumeister, R. F. (1989). The optimal margin of illusion. *Journal of Social and Clinical Psychology, 8,* 176–189.

Baumeister, R. F. (1991a). *Meanings of life.* New York: Guilford.

Baumeister, R. F. (1991b). *Escaping the Self: Alcoholism, spirituality, masochism, and other flights from the burden of selfhood.* New York: Basic Books.

Baumeister, R. F. (1991c). On the stability of variability: Retest reliability of metatraits. *Personality and Social Psychology Bulletin, 17,* 633–639.

Baumeister, R. F., Tice, D. M., & Hutton, D. G. (1989). Self-presentational motivations and personality differences in self-esteem. *Journal of Personality, 57,* 547–579.

Baumgardner, A. H. (1990). To know oneself is to like oneself: Self-certainty and self-affect. *Journal of Personality and Social Psychology, 58,* 1062–1072.

Baumgardner, A. H., Kaufman, C. M., & Levy, P. E. (1989). Regulating affect interpersonally: When low self-esteem leads to greater enhancement. *Journal of Personality and Social Psychology, 56,* 907–921.

Campbell, J. D. (1990). Self-esteem and clarity of the self-concept. *Journal of Personality and Social Psychology, 59,* 538–549.

Fleming, J. S., & Courtney, B. E. (1984). The dimensionality of self-esteem: II. Hierarchical facet model for revised measurement scales. *Journal of Personality and Social Psychology, 46,* 404–421.

Harris, R. N., & Snyder, C. R. (1986). The role of uncertain self-esteem in self-handicapping. *Journal of Personality and Social Psychology, 51,* 451–458.

Heatherton, T. F., & Polivy, J. (1991). Development and validation of a scale for measuring state self-esteem. *Journal of Personality and Social Psychology, 60,* 895–910.

Janis, I. L., & Field, P. (1959). Sex differences and personality factors related to persuasibility. In C. Hovland & I. Janis (Eds.), *Personality and persuasibility* (pp. 55–68 and 300–302). New Haven, CT: Yale University Press.

McFarlin, D. B., & Blascovich, J. (1981). Effects of self-esteem and performance feedback on future affective preferences and cognitive expectations. *Journal of Personality and Social Psychology, 40,* 521–531.

Shrauger, J. S. (1975). Responses to evaluation as a function of initial self-perceptions. *Psychological Bulletin, 82,* 581–596.

Steele, C. M. (1988). The psychology of self-affirmation: Sustaining the integrity of the self. In L. Berkowitz (Ed.), *Advances in experimental social psychology, vol. 21* (pp. 261–302). New York: Academic Press.

Swann, W. B. (1987). Identity negotiation: Where two roads meet. *Journal of Personality and Social Psychology, 53,* 1038–1051.

Swann, W. B., Griffin, J. J., Predmore, S. C., & Gaines, B. (1987). The cognitive-affective crossfire: When self-consistency confronts self-enhancement. *Journal of Personality and Social Psychology, 52,* 881–889.

Taylor, S. E., & Brown, J. D. (1988). Illusion and well-being: A social psychological perspective on mental health. *Psychological Bulletin, 103,* 193–210.

CHAPTER 12

SELF-ESTEEM AND EXPECTANCY-VALUE DISCREPANCY

THE EFFECTS OF BELIEVING THAT YOU CAN (OR CAN'T) GET WHAT YOU WANT

JOEL BROCKNER, BATIA M. WIESENFELD, AND DAPHNA F. RASKAS

This volume consists of chapters that provide rich theoretical insights into the nature of self-esteem. Each chapter describes an impressive program of research; in these, self-esteem is shown to relate to diverse outcomes ranging from task performance to suicidal ideation. The purpose of this chapter is twofold: (a) to highlight the empirical trends that emerge across the preceding chapters and offer the beginnings of a unified explanation, and (b) to discuss the implications of the contributors' theory and research (and our unified explanation) for behavior in organizational settings.

JOEL BROCKNER, BATIA M. WIESENFELD, AND DAPHNA F. RASKAS • Graduate School of Business, Columbia University, 715 Uris Hall, New York, NY 10027.

Self-Esteem: The Puzzle of Low Self-Regard, edited by Roy F. Baumeister. Plenum Press, New York, 1993.

TOWARD EXPLANATION OF THE EMERGING TRENDS

Expectancy theory offers a fundamental explanation of behavior, particularly in organizational settings (Vroom, 1964). According to the theory, behavior is a function of (a) people's beliefs that they can successfully perform the desired behavior, (b) the perception that certain outcomes are contingent upon the successful performance of the behavior, and (c) the judgment that the performance-contingent outcomes are valued. The first two of these three components are expectancies. The former is similar to Bandura's notion (1977) of self-efficacy, and the latter refers to the perceived relationship between behavior and outcome. Although behavior and outcome are conceptually distinct, in practice they often are inextricably linked; when this is so, the first belief refers to the expectation of being able to perform a behavior and thereby elicit its associated outcomes. The third component describes the motivational value of the outcomes associated with the behavior. Therefore, whether someone will behave in an esteem-building way (e.g., performing well in an athletic, intellectual, or social situation) depends upon the individual's expectations that he or she can perform the behavior, the belief that the behavior leads to certain outcomes, and the value that he or she places on the outcomes.

How is self-esteem related to the expectations and values that are central to expectancy theory? According to several contributors to this volume, high and low self-esteem people differ much more on the expectancy than the value dimension. Both groups want to feel good about themselves (i.e., both value outcomes that will heighten their self-esteem); however, low self-esteem people have lower expectations than their high self-esteem counterparts that they will be able to perform esteem-heightening behaviors.

Given that low and high self-esteem individuals diverge more on expectations than on values, it is tempting to conclude that self-esteem differences in belief and behavior are mediated by expectations. Expectations may well be a partial determinant of self-esteem effects. Within the context of expectancy theory, however, we offer a somewhat different explanation: Specifically, *it is individuals' perceptions of the discrepancy or tension between expectancies and values that account for the consequences of self-esteem*. Expectations and values are matched at a high level for those with high self-esteem. They believe that they can act in an esteem-enhancing way, and they want to do so. A very different picture emerges of persons with low self-esteem. The latter covet esteem-enhancing outcomes, but do not believe that they can elicit those outcomes. Indeed, it is the very realization that they cannot get what they want that lies at the core of their low self-esteem.

Harter, in Chapter 5, implies that expectancy-value discrepancy is one antecedent of self-esteem. Drawing from the seminal theorizing of James (1890), Harter found that self-esteem depends upon being successful in domains of psychological significance. Low self-esteem arises when people judge themselves as incompetent (i.e., they have low expectations) in areas in which they value being competent.

Differences between high and low self-esteem persons in their perceptions of the expectancy-value discrepancy may also account for four empirical trends cited in previous chapters: (a) Self-consistency and self-enhancement work together for high self-esteem persons, but not for those low in self-esteem (Brown, Chapter 6; De La Ronde & Swann, Chapter 8); (b) self-enhancement effects typically are found on affective measures, whereas self-consistency effects generally are observed on cognitive measures (Blaine & Crocker, Chapter 4); (c) high self-esteem persons are more certain about their self-knowledge than are low self-esteem individuals (Campbell & Lavallee, Chapter 1); and (d) high self-esteem people are more likely to practice self-enhancement, whereas those low in self-esteem are more apt to engage in self-protection (Tice, Chapter 3).

Self-Enhancement and Self-Consistency

Self-enhancement refers to the tendency to think and act in ways that allow people to feel good about themselves, whereas self-consistency refers to the tendency to think and act in ways that reinforce peoples' existing self-views. These two tendencies push high (or low) self-esteem persons in the same (or opposite) direction. Most of the contributors to this volume treat self-enhancement and self-consistency as motivations. For example, the chapter by De La Ronde and Swann speaks of positivity (self-enhancement) and self-verification (self-consistency) *strivings*, whereas Brown in Chapter 6 noted that low self-esteem people act in ways that enable them "to fulfill their *desire* for self-enhancement without sacrificing their *need* for self-consistency" (emphasis added).

As other contributors note, however, the tendencies to be self-consistent and self-enhancing have cognitive (i.e., information processing) as well as motivational substrates. For example, Blaine and Crocker (Chapter 4), in noting that low self-esteem persons assign greater credibility to negative feedback, suggest that "one need not assume a *motive* for self-consistency; one need only assume that reasonable, logical thought processes can lead high and low self-esteem people to different conclusions regarding positive and negative feedback." Miller and Ross (1975) were among the first to set forth an information-processing explanation of the self-serving bias in attributions for successes and failures. Because expected (or unexpected) outcomes are generally attributed to internal (or external) causes, and because high self-esteem people have higher expectancies for success than those low in self-esteem, the former are more likely to attribute success internally and failure externally than are the latter.

Thus, from a purely cognitive perspective, outcomes should be more easily processed and accepted (i.e., attributed internally, remembered better, and assigned greater credibility) if they are consistent with individuals' prior expectations. It is not only that the motives for self-enhancement and self-consistency are less congruent for low self-esteem persons, but also that the latter experience greater tension between the expectation for self-enhancement and the desire for self-enhancement relative to their high self-esteem counterparts.

Although our primary focus is on the perception of the tension between the expectation and desire for self-enhancement (hereafter referred to as the *expectancy-value discrepancy*), the level of congruence between self-enhancement and self-consistency motives offers a partial explanation of the consequences of self-esteem. Spencer, Josephs, and Steele (Chapter 2) suggest that people seek to maintain "an image of self-integrity, that is, overall moral and adaptive adequacy." Self-integrity may be achieved through self-verification (the motivated process by which people think, act, or elicit behaviors from others in ways consistent with their prior self-image) and/or self-enhancement (the motivated process by which people elicit or perceive outcomes in ways that allow them to feel better about themselves). Spencer et al. show that high self-esteem individuals are less bothered by esteem-threatening feedback because they have more self-enhancing (and hence self-affirming) resources inherent in their self-esteem.

These two routes to self-integrity work together for high self-esteem people, but not for low self-esteem persons. When confronted with positive feedback, low self-esteem individuals may have to choose between feeling good about themselves (and accepting the feedback) or preserving their self-identity (and rejecting the feedback). Brown (Chapter 6) also has discussed the consequences of this strictly motivational crossfire, which low self-esteem persons are more apt to experience. Thus, low self-esteem people are more likely than their high self-esteem counterparts to be buffeted by two sources of psychological tension: the perception of the discrepancy between their expectation and desire for self-enhancement, and the opposition of the motive for self-enhancement to the motive for self-consistency. One difference between these two sources of tension is the long-standing distinction between cognitive and motivational explanations of behavior. The former discrepancy combines cognitive (expectation for self-enhancement) and motivational (desire for self-enhancement) elements; the latter tension is entirely motivational. Both may explain why the tendencies toward self-enhancement and self-consistency are united for high self-esteem persons and divided for low self-esteem individuals. If so, then these tendencies are most appropriately viewed as resulting from a *combination* of information processing and motivated activity, rather than as being dominated by one type or the other.

Although these two sources of tension are conceptually distinct, they are sometimes (and mistakenly) used interchangeably. For example, in explaining different modes of self-enhancement for high versus low self-esteem people, Brown says in Chapter 6 that "high self-esteem people, *being confident of their abilities and positive qualities*, seek self-enhancement in ways that directly implicate the self. Low self-esteem people, *lacking confidence in their own abilities and qualities*, seek self-enhancement in ways that do not directly involve the self" (emphasis added). This explanation focuses on differences between low and high self-esteem people in their expectations and, therefore, possible discrepancies between their expectation and desire for success (i.e., that low self-esteem individuals perceive a greater discrepancy). Yet almost immediately thereafter, Brown explains the same phenomenon in the following way: "*motivational* ambivalence might underlie the conservatism of people with low self-esteem. Caught between an affectively based desire to enhance feelings of self-worth and a cognitively based need to maintain their existing self-conceptions . . . people with low self-esteem must fashion a compromise. This compromise takes the form of a conservative middle ground" (emphasis added). This latter explanation focuses on the tension between self-enhancement and self-consistency motives among low self-esteem people, and not on the perceived discrepancy between their expectation and desire for success.

It may even be the case that the expectancy-value discrepancy subsumes the motivational tension between self-enhancement and self-consistency. Several studies have shown that in those instances in which people with negative self-views (e.g., low self-esteem persons, depressives) have positive beliefs or expectations about themselves, they act in esteem-enhancing or self-serving ways (Brockner, 1988; Pelham, Chapter 10). That is, the reduction of the expectancy-value discrepancy among low self-esteem people causes them to respond in the customary ways of persons high in self-esteem. Moreover, on logical grounds it seems that the reduction of the motivational tension between self-enhancement and self-consistency for low self-esteem persons requires that their expectations become more positive; note, however, that raised expectations would also reduce the expectancy-value discrepancy among this group.

EFFECTS ON AFFECTIVE AND COGNITIVE MEASURES

Considerable evidence from an older literature review (Shrauger, 1975) and more recent empirical findings (Blaine & Crocker, Chapter 4) suggest that self-enhancement effects are generally found on affective dependent variables (e.g., liking for an evaluator), whereas self-consistency effects are obtained on cognitive measures (e.g., causal attributions for, memory of, and credibility judgments of evaluative feedback). If self-enhancement and self-consistency tendencies reflect a mixture of cognitive processes and motivational forces—and are not simply viewed as motives—then differences in the expectancy-value discrepancy between high and low self-esteem persons may account for the emergence of self-enhancement effects on affective measures and self-consistency effects on cognitive measures.

The typical way that the above results are described is that on affective measures, all people show greater preference for positive than negative feedback. In some instances this tendency is more pronounced among low than high self-esteem persons (S. C. Jones, 1973), presumably because the former are more needy of positive evaluations. On cognitive measures, persons high in self-esteem show greater acceptance of positive than negative feedback, relative to their low self-esteem counterparts. An alternative way to describe the same results is that on both affective and cognitive measures, high self-esteem people tend toward self-enhancement (and/or self-consistency, given that for them both tendencies work in concert). People with low self-esteem, in contrast, exhibit self-enhancement on affective measures and self-consistency on cognitive measures.

It seems unlikely that the reactions of low self-esteem individuals simply reflect motivational forces. If they did, then we would be hard-pressed to explain why one motivational force is predominant on one type of dependent measure, whereas another is salient on the other type of measure. Moreover, Blaine and Crocker state that to *"muddy the waters further,* it should also be noted that although both self-consistency and self-enhancement theories are framed in motivational terms, data consistent with self-consistency theory can also be interpreted in cognitive terms" (emphasis added).

From our perspective, the quote is potentially clarifying rather than muddying. Low self-esteem people have negative expectations. Therefore, from a strictly cognitive (rather than motivational) perspective, they are likely to respond to negative feedback (i.e., that is consistent with their self-image) by attributing it more internally, remembering it better, and assigning it greater credibility, relative to their high self-esteem counterparts. In short, the perceived discrepancy between what low self-esteem persons want (to receive esteem-enhancing feedback) and what they expect (to not be able to elicit esteem-enhancing feedback) leads them to show different tendencies on affective versus cognitive measures. Their negative expectations set the stage for self-consistency effects on cognitive measures, and their desire to feel good about themselves leads to self-enhancing tendencies on affective measures. For high self-esteem individuals, self-enhancement and self-consistency tendencies—whether mediated by cognitive or motivational processes—work hand in hand. As a consequence, they are more likely to be self-enhancing or self-consistent on both cognitive and affective measures.

CLARITY OF SELF-KNOWLEDGE

In Chapter 1, Campbell and Lavallee provide impressive evidence that low and high self-esteem people differ in the clarity of their self-knowledge. This difference may be attributable in part to the tendency of persons with low self-esteem to perceive more of an expectancy-value discrepancy than those high in self-esteem. People come to know themselves via introspection, a state of self-focused attention. If introspection makes salient the negative discrepancy between what people expect from themselves and what they want, then they may have difficulty coming to know themselves. One way to deal with the discomfort of introspection is avoidance. It has been shown that low self-esteem people are made more anxious by, and are more motivated to avoid, the state of self-focused attention (Brockner & Wallnau, 1981). The present reasoning may help explain *why* they find self-focused attention an unpleasant experience to be avoided: It makes salient a painful discrepancy between expectations and desires.

Not all people low in self-esteem avoid self-focused attention. Psychotherapy is a self-focusing experience undertaken by millions of people seeking to improve their opinions of themselves. The expectancy-value discrepancy experienced during introspection, however, may distract low self-esteem people from coming to know themselves. For these people, the truth about themselves hurts. Consequently, they may be reluctant to face what they think is the truth, and thereby may minimize the certainty of their self-knowledge. Campbell and Lavallee offer a similar viewpoint:

> When the current self-view is less positive . . . people are caught . . . between what they *want* to believe is true of them and what they *think* might be true of them. These conflicting . . . reactions . . . can lead in turn to increased self-concept uncertainty . . . Studies have shown that when people are led to believe that they might possess some negative attribute, they seem to seek uncertainty in that they actively avoid acquiring certain diagnostic information about the attribute.

Although the perceived discrepancy between expectations and values may account for a number of differences between persons who are high and low in self-esteem, the causal arrow can also run in the opposite direction. Just as greater expectancy-value discrepancy may cause low self-esteem people to be more avoidant of self-focused attention and to be less self-knowledgeable as a result, people who are less self-knowledgeable may be more likely to avoid self-focused attention. Dixon and Baumeister (1991) examined the relationship between self-complexity and avoidance of self-focus. *Self-complexity* is operationalized as the number of different categories of adjectives people use to describe themselves, as well as the diversity of those categories. It seems likely that less self-knowledgeable people are lower in self-complexity. Dixon and Baumeister discovered that low self-complexity people were more avoidant of self-focused attention, particularly if they had just received negative performance feedback. Thus, self-knowledge and self-focus avoidance may be reciprocally related.

Self-Enhancement Versus Self-Protection

Self-enhancement refers to the tendency to think and act in ways that allow people to feel good about themselves. These tendencies can be further subdivided into two categories: acting and perceiving in ways that maximize positive boosts to self-esteem, and acting and perceiving in ways that minimize negative threats to self-esteem. Several contributors to this volume (see Chapters 1, 2, and 3) have noted that high self-esteem people are more likely to exhibit the first of these two tendencies, whereas low self-esteem people are more likely to exhibit the second. (The former tendency has been dubbed *self-enhancement* and the latter has been called *self-protection*.)

Although self-enhancement and self-protection are similar in certain ways, they do differ in a number of important respects. Self-enhancement refers to the tendency to think and act in ways that enable favorable things to occur (i.e., to feel good about oneself), whereas self-protection refers to a tendency to think and act in ways that minimize bad things that may happen (i.e., to avoid feeling bad about oneself). Self-enhancement also is more psychologically "risky" than self-protection. The behaviors needed to bring about self-enhancement typically have greater reward value, but also have a lower probability of success relative to those needed to produce self-protection.

We refer to self-enhancement and self-protection as behavioral and psychological tendencies resulting from a combination of motivational and cognitive processes. The contributors to this volume generally speak of these tendencies in largely motivational terms. We agree that the two tendencies result from motivational forces in part, but we do not wish to take the position that they are entirely the result of motivated activity; this position parallels the one we took earlier in discussing self-enhancement and self-consistency.

Tice (1991) neatly illustrates self-esteem differences in self-enhancement versus self-protection in the context of self-handicapping. As originally conceptualized (E. E. Jones & Berglas, 1978), *self-handicapping* refers to the process whereby people create obstacles for themselves in the service of heightening the esteem-protecting or -enhancing value of the feedback. In response to negative feedback, people can protect their self-esteem by attributing their poor performance to the self-imposed obstacle; in response to positive feedback, people can enhance their self-esteem by attributing their favorable performance to internal qualities that enabled them to overcome the self-imposed obstacle. Self-handicapping thus combines self-protective and self-enhancing tendencies (which are, of course, conceptually distinct).

Tice (1991) found that self-esteem was associated with preferences in peoples' self-handicapping behavior. When the performance situation was described as one that could only identify exceptionally poorly qualified people, low self-esteem individuals showed a greater tendency to self-handicap. Self-handicapping in this situation served self-protective purposes, in that it enabled people to attribute their poor performance (if it materialized) to the handicap. When the performance situation was described as one that could only identify highly qualified people, however, high self-esteem persons were more likely to self-handicap. By doing so, they could experience self-enhancement by attributing any favorable outcome to their internal qualities. Numerous other studies (see Chapters 1, 2, and 3) have shown the conceptually analogous findings that low (or high) self-esteem persons are more likely to self-protect (or self-enhance).

Differences between high and low self-esteem people in the expectancy-value discrepancy may account for these tendencies, in at least two ways. The first explanation is simpler than the second. First, let us assume that self-enhancement reflects a relatively dramatic (or, as noted earlier, risky) attempt at self-aggrandizement rather than self-protection. All people want to think and act in ways that will enable them to feel good about themselves. Relative to low self-esteem people, however, those high in self-esteem expect that they will be able to perform the behaviors that allow them to feel good about themselves. Low self-esteem people set more "modest" self-aggrandizement goals than high self-esteem individuals, translating into a greater tendency toward self-protection for the former group and self-enhancement for the latter.

Second, in the previous section of this chapter, we speculated that differences between high and low self-esteem people in the expectancy-value discrepancy led to differences in the certainty of their self-knowledge (i.e., low self-esteem people have a less clear sense of who they are). We now hypothesize that the joint combination of expectancy-value discrepancy (shown more by low than high self-esteem individuals) and self-knowledge uncertainty (also found more among the former group) leads to the tendencies for low self-esteem persons to be self-protective and for high self-esteem individuals to be self-enhancing. If expectancy-value discrepancy and self-knowledge uncertainty are related, then most people will fall into two groups: those having high discrepancy and high uncertainty (low self-esteem persons), and those having low discrepancy and low uncertainty (high self-esteem individuals). The combination of high discrepancy and high uncertainty should lead to self-protection.

With high discrepancy, people are likely to set modest self-aggrandizement goals, as mentioned in the first explanation. Furthermore, high uncertainty enables people to think that the "jury is still out" on whether they can act or think in ways that enable them to feel good about themselves. Indeed, it is this very uncertainty that may allow the individual to strive toward self-improvement. So, just as Campbell and Lavallee suggested in Chapter 1 that people seek uncertainty when they believe that they might possess some negative attribute, the reverse causal sequence may also apply: The presence of uncertainty provides hope to people that they may be able to feel good (or at least better) about themselves in the end, so they should not yet give up the fight. In short, we suggest that the self-protective tendencies of people with low self-esteem reflect a compromise. Uncertainty allows them to seek self-improvement, but modest beliefs about their capabilities lead to a dampening of their quest for self-improvement.

The self-enhancing tendencies of high self-esteem people reflect the firm conviction that they can succeed in their risky, esteem-building ventures. They have little expectancy-value discrepancy (i.e., they think that they can live up to what they want), and they are fairly certain of their belief in themselves.

Even if expectancy-value discrepancy and self-knowledge uncertainty are positively correlated, there should be a nontrivial number of individuals who fall in two other categories: those who are high in discrepancy and low in uncertainty, and those who are low in discrepancy and high in uncertainty. The former refers to low self-esteem people who are certain in their self-knowledge, whereas the latter describes high self-esteem persons who are not so sure in what they know about themselves. The former group would be expected to show the fewest attempts at self-improvement; that is, they should be relatively unlikely to exhibit self-protection or self-enhancement, because they firmly believe that there is little hope for them. The results of a handful of studies are consistent with this speculation. Marecek and Mettee (1972) gave all subjects positive feedback, but varied whether that feedback was attributable to luck (a self-irrelevant factor) or skill (a self-enhancing factor). Subjects varied not only in their level of self-esteem, but also in the certainty with which they maintained their self-evaluations. All groups improved their performance on a subsequent task, save one—low self-esteem individuals who were certain of their self-appraisals and who also believed that their prior success was the result of skill. Put differently, this group failed to capitalize on its self-enhancing success.

Kernis's remarks in Chapter 9 on the joint effects of self-esteem level and stability also may be germane. Stability refers to the consistency in peoples' situation-specific judgments of their self-esteem. To assess stability, subjects complete a self-esteem scale with regard to how they are feeling at that particular moment; this procedure is performed on multiple occasions over a 5- to 7-day period. Stability is inversely related to the size of the standard deviation of these judgments. It seems reasonable that self-knowledge certainty will manifest itself in the stability with which people describe their self-esteem; that is, one of the determinants of how consistently people describe themselves is the depth with which they know themselves. People with a confused sense of self may find their state self-esteem to be more situationally influenced, and hence less stable over time.

If this reasoning is correct, then several of Kernis's findings are consistent with the notion that people with high expectancy-value discrepancy and low uncertainty in their self-knowledge will be particularly unlikely to self-protect. In one study, Kernis, Grannemann, and Mathis (in press) found that low self-esteem/high stability people—who map onto those high in expectancy-value discrepancy and low in self-knowledge uncertainty—were unlikely to make self-protective excuses for failure feedback. As Kernis puts it in Chapter 9, "Individuals with unstable low self-esteem appear to engage in excuse making primarily as a way of diminishing the negative implications of a poor performance."

In another study, Kernis examined the relationship between self-esteem and overgeneralization following failure, the tendency to allow negative feedback to call to mind other negative thoughts about oneself (Carver & Ganellen, 1983). Although previous research has shown that low self-esteem is strongly related to overgeneralization following failure (Kernis, Brockner, & Frankel, 1989), this seems to be particularly true among those with stable low self-esteem. Thus, stable low self-esteem people react to failure in a particularly nonself-protective fashion; failure triggers the process of bringing other self-critical thoughts to mind.

Kernis, Grannemann, and Mathis (1991) also found that stability of self-esteem moderates the relationship between self-esteem and depression. The most depressed individuals are those who are low in self-esteem and high in stability. The fact that this group acts in the least self-protective fashion may account for their high levels of depression.

What about the people who are low in expectancy-value discrepancy and high in self-knowledge uncertainty? Like the presumably larger group of people who are low in expectancy-value discrepancy and low in self-knowledge uncertainty, these people should exhibit self-enhancement. Unlike the low expectancy-value discrepancy/low uncertainty people, however, they are not quite certain that they deserve their low expectancy-value discrepancy status. Thus, they may strive toward self-enhancement more than the low expectancy-value discrepancy/low uncertainty people. For example, Kernis, Grannemann, and Mathis (in press) found that unstable high self-esteem people were more likely to self-enhance (i.e., explain the cause of positive feedback in a way that shined favorably upon them) than their stable high self-esteem counterparts.

Moreover, even if these two groups do not differ in their degree of self-enhancement, they may differ in the nature of the underlying process. For example, Marecek and Mettee (1972) found that high self-esteem persons reacted in a self-enhancing way to success feedback, regardless of their level of self-esteem certainty. It is possible that this tendency required little psychological effort for those high in certainty;

they were merely doing what came naturally. The high self-esteem/ uncertain individuals may have been hypothesis testing in their self-enhancing reactions, however, wanting to convince themselves that they were indeed worthy of their positive (albeit tentative) beliefs about themselves. Clearly, these speculative comments await further research.

Adaptivity of Self-Enhancement Versus Self-Protection

Although high (or low) self-esteem people generally self-enhance (or self-protect), we are not saying that one tendency is uniformly more adaptive than the other. Heatherton and Ambady (Chapter 7) define complex self-regulation (i.e., adaptive functioning) as the ability to make accurate predictions about one's capabilities; commit oneself to reachable, appropriate goals; and manage performance so as to reach the goals. According to Heatherton and Ambady, both low and high self-esteem persons may have difficulty self-regulating, but for different reasons. Although persons with low self-esteem want to do well, the combination of low expectations and low self-clarity may lead them to set modest goals. Self-regulation failure may occur if these goals are too modest (i.e., if the persons sell themselves short).

People with high self-esteem have less expectancy-value discrepancy and are more certain of who they are and what they can accomplish. Self-regulation failure may occur, however, if their high expectations and certainty are unrealistic. Heatherton and Ambady report that these people may be maladaptively overconfident in the face of challenging conditions, such as when they were told to "set low goals because they might not be able to perform effectively under pressure." In their quest for self-enhancement, high self-esteem individuals were shown to set risky, inappropriate goals, which led them to perform more poorly than their low self-esteem counterparts. We speculate that the high self-esteem people who showed this tendency were at least somewhat uncertain of their high self-esteem status (i.e., unstable high self-esteem people, in Kernis's framwork). Heatherton and Ambady suggested that high self-esteem people may fail to self-regulate "when their abilities are questioned." It is possible that situations which force them to question their abilities elicit the hypothesis-testing mode of self-enhancement in which unstable high self-esteem people may engage.

ORGANIZATIONAL IMPLICATIONS

The tendency of low self-esteem persons to perceive a greater expectancy-value discrepancy than their high self-esteem counterparts may account for a variety of phenomena described in the present volume. It is useful to discuss how the various phenomena, in turn, may shed light on some important and unresolved issues in organizational behavior.

SELF-ENHANCEMENT AND SELF-CONSISTENCY

These two tendencies pull low self-esteem persons in opposite directions. The fact that self-consistency may be at odds with self-enhancement for some people may help explain why attempts to uplift employee performance or morale often meet with mixed success at best. Consider self-fulfilling prophecies as a case in point. Organizational scholars have argued that managers should take advantage of the fact that people often behave consistently with how they are expected to behave. The prescription is for managers to communicate high expectations to their subordinates to elicit greater performance; indeed, several studies have shown that managers or organizations who expect more from their workers do engender greater productivity (Eden, 1990).

Given the apparent simplicity of the notion that managers may elicit greater performance through high expectations, it is perplexing that they do not capitalize on it to a greater extent. One possible explanation, at least among workers with relatively low self-esteem, resides in the tension between self-enhancement and self-consistency. Although self-enhancement tendencies may lead low self-esteem people to conform with their managers' high expectations, their self-consistency tendencies push them in the opposite direction. From an information-processing perspective, these people may have difficulty believing that they can live up to the high expectations set for them. From a motivational vantage point, they run the risk of having their identities disrupted (Brown, Chapter 6) by conforming to their managers' high expectations.

EFFECTS ON AFFECTIVE AND COGNITIVE MEASURES

Social psychologists have noted that attitudes and behaviors often are related weakly, if at all. The organizational counterpart to attitude-behavior relationships (or the lack thereof) is the literature examining the linkage between job satisfaction and performance. Contrary to the intuitive belief that "the happy worker is the productive worker," many studies have found very slight correlations between job satisfaction and performance.

The causes of self-enhancement effects on affective measures and self-consistency effects on cognitive measures may provide at least a partial explanation of satisfaction-performance inconsistency. If people with low self-esteem are given positive feedback about their job performance, they are likely to show self-enhancement on affective measures. For example, they should express liking for the evaluator. Their cognitive reactions however (e.g., expectations for future performance, attribution for their past performance, and the credibility of the feedback), are likely to lag behind, showing self-consistency effects instead. Thus, these people may like a positive evaluator more than a negative evaluator, but their cognitive appraisals will not tend toward self-enhancement nearly as much.

We make the assumption that cognitive reactions are very relevant to performance. For example, if persons low in self-esteem respond to positive evaluations by not raising their expectations for future performance, or by attributing the success to nonself-enhancing causes, then their subsequent performance is not likely to improve. In short, at least within the context of the reactions of low self-esteem persons to positive feedback, we see the possibility for satisfaction-performance inconsistency.

In-Group Bias

Intergroup relations are a ubiquitous aspect of organizational life. Smooth coordination between interdependent groups is necessary for effective performance. One intergroup phenomenon that could influence how well groups work together is in-group bias: the tendency for groups to evaluate or treat members of their own group more favorably than members of out-groups. The fact that people usually exhibit self-enhancement on affective measures but self-consistency on cognitive dimensions could account for an interesting paradox of group behavior noted by Luhtanen and Crocker (1991). On the one hand, in-group bias does seem to heighten self-esteem. Thus, one might expect people to exhibit in-group bias after negative feedback, particularly if they are low in chronic self-esteem. These are the conditions under which people should be most in need of esteem-enhancing (or esteem-protecting) experiences. On the other hand, Crocker, Thompson, McGraw, and Ingerman (1987) found that following negative feedback, high self-esteem people showed more in-group bias. They rated others who had performed poorly (like themselves) much more favorably than did their low self-esteem counterparts.

If in-group bias heightens self-esteem, then why did the more needy group show less in-group bias? Heightened self-esteem resulting from in-group bias seems to be an example of self-enhancement on affective measures. Low self-esteem people, however, may have difficulty *believing* that their group is better than the out-group. Their reaction is reminiscent of a remark made by Woody Allen, who in the film *Annie Hall* quoted Groucho Marx as saying that he wouldn't want to join any club that would have him as a member. Although their esteem stands to benefit from in-group bias, the cognitive judgments of low self-esteem people push them toward self-consistency, thereby making it more difficult to exhibit in-group bias.

It is also possible, as Brown (Chapter 6) suggests, that low self-esteem people will exhibit in-group bias, albeit indirectly. Whereas persons high in self-esteem self-enhance directly by rating favorably groups of which they are members, low self-esteem people self-enhance indirectly by rating favorably groups to which they do not belong, but that are similar to groups of which they are members. These tendencies could be manifested, for example, in an organization grouped on the basis of the product or service provided. In such an organization, people working in similar functional areas (e.g., marketing, manufacturing, sales, research and development) are assigned to different product or service teams. Thus, members of a product team in a functional area have counterparts working on a different product team. Consider how people in a functional area (e.g., marketing) in team A might respond as a function of their self-esteem. High self-esteem people may self-enhance directly by rating their product team as better than team B. Low self-esteem individuals in marketing in team A may self-enhance indirectly by rating favorably the members of the marketing function in team B.

CLARITY OF SELF-KNOWLEDGE

Brockner (1988) reported that low self-esteem people are more "behaviorally plastic" than their high self-esteem counterparts (i.e., they are more likely to be influenced in the direction of a variety of external cues). These plasticity effects have been demonstrated under controlled laboratory conditions and in organizational settings. Organizational examples of self-esteem differences in behavioral plasticity include (a) the tendency for low (but not high) self-esteem people to vary their supervisory style as a function of their own supervisor's competence, success, and reward power (Weiss, 1977); (b) the tendency of low self-esteem people to be more influenced by the organization's socialization practices (G. R. Jones, 1986); and (c) the fact that the performance and satisfaction of persons low in self-esteem vary as a function of the supportiveness of their peer group (greater supportiveness leads to higher performance and satisfaction), which is not the case for persons with high self-esteem (Mossholder, Bedeian, & Armenakis, 1982).

Brockner explained these and many other examples of behavioral plasticity as attributable to the tendency of low self-esteem people to be less sure of themselves (i.e., to be less confident in the correctness of their behaviors and beliefs), thereby rendering them more susceptible to influence by external cues. The present conceptualization offers a possible explanation of their tendency to be less certain about the correctness of their behaviors and beliefs. The perceived discrepancy between what they believe they can accomplish and what they want to accomplish leads to greater self-concept confusion. Not having as clear a sense of who they are, they are more likely to be influenced by external cues for appropriate thoughts, feelings, and behavior.

SELF-ENHANCEMENT VERSUS SELF-PROTECTION

People high in self-esteem attempt to capitalize on situations that provide them with the opportunity for self-enhancement, whereas persons having low self-esteem are more likely to respond in situations that pose a threat to their self-esteem. As Tice demonstrates in Chapter 3, situations differ in the extent to which they provide opportunities for self-enhancement or pose threats to self-esteem. For example, imagine two very different managerial or organizational reactions to employee performance. In the first organization, the culture is one in which successful performance is celebrated; unsuccessful performance, though not taken lightly, does not elicit strict, punitive reactions. In the second organization, there is little reaction to (i.e., celebration of) positive performance, but there are harsh reactions to negative employee performance. The first organization mainly provides opportunity for self-enhancement, whereas the second one primarily presents a threat to self-esteem. All else being equal, we predict that high self-esteem individuals would be more responsive in the first situation, and low self-esteem people would be more responsive in the second situation.

Although organizations (or situations) may differ in the extent to which they provide opportunities for self-enhancement versus threats to self-esteem, it is likely that the same organization (or situation) combines elements of both. For example, suppose that external cues suggested that although it was by no means certain, employees should not expect to perform well in a given situation. High self-esteem people may experience this as a challenge, or an opportunity for self-enhancement. Low self-esteem persons may interpret the situation as a threat against which they need to protect themselves. Thus, both groups may be motivated to perform, and both may even perform at the same level. The underlying process driving motivation and performance, however, could be very different; moreover, unless the investigator included measures in addition to motivation and performance, this difference in the underlying process would go unnoticed.

Factors other than the individuals' self-esteem may affect whether the situation is framed as providing opportunity for self-enhancement or a possible threat to self-esteem. In the example of people believing that it is likely but not certain that they will not perform well, suppose that some people were given the choice about whether they wanted to undertake the task, whereas others were forced to work on the task. Through a self-perception process, those who chose to work on the task may have inferred that there must have been something positive about the undertaking, such as the opportunity for self-enhancement. Or the act of choosing may have been a self-affirming experience (Steele, 1988), in which people experienced a temporary boost to self-esteem. If the perception of choice leads people to frame the situation as providing opportunity for self-enhancement, then high self-esteem people may be particularly responsive (i.e., they may work harder at the task).

If people are coerced to work on this very same task, however, they may frame the situation as one that threatens their self-esteem, through either a self-perception or a self-(dis)affirmation process. If so, then low self-esteem people may be more responsive than if the same situation were framed as an opportunity. In summary, predictions about the motivation levels of high or low self-esteem persons in a given situation may depend upon whether the self-threatening aspects are salient (which should prompt low self-esteem individuals into action via self-protection) or the opportunity for self-enhancement is present (which should elicit greater striving among high self-esteem people).

COLLECTIVE SELF-ESTEEM

There is growing interest in the role of self-evaluative variables and processes in work organizations. The book *Self-Esteem at Work* (Brockner, 1988) explores the causes and consequences of employee self-esteem. Others have applied Bandura's work (1977) on self-efficacy to individual behavior in organizations (Gist, 1987). Furthermore, several scales of work-related self-concept have been published recently, including one concerning *organization-based self-esteem*. This measure refers to the extent to which people believe that "they are valuable, worthwhile, effectual members of their employing organizations" (Pierce, Gardner, Cummings, & Dunham, 1989, p. 634). The present volume provides an impressive array of theory and research that may help explain individual behavior in organizations.

Furthermore, because so much activity in organizations is undertaken in a group context, organizations may provide particularly fertile ground in which to study collective self-esteem. Collective self-esteem can be conceptualized in several ways, varying along the dimension of unit of analysis. *Social identity* relates to one form of collective self-esteem, referring to "that part of the individuals' self-concept which derives from their knowledge of their membership in a social group (or groups) together with the value and emotional significance of that membership" (Tajfel, 1981, p. 255). Note that the individual is the unit of analysis in social identity theory. Individuals who have more of their self-identity invested in their group memberships will be more influenced by group actions having self-evaluative implications. For example, Brockner, Tyler, and Cooper-Schneider (1992) discovered that the perceived fairness of an institution's actions had greater impact on individuals who were more committed to the institution prior to the action. In several settings, it was found that people reacted particularly negatively when they were highly committed to the institution beforehand, but felt that they had been treated unfairly in some recent encounter with the institution.

An important question for further research is whether collective self-esteem is related to behavior in ways that parallel the relationship of an individual's self-esteem to his or her own behavior. A recent study by Crocker and Luhtanen (1990) suggests that parallelism may exist. In their study, individuals high in collective self-esteem showed greater in-group bias in the face of a threat to the collective's self-esteem. Specifically, high collective self-esteem individuals whose *group* performed poorly rated below-average performers (like themselves) more favorably and above-average performers less favorably, relative to high collective self-esteem individuals whose group performed well. These findings are strikingly similar to those obtained by Crocker et al. (1987), who examined the role of personal self-esteem and threat on in-group bias.

To evaluate the role of perceived expectancy-value discrepancy in the context of collective self-esteem, it is necessary to measure both the individuals' level of attachment to the group (which corresponds to the importance people place on the group performing well) and their beliefs about the group's efficacy (which correspond to their expectations for the group's performance). Existing measures have tapped the former dimension quite well; constructs such as group cohesion, collectivism, and organizational commitment seem related to the value people attach to successful collective performance. There is a need, however, to develop measures of collective expectations or efficacy to determine whether expectancy-value discrepancy mediates the effects of collective self-esteem.

Collective self-esteem may also influence behavior at the group or even organizational level of analysis. To evaluate the possibility that the expectancy-value discrepancy mediates the effects of self-esteem at the collective level of analysis, it probably is necessary to aggregate the expectations of individual members for the collective's performance, as well as the importance members attach to successful collective performance. Based upon the results presented in the first half of this chapter, it may be that groups who believe that they can get what they want have a clearer sense of group identity than those who believe that they cannot. For example, the latter group may agree less on the collective's values, strategies, and goals, as a result of their confused sense of self-identity. Furthermore, groups with a less clear sense of who they are may be more likely to self-protect (and less likely to self-enhance) compared to groups with a more clearly defined sense of self. For example, low-clarity groups may shy away from negative feedback that provides valuable opportunities for learning, whereas high-clarity groups, seeking to self-enhance, may relish those situations.

U.S. corporations have come under great competitive pressures in the past two decades, and there is every indication that this trend will continue as we head toward the 21st century. Now more than ever, organization members need to work together. Many organizations have redesigned the nature of their work; activities previously done by individuals are now performed by groups. Therefore, for both theoretical and practical reasons, it is important to understand constructs such as collective self-esteem. Future research should evaluate whether perceptions of the expectancy-value discrepancy—which appears to provide a parsimonious explanation of self-esteem effects at the individual level—will be useful in explaining the antecedents and consequences of collective self-esteem.

ACKNOWLEDGMENTS

We thank Roy Baumeister for his helpful comments on a previous draft of the chapter.

REFERENCES

Bandura, A. (1977). Self-efficacy: Toward a unifying theory of behavioral change. *Psychological Review, 84*, 191–215.

Brockner, J. (1988). *Self-esteem at work: Research, theory, and practice*. Lexington, MA: Lexington Books.

Brockner, J., Tyler, T. R., & Cooper-Schneider, R. (1992). The influence of prior commitment to an institution on reactions to perceived unfairness: The higher they are, the harder they fall. *Administrative Science Quarterly. 37*, 241–261.

Brockner, J., & Wallnau, L. B. (1981). Self-esteem, anxiety, and the avoidance of self-focused attention. *Journal of Research in Personality, 15*, 277–291.

Carver, C. S., & Ganellen, R. J. (1983). Depression and components of self-punitiveness: High standards, self-criticism, and overgeneralization. *Journal of Abnormal Psychology, 92*, 330–337.

Crocker, J., & Luhtanen, R. (1990). Collective self-esteem and in-group bias. *Journal of Personality and Social Psychology, 58*, 60–67.

Crocker, J., Thompson, L. J., McGraw, K. M., & Ingerman, C. (1987). Downward comparison, prejudice, and evaluations of others: Effects of self-esteem and threat. *Journal of Personality and Social Psychology, 52*, 907–916.

Dixon, T. M., & Baumeister, R. F. (1991). Escaping the self: The moderating effects of self-complexity. *Personality and Social Psychology Bulletin, 17*, 363–368.

Eden, D. (1990). *Pygmalion in management*. Lexington, MA: Lexington Books.

Gist, M. E. (1987). Self-efficacy: Implications for organizational behavior and human resource management. *Academy of Management Review, 12*, 472–485.

James, W. (1890). *Psychology: The briefer course*. New York: Henry Holt.

Jones, E. E., & Berglas, S. (1978). Control of attributions abut the self through self-handicapping strategies: The appeal of alcohol and the role of underachievement. *Personality and Social Psychology Bulletin, 4*, 200–206.

Jones, G. R. (1986). Socialization tactics, self-efficacy, and newcomers' adjustments to organizations. *Academy of Management Journal, 29*, 262–279.

Jones, S. C. (1973). Self and interpersonal evaluations: Esteem theories vs. consistency theories. *Psychology Bulletin, 79*, 185–199.

Kernis, M. H., Brockner, J., & Frankel, B. S. (1989). Self-esteem and reactions to failure: The mediating role of overgeneralization. *Journal of Personality and Social Psychology, 57*, 707–714.

Kernis, M. H., Grannemann, B. D., & Mathis, L. C. (1991). Stability of self-esteem as a moderator of the relation between level of self-esteem and depression. *Journal of Personality and Social Psychology, 61*, 80–84.

Kernis, M. H., Grannemann, B. D., & Mathis, L. C. (in press). Stability of self-esteem: Assessment, correlates, and excuse making. *Journal of Personality.*

Luhtanen, R., & Crocker, J. (1991). Self-esteem and intergroup comparisons: Toward a theory of collective self-esteem. In J. Suls & T. A. Wills (Eds.), *Social comparison: Contemporary theory and research* (pp. 211–234). Hillsdale, NJ: Lawrence Erlbaum Associates.

Marecek, J., & Mettee, D. R. (1972). Avoidance of continued success as a function of self-esteem, level of esteem certainty, and responsibility for success. *Journal of Personality and Social Psychology, 22*, 98–107.

Miller, D. T., & Ross, M. (1975). Self-serving biases in attribution of causality: Fact or fiction? *Psychological Bulletin, 82*, 213–225.

Mossholder, K. W., Bedeian, A. G., & Armenakis, A. A. (1982). Group process-work outcome relationships: A note on the moderating impact of self-esteem. *Academy of Management Journal, 25*, 575–585.

Pierce, J. L., Gardner, D. G., Cummings, L. L., & Dunham, R. B. (1989). Organization-based self-esteem: Construct definition, measurement, and validation. *Academy of Management Journal, 32*, 622–648.

Shrauger, J. S. (1975). Responses to evaluation as a function of initial self-perceptions. *Psychological Bulletin, 82*, 581–596.

Steele, C. M. .(1988). The psychology of self-affirmation: Sustaining the integrity of the self. In L. Berkowitz (Ed.), *Advances in experimental social psychology, vol. 21* (pp. 261–302). New York: Academic Press.

Tajfel, H. (1981). *Human groups and social categories: Studies in social psychology.* Cambridge, England: Cambridge University Press.

Tice, D. M. (1991). Esteem protection or enhancement? Self-handicapping motives and attributions differ by trait self-esteem. *Journal of Personality and Social Psychology, 60*, 711–725.

Vroom, V. H. (1964). *Work and motivation.* New York: John Wiley.

Weiss, H. M. (1977). Subordinate imitation of supervisory behavior: The role of modeling in organizational socialization. *Organizational Behavior and Human Performance, 19*, 89–105.

CHAPTER 13

THE PUZZLES OF SELF-ESTEEM
A CLINICAL PERSPECTIVE

HOWARD TENNEN AND GLENN AFFLECK

In the clinical setting we recognize that cognition, affect, and behavior are determined by varied, interdependent, and complex processes. The theories and findings presented in this volume are important to clinical practice because they address just such processes among individuals with low self-regard. Basic theory and research on competing motives (De La Ronde & Swann, Chapter 8; Brown, Chapter 6), on offsetting threats to one dimension of esteem by affirming other aspects of the self (Spencer, Josephs, & Steele, Chapter 2; Heatherton & Ambady, Chapter 7), on indirect forms of self-enhancement (Brown, Chapter 6), and on daily fluctuations in self-esteem (Kernis, Chapter 9) should be welcomed by clinicians. In turn, clinical theory and research have much to offer investigations of self-esteem. In this chapter, we address points of contact and contrast between the models described in this volume and modern clinical theory and research.

We begin by summarizing issues on which the contributors agree, those issues that remain unresolved, and new directions suggested by these contributions. Because self-esteem is linked to depression in several chapters, we review briefly what is known—and what is frequently assumed but not known—about self-esteem as a vulnerability marker

HOWARD TENNEN AND GLENN AFFLECK • Department of Psychiatry, University of Connecticut Health Center, Farmington, CT 06030.

Self-Esteem: The Puzzle of Low Self-Regard, edited by Roy F. Baumeister. Plenum Press, New York, 1993.

for depression. We then discuss four strategies of esteem maintenance employed by those with high self-esteem and explore why they are puzzling to clinicians. Finally, we question proposed relations among self-esteem, positive illusions, and well-being, and we point to limitations in our knowledge of how esteem is maintained across the life span.

POINTS OF CONVERGENCE, UNRESOLVED ISSUES, AND NEW DIRECTIONS

There are three areas relevant to clinical practice about which the contributors agree. One is that individuals with low self-esteem are not self-loathing people. Rather, their descriptions of themselves are neutral, not self-effacing (Tice, Chapter 3). A second area of convergence is that people with low self-esteem maintain conservative social motives: They act to minimize potential losses (Chapter 3), set unchallenging goals to avoid failure (Heatherton & Ambady, Chapter 7), and are motivated by self-protection rather than self-enhancement (Campbell & Lavallee, Chapter 1). Third, low self-esteem individuals appear to be more sensitive and reactive to their social environments (Chapters 1 and 7). Whether this makes them more vulnerable to life's slings and arrows or better able to respond to others and thus learn from experience has not yet been determined.

Alongside these areas of agreement, there remain important unsettled questions. Most salient is how best to depict the motives of the person with low self-regard. Three apparently incompatible motivational structures have been hypothesized. One model portrays low self-esteem individuals as having fewer esteem resources from which to draw in the face of threat (Spencer et al., Chapter 2); thus, when threatened, they have a *greater* need to use self-enhancement strategies (Chapter 1). Another model has the extremely low esteem individual *lacking* the motivation for self-enhancement (Blaine & Crocker, Chapter 4). The third perspective, captured in Chapter 8 by De La Ronde and Swann, is that people with low self-esteem are caught between the wish to be evaluated favorably and the simultaneous wish to receive self-confirming (i.e., negative) evaluations. Although these depictions lead to distinct predictions about the behavior of low self-esteem individuals, direct tests of these predictions require an as-yet-unreached consensus regarding what behaviors reflect self-enhancement (Wills, 1991).

Another unresolved issue is the role of positive attributes in the self-concepts of people with low self-esteem. Blaine and Crocker state that low self-esteem individuals "are not at all certain that they have positive attributes," and Brown (Chapter 6) believes that "almost by definition, these people are unaccustomed to thinking about themselves in positive terms." On the other hand, Pelham (Chapter 10) argues convincingly that even people with extremely low self-regard believe they have at least one very important and very positive attribute. Clearly, the place of positive attributes in the self-concepts of low self-esteem individuals remains unsettled.

These chapters also hold great promise for theory elaboration and new research directions. Promising directions include the idea that both high and low self-esteem individuals want to affirm themselves (Spencer et al., Chapter 2) and desire positive feedback (De La Ronde & Swann, Chapter 8); that low self-esteem individuals might enhance their esteem indirectly through their association with others (Brown, Chapter 6); that self-esteem variability might be as important to well-being as level of esteem (Kernis, Chapter 9); that individuals with low self-esteem have an unstable self-concept (Campbell & Lavallee, Chapter 1); that in situations that threaten esteem, people with high self-esteem may be the ones who show self-regulatory failures (Heatherton & Ambady, Chapter 7); and that by maintaining their most positive self-appraisals, low self-esteem individuals may create the conditions for self-limiting depression (Pelham, Chapter 10). It is to the relation of depression to self-esteem that we now turn.

SELF-ESTEEM AS A RISK FACTOR FOR DEPRESSION

Depression plays a prominent role in the theories and investigations described in this volume. Blaine and Crocker discuss the association between low self-esteem and depression, citing evidence that severely depressed individuals show a self-deprecating explanatory style in which they accept more responsibility for bad outcomes than for good outcomes. Harter (Chapter 5) and Pelham suggest that persons having low self-regard may be particularly vulnerable to depression, and Kernis reviews evidence from his own work (Kernis, Grannemann, & Mathis, 1991) to support this hypothesis. Interventions for individuals with low self-esteem are offered by De La Ronde and Swann and by Heatherton and Ambady. But as Tice (Chapter 3) and Campbell and Lavallee remind us, the low self-esteem described in these chapters is not self-hate, self-loathing, or even low self-regard in the absolute sense. Are the low self-esteem participants in these studies at risk for clinical depression? We think not, for several reasons.

The poor concordance between depth of depression measured by depression inventories and actual major depressive disorder (Golin & Hartz, 1979; Hammen, 1980; Hesselbrock, Hesselbrock, Tennen, Meyer, & Workman-Daniels, 1983; Lewinsohn & Teri, 1982) is reason enough to suspect that the moderate levels of self-esteem and depression reported by student subjects do not represent clinical disturbance. Even the assumption that depression seen in student samples is quantitatively (if not qualitatively) different from what is found in clinical populations may be unwarranted (Coyne & Gotlib, 1983; Depue & Monroe, 1978).

Personal narratives of genuine depressive episodes provide an even more compelling argument for distinguishing the despair and self-loathing seen in clinical settings from the sadness and moderate self-regard shown among depressed students. Consider this account:

> The pain . . . is quite unimaginable to those who have not suffered it. . . . Loss of self-esteem is a celebrated symptom, and my own sense of self had all but disappeared, along with any self-reliance. This loss can quickly degenerate into dependence, and from dependence into infantile dread. One dreads the loss of all things, all people close and dear. (Styron, 1990, pp. 16, 33, 56)

Although far from the abysmal esteem described by Styron, moderate self-esteem might still predict the occurrence of depressive episodes. It can do so directly (as described by Kernis) or indirectly as a diathesis that is activated only in threatening circumstances. The direct relation between esteem and subsequent depressed mood has been reported among adolescents (Allgood-Merten et al., 1990) and among drug users (Buckner & Mandell, 1990).

Support for low self-esteem as a depressive diathesis is advocated most strongly by Brown, Harris, and colleagues (Brown, Andrews, Harris, Adler, & Bridge, 1986; Brown & Harris, 1978). Three strategies have been employed to test the esteem-as-vulnerability hypothesis. One strategy is to study individuals who were formerly depressed; if low self-esteem is not merely a symptom of depression but a trait making one vulnerable to depression, formerly depressed persons should maintain low levels of self-esteem. Wittenborn and colleagues (Altman & Wittenborn, 1980; Cofer & Wittenborn, 1980) indeed found that formerly depressed women reported lower self-esteem than matched controls. A second strategy is to study individuals from depression through recovery. Studies of this type (Caine, 1970; Hamilton & Abramson, 1983; Mayo, 1967), however, have failed to support the notion of self-esteem as a depressive diathesis.

The third and most direct test of the esteem-as-vulnerability hypothesis comes from longitudinal studies comparing nondepressed individuals who eventually become depressed with individuals who remain free of depression. Although Brown (1984; described in Ingham, Kreitman, Miller, Sashidharan, & Surtees, 1986) found that he could predict subsequent depression from negative self-evaluation prior to the onset of depression, Lewinsohn, Steinmetz, Larson, and Franklin (1981) and Ingham, Kreitman, Miller, Sashidharan, and Surtees (1987) found no evidence that low self-esteem predicted future depressive episodes. So although low self-esteem—and particularly unstable low self-esteem—may anticipate later depressed *mood* directly (Kernis, Chapter 9), or indirectly (Hobfoll & Lieberman, 1987), there is little evidence that level of esteem predicts the onset of depressive *disorders.*

Kernis's concept of self-esteem stability offers a possible explanation for previous failures of community and clinical samples to support the esteem-as-vulnerability model. If, as Kernis suggests, unstable self-esteem makes high self-esteem individuals vulnerable to threatening events but buffers low self-esteem individuals from threat, the prediction of depressive episodes requires knowledge of both self-esteem level and stability. Only if one samples stable high and low self-esteem persons (which is what most investigators presume they are doing) is self-esteem likely to predict depression. By considering both self-esteem level and stability, clinical researchers may finally be able to establish empirically a link between self-esteem and vulnerability to depression.

Unstable self-esteem actually plays a prominent role in clinical theorizing about vulnerability to depression. Bibring (1953), Chodoff (1973), Fenichel (1945), and Jacobson (1975) have argued that individuals prone to depression experience vulnerable rather than low self-esteem prior to becoming depressed. For Bibring, the depressive-to-be is vulnerable to deflated esteem because she or he cannot live up to aspirations. Fenichel and Chodoff maintain that self-esteem regulation for some depression-prone individuals is contingent on being loved and, for others, on acting correctly. Jacobson believes that stable self-esteem requires that one's mental representations of self be independent of one's representations of others (see Becker, 1979). What all these conceptions assert is that the depression-prone individual is susceptible to fluctuations in self-esteem in reaction to life's inevitable misfortunes. The idea that many individuals with low self-regard are also uncertain of their self-conceptions (Campbell & Lavallee, Chapter 1; Linville, 1987) and that even those with high esteem may be vulnerable to depression if their esteem is unstable (Kernis, Chapter 9) offers a promising conceptual bridge between clinical theory and empirical investigation into the antecedents of depressive disorders.

PUZZLES AND POSSIBLE PITFALLS OF HIGH SELF-REGARD

Although the focus of this volume is low self-regard, we, like Baumeister (1989), are concerned that the psychological literature retains an assumption that people with high self-esteem present no conceptual puzzles and that their efforts to maintain self-esteem are more adaptive than the efforts of those with low self-esteem. Baumeister and Heatherton (1991) have already found that in certain esteem-threatening situations, individuals with high self-esteem may show self-regulatory failures. Similarly, Heatherton and Ambady (Chapter 7) speculate that despite evidence that unrealistic views can enhance well-being (e.g., Taylor & Brown, 1988), individuals with very high self-esteem may pursue paths that are not in their best interests. We now examine four strategies of esteem maintenance used by high self-esteem individuals; we argue that they may be shortsighted and that they present genuine conceptual puzzles for self-esteem theory. The four strategies are attributional self-enhancement, adaptive preferences, active downward comparisons, and derogation of others.

ATTRIBUTIONAL SELF-ENHANCEMENT

It wasn't my fault. I ran out of gas; I had a flat tire; I didn't have enough money for cab fare; my socks didn't come back from the cleaners; an old friend came in from out of town; someone stole my car; there was an earthquake; a terrible flood; locusts. It wasn't my fault! (Joliet Jake in the film *The Blues Brothers*)

Perhaps the most widely investigated characteristic of people with high self-regard is their pervasive way of explaining untoward events. The self-esteem literature (Tennen & Herzberger, 1987; Tennen, Herzberger, & Nelson, 1987) and the depression literature (Brewin, 1985; Peterson, Villanova, & Raps, 1985) are now replete with studies demonstrating that unlike their low self-esteem peers, who accept credit and blame equally, individuals with high self-esteem accept credit for good outcomes comparably to those with low self-esteem but ascribe bad outcomes to external causes. Blaine and Crocker (Chapter 4), Heatherton and Ambady (Chapter 7), and Kernis (Chapter 9) have documented and extended the role these self-enhancing explanations have in regulating self-esteem.

This consistent pattern of causal explanations would disarm most clinicians, because it seems to contradict everyday experience, clinical lore, and the dynamics of interpersonal relationships. In everyday life, people who consistently disavow responsibility make unpleasant colleagues, friends, and spouses. Joliet Jake, quoted above, is the quintessential attributional self-enhancer. That we find his causal explanations humorous is evidence that such externalizations hold little currency in everyday life; people see them for what they are. That they are exaggerated in Jake, who has a long prison record, blatant antisocial characteristics, and an uncanny ability to repeat grave errors of judgment, is in keeping with most people's experience that people who employ this "explanatory style" (Peterson, 1991; Peterson & Seligman, 1984) are unreliable, unempathic, and self-centered. Lest the Blues Brothers appear a frivolous source of psychological data, consider the following example provided by Kiecolt-Glaser and Williams (1987). They describe

> a subject who, angered by his father-in-law, set himself on fire and attributed all blame for the accident to his father-in-law. This 20-year-old man was a terror on the unit; he frequently yelled at the staff and threw things at them, providing an extreme example of non-compliance. His inability to assign any blame to himself either for his accident or for his disruptive behavior in the hospital was quite consistent with his long personal history of impulsive behavior and his regular disavowal of responsibility for any unfortunate consequences. (p. 23)

This example supports conventional wisdom about individuals who consistently externalize responsibility for untoward events: They appear shallow, irresponsible, and unpleasant. Yet, according to current psychological theories (as well as evidence from the laboratory), such externalization is an indicator of high self-regard, less distress in the face of failure (Follette & Jaconbson, 1987), a relative invulnerability to depression (Metalsky, Halberstadt, & Abramson, 1987), and better health, school achievement, and enhanced psychotherapeutic outcomes (Snyder & Higgins, 1988). In fact, according to one prominent theory (Abramson, Seligman, & Teasdale, 1978), Joliet Jake's explanations are particularly adaptive because they are not only external but quite specific to the immediate situation!

Unlike the social psychological theories that drive most research relating causal explanations to self-esteem, a number of prominent psychodynamic clinical theories propose that external explanations for bad events are neither indicators of high self-regard nor precursors of positive adaptation. According to Sullivan (1956), a feeling of inferiority is what leads one to transfer blame to others or to the environment: "One is the victim, not of one's own defects, but of a devilish environment. One is not to blame; the environment is to blame" (p. 146). In keeping with his interpersonal theory, Sullivan argues that external explanations for negative events are maladaptive because they are not validated by others and lead to social alienation.

Another clinical account linking externalization to maladaptation was proposed by Phillips (1968), who states explicitly that "those who feel others are to blame for the vicissitudes of their existence, should either tend to turn destructively against others, or avoid others who threaten them" (p. 146). Phillips presents evidence that individuals with lower levels of social competence blame others for their circumstances and, when symptomatic, either turn against others or avoid others. Whereas Sullivan attributed the hypothesized externalization-maladaptation link to an unfavorable response from the social environment, Phillips views both external causal explanations and psychosocial disruption as derivatives of developmental arrest.

This apparent conflict between clinical theory and evidence and social psychological theory and evidence has not gone unnoticed (Tennen & Affleck, 1990). In an attempt to reconcile these differences, Thompson and Janigian (1988) proposed that in ego-relevant achievement situations like those examined in the laboratory, externalizing blame may be more adaptive. But for many other situations described in the clinician's consulting room, where it is not one's ability that is threatened but one's view of the world, externalizations may be harmful. Do people with high self-esteem shift from construing external causes for achievement events to more internal causes for situations that threaten their view of a benevolent world? This would represent a rather remarkable extension of the flexibility of illusions (Baumeister, 1989; Taylor, 1989).

We (Tennen & Affleck, 1991a) have reasoned that the adaptive or maladaptive qualities of external attributions cannot be divorced from an individual's values and agendas. People who make external (and particularly external and circumscribed) attributions for negative events may be people who feel good about themselves and who produce. But *what* they produce, and how *others* feel about them, depends on their goals or values. A relentless salesperson may attribute failures to tough customers and may persevere and succeed in selling his or her wares (Seligman & Schulman, 1986). He or she may also be able to maintain a high level of self-esteem. But we are reluctant to interpret high self-esteem or meeting one's goals as a proxy for satisfactory adjustment, nor would we accept short-term satisfaction as a proxy for social functioning over the long haul (Fincham & Bradbury, 1988).

Sour Grapes: The Deployment of Adaptive Preferences

Another way that high self-esteem individuals maintain their self-esteem is by discounting the importance of negative outcomes and personal failures. Spencer et al. (Chapter 2) and Heatherton and Ambady (Chapter 7) describe how people with high self-esteem are able to counteract esteem threats by focusing on self-affirmational resources, thereby diminishing the significance of the threat. Blaine and Crocker (Chapter

4) and Harter (Chapter 5) demonstrate how people with high self-regard show a facility for diminishing the significance of goals beyond their grasp. Put another way, high self-esteem individuals are able to discount the importance of aspirations that cannot be achieved.

We have all at one time or another decided "that what we cannot have we didn't really want in the first place" (Ryan, 1991), and through this decision eliminated our longing for previously sought goals. Both conventional wisdom and psychological inquiry affirm that knowing when to persevere and when to disengage from incentives is important to successful achievement and social adaptation (Klinger, 1975; Seligman, 1975; Taylor, 1989; Weiner, 1981). Nonetheless, we wonder if despite their emotional benefits, such strategic disengagement might take its toll in other ways. Perhaps these decisions among high self-esteem individuals require more careful examination.

Elster (1983) refers to such strategies as "sour grapes" or, more formally, "adaptive preferences," inasmuch as one is adapting one's preferences to what seems possible. He argues cogently that such strategies are preferable to "counteradaptive strategies" where what is wanted is only what *cannot* be had. To our knowledge, there is no evidence that individuals with low self-esteem chronically engage in the counteradaptive "grass is greener on the other side" (Ryan, 1991) strategy; they are simply less likely to engage in sour grapes. Should we interpret this as a psychological deficit—a defect in need of intervention?

Consider the example offered by Spencer et al. in Chapter 2 of a high self-esteem individual who is having difficulties with his roommate. The "roommate eventually decides the person is a slob and an awful roommate." Having high self-regard, our protagonist counteracts this threat by saying to himself, "Oh well, I am a good student and have lots of other friends." This certainly bolsters his esteem, probably brightens his mood, and allows him to study for an upcoming exam unburdened by intrusive thoughts of what transpired. Imagine now that our protagonist has low self-regard. He does not have the resources to affirm himself in other areas or to discount the importance of his relationship with his roommate. Instead, he is troubled by his roommate's comments. Inclined to self-focus (Pyszczynski & Greenberg, 1987), he reflects upon his own actions and realizes that he *has* been an awful roommate. He has not contributed to chores, has played his stereo late into the evening, and has invited other friends to his room without checking first with his roommate. Although he realizes that the roommate could have mentioned these things as they arose rather than simply deciding to leave, our low self-esteem protagonist appreciates that he must accept responsibility for his actions. He experiences sadness, remorse, a drop in his self-regard, and a desire to make amends. Because he is preoccupied by his misdeeds, he is unable to prepare very well for his exam. His performance suffers. He calls his former roommate, apologizes for his inconsiderate behavior, and suggests that they give another try to being roommates. When refused, he offers to pay any moving costs incurred.

Were both the high and low self-esteem protagonists participants in a psychological study of self-regard and well-being, the high self-esteem student would appear by all indicators to be functioning better. His scores on affect rating scales would reveal little or no distress, and these ratings would be linearly and strongly correlated with his self-esteem. If the study were examining daily stress (Tennen, Suls, & Affleck, 1991), our high self-esteem protagonist would report fewer negative events and might not even construe the roommate incident as negative (and, if so, certainly not as important). Undaunted by such incidents, he would show considerable stability in his esteem (Kernis, Chapter 9) and little variability in his mood (Campbell & Lavallee, Chapter 1). And if academic achievement were the indicator of well-being, his high self-esteem would no doubt be interpreted as a resource that fosters problem-focused coping and, consequently, good grades.

From both clinical and lay perspectives, this analysis is flawed. A number of clinical theories view the capacity for remorse (Kernberg, 1980) and the ability to make reparation (Klein, 1964) as critical to psychosocial positive adjustment. Most laypeople, we believe, would also see remorse and reparative efforts as indicators of maturity. Although the high self-esteem student depicted in the Spencer et al. vignette was not sad, neither was he wise. As long as we equate adaptation with happiness, persistence, and productivity unburdened by concern, those people who are able to discount the importance of negative outcomes and personal failures will emerge as paragons of mental health. But if we look beyond subjective well-being and productivity as indicators of mental health, what may emerge is a richer and even more interesting picture of both high and low self-esteem people.

We are by no means arguing that individuals with high self-regard are incapable of self-reflection, remorse, reparative gestures, or the capacity to mourn losses. Such a position would be ludicrous. Nonetheless, current theories of self-esteem maintenance make it difficult to imagine how someone with high self-esteem discounts the significance of lost opportunities and simultaneously has the painful, sobering, and often humbling experiences inevitable among those who are less willing or less able to engage in such "adaptive" preferences.

Taylor (1989) suggests several mechanisms that might limit positive illusions and perhaps keep in check the strategies maintaining them. One such mechanism is the ability to incorporate negative information usefully without acknowledging all of its implications (see Janoff-Bulman, 1989; Lazarus, 1983). Perhaps the high self-esteem student depicted by Spencer et al. can simultaneously appreciate his misdeeds, experience remorse, *and* discount the significance of his relationship with his roommate without undue distress or performance decrements. It is not yet clear if and how people actually carry out these appraisals simultaneously, nor is it clear why discounting is *needed* to bolster the esteem of genuinely high self-esteem individuals. One would think it possible to acknowledge wrongdoing without feeling so threatened as to turn to sour grapes (Epstein, 1983). Kernsis's concept of unstable self-esteem and clinical notions of vulnerable self-esteem may help us better identify those high self-esteem individuals who find it necessary to create adaptive preferences.

Another reason why the adaptive preferences of high self-esteem individuals may stay within reasonable limits is that they are responsive to correction from the social environment (Taylor, 1989). Perhaps others would remind our high self-esteem protagonist that he had acted poorly and should make amends; someone might even call him on his sour-grapes reappraisal. But if this and other esteem-maintaining strategies are responsive to social correction, why are they needed at all? If one feels impelled to discount the importance of a relationship so as to maintain a positive self-image, what proxy mechanism maintains that image after social correction? To argue that no further mechanism is needed only begs the question of why the discounting was needed from the start. Although Taylor's notion (1989) of self-correcting esteem maintenance and Baumeister's concept (1989) of an "optimal margin of illusion" are provocative and provide a process-oriented context in which to study self-steem, they remain essentially untested and will require that researchers pursue the puzzles of high self-regard as vigorously as they have pursued the complexities of low self-regard. We will return shortly to the issue of self-correcting illusions.

DOWNWARD COMPARISONS

There is abundant evidence that when threatened, high self-esteem individuals are more likely to find or create others who are worse off and thus make themselves appear fortunate by comparison. Crocker (Crocker & Schwartz, 1985; Crocker, Thompson, McGraw, & Ingerman, 1987) has shown that unlike those with low self-esteem, people with high self-regard compare themselves favorably to out-group members (see Brown, Chapter 6; Wood & Taylor, 1991). Comparable findings have emerged in the depression literature. Whereas depressed subjects view themselves as comparable to others or view others more favorably than they view themselves, nondepressed subjects consistently engage in self-enhancing (i.e., downward) social comparisons (Ahrens, Zeiss, & Kanfer, 1988; Alloy, Albright, & Clements, 1987; Campbell, 1986; see Swallow & Kuiper, 1988, for a review).

Recent studies clarify further how high and low self-esteem individuals take advantage of information about less fortunate others and may even create those others through active derogation. It appears that whereas people with high self-esteem are better able than their low self-esteem counterparts to enhance themselves through both upward and downward comparisons (Buunk, Collins, Taylor, VanYperen, & Dakof, 1990; Collins & Trobst, 1992), and those with low self-esteem select others who are worse off for comparison (Spencer et al., Chapter 2; DeVellis et al., 1990; Wood & Taylor, 1991), only high self-esteem individuals actively derogate others ("active downward comparison"; Wills, 1981, 1987) to enhance their esteem following a threat (Blaine & Crocker, Chapter 4; Gibbons & Gerrard, 1989; Gibbons & McCoy, 1991).

Gibbons and McCoy (1991) speculate that derogating others to enhance one's esteem may be a barometer of therapeutic success among individuals who begin therapy with low self-esteem. Following our caution regarding the potential costs of externalizing untoward events, we are concerned about the detrimental effects of derogating others to enhance oneself. Such derogation, or active downward comparison, is qualitatively different from feeling comforted by existing evidence of less fortunate others. As Elster (1983) argues, "We need to distinguish between taking the achievement of others as a parameter and one's own as the control variable, and manipulating the achievements of others so that they fall short of one's own" (see also Tesser, 1991).

One potential drawback of derogating others is that they may withdraw and be unavailable as support providers (Brickman & Bulman, 1977; Swallow & Kuiper, 1988). This may become a particularly thorny problem, because high self-esteem individuals derogate others when they are feeling threatened—precisely when they might benefit most from others' support. But even if others are available to provide support, high self-esteem individuals may for two reasons be less able to take advantage of available support resources. First, one's ability to depend on others is compromised when others have been derogated (Bakan, 1966). Second, precisely because they view themselves as capable and self-reliant, high self-esteem individuals "are more sensitive to the self-threatening implications involved in receiving help (e.g., information about inferiority and dependency) than are those with low self-esteem" (Nadler & Fisher, 1986, p. 86; see also DePaulo, Brown, Ishii, & Fisher, 1981). Nadler and Fisher (1986) review impressive evidence that for individuals with high self-esteem, help from another (particularly a similar other) results in lowered self-appraisals and more negative affect. In fact, they demonstrate that when support is needed in an area central to self-esteem, a close friend may be most threatening and, ironically, least able to provide needed support to someone with high self-esteem (Nadler, Fisher, & Ben-Itzhak, 1983; Tesser, 1980).

These findings are intriguing from several perspectives. First, they imply that when we look carefully, high self-esteem individuals are as puzzling as are those with low esteem. They, too, may be caught in certain "crossfires" (De La Ronde & Swann, Chapter 8), such as maintaining their threatened self-esteem without alienating their well-intentioned friends. Second, although Campbell (Campbell, Chew, & Scratchley, 1991; Campbell & Lavallee, Chapter 1) finds that people with low self-regard are frequently more reactive to self-relevant events, the findings we have reviewed related to derogating others and response to supportive gestures suggest that high self-esteem individuals are *exquisitely* sensitive to the esteem implications of their interpersonal environment. Although they may not be as affectively or behaviorally reactive as their low self-esteem counterparts, they are intrapsychically reactive, engaging in a wide variety of cognitive strategies to ward off esteem threats. These findings also suggest limiting conditions of Taylor's speculation (1989) that the social environment will correct positive illusions and their manifestations. Surely, verbalized derogation by someone with high self-esteem will be confronted at some point, as will spiteful attempts to interfere with others' success so as to protect one's self-regard. But unspoken derogation—which is far more common—breeds silent contempt and an inability to take advantage of a potentially supportive environment. Attempts by close friends to provide support will be rebuffed because their implications of inferiority and dependency further threaten self-esteem. This may actually introduce strain into what may have been an amiable relationship (Nadler & Fisher, 1986).

Derogation, Identification, and Self-Esteem Regulation

Another puzzling aspect of the high self-esteem individual's derogation of others is that it would seem to interfere with opportunities to identify with people who are helpful, empathic, and compassionate. Harter (Chapter 5) identifies five sources of self-esteem in childhood:

scholastic competence, athletic competence, physical attractiveness, social competence, and socially appropriate behavior. White (1963) and Pine (1985) agree that actual accomplishments and the social world's response to those accomplishments are important sources of self-esteem. But Kernberg (1975), Schafer (1968), and Westen (1990) remind us that identifications are also crucial to the formation and maintenance of self-regard. In fact, Westen surmises that therapeutic changes in self-esteem may come about through identification with the therapist's attitudes toward the self. But if, when faced with threats to their self-esteem, high self-esteem individuals derogate others (particularly similar others offering help), decide the source of the threat is not credible, or focus on negative information about others (Blaine & Crocker, Chapter 4), they miss important opportunities to learn about themselves and, perhaps more important, to identify with now-disparaged others as a source of self-esteem. Although the act of derogation may transiently bolster self-esteem, it strikes us as a shortsighted solution to feeling threatened; a solution that impedes the potentially beneficial consequences of identifying with a caring other. Certainly high self-esteem individuals have the capacity to make positive affective ties and identifications with helpful caretakers and friends. Their capacity to do so may be key to their high self-esteem. *How* they make these identifications without experiencing an increased threat to their self-esteem and without derogating the potential source of enhanced esteem is unclear from current social psychological models of self-esteem maintenance.

SELF-ESTEEM, POSITIVE ILLUSIONS, AND WELL-BEING: A CALL TOO EARLY TO MAKE

Recent theory (Janoff-Bulman, 1989; Taylor, 1989) and evidence (Taylor & Brown, 1988) point to the adaptational benefits of positive illusions precisely like those demonstrated by people with high self-esteem, including inflated self-appraisals and optimistic expectations about the future. This theorizing and the findings it has spawned provide a genuine challenge for traditional clinical theories, which assume that the most adaptive appraisals are those that remain true to reality. Despite the intuitive appeal of the argument, we believe the final word on the benefits of illusions will have to await investigations designed to evaluate illusions' possible harm (see Heatherton & Ambady, Chapter 7; Baumeister, 1989; Snyder, 1989).

A particularly influential argument for the unalloyed benefits of positive illusions is that there are natural mechanisms that limit them and thus render them benign. One such mechanism is proposed by Janoff-Bulman (1989; see Epstein, 1983), who proposes that people can maintain their broad illusory assumptions about themselves while accepting more concrete evidence of their limitations. Although we agree with this proposition in principle, the findings reported in this volume indicate that students with high self-esteem are not readily able to accept even specific threats to their self-esteem without employing self-enhancing counterappraisals. For example, after completing a self-esteem scale, high self-esteem students feel compelled to reaffirm their positive views of themselves (Spencer et al., Chapter 2). Failing a social sensitivity test in a psychology experiment prompts those with high self-esteem to remember three times as many negative attributes of others compared to when they succeeded on the test (Blaine & Crocker, Chapter 4). And when faced with concrete evidence of a negative attribute, high self-esteem subjects are impelled to view that attribute as relatively unimportant (Chapter 4). Individuals with high self-regard seem *not* to accept concrete evidence of their limitations readily. Rather, they counter such evidence with self-enhancing thoughts, derogation of others, and adaptive preferences. As we suggested earlier, these self-protective efforts may have maladaptive consequences independent of the illusions they serve.

Collins, Skokan, and Aspinwall (1989) propose that the limits of positive illusions derive not from the individual but from his or her social environment, which will subtly hold in check any but the most benign illusions. Should someone hold too positive a view of himself or herself or too much self-confidence, others will intervene to provide a natural feedback loop. Although it seems plausible that others might attempt to interdict a self-inflating spiral, there is little reason to believe that individuals with high self-esteem respond to such efforts. Why, for example, should they be responsive to social feedback when they are relatively unresponsive to social norms for humility and personal responsibility for failures?

In a less speculative vein, there is abundant evidence reviewed in this volume that high self-esteem individuals are in fact unresponsive to interpersonal feedback, particularly regarding their own behavior. Campbell and Lavallee (Chapter 1) summarize considerable evidence that people with high self-esteem are not particularly responsive to their social environment. Rather, whereas people with *low* self-esteem "are more dependent on, and hence more susceptible to, external cues that convey self-relevant information," high self-esteem individuals "accept only those environmental cues that convey the affectively preferred positive information." Similarly, Heatherton and Ambady (Chapter 7) note that "low self-esteem subjects make better use of external guides for performance (Brockner, 1983) and therefore, when the advice is useful . . . low self-esteem subjects outperform high self-esteem subjects." Considering these summaries of the literature, it is difficult to imagine high self-esteem people responding readily to comments from others challenging their illusions.

We believe the available evidence does not support the premise that intraindividual or interpersonal mechanisms limit the self-enhancing illusions of high self-esteem individuals. Moreover, we need to differentiate these illusions from people's efforts to maintain them. We suspect that these efforts become "problem-maintaining solutions" (Tennen & Affleck, 1991b; Watzlawick, 1978) that may be more problematic than the illusions themselves. Although there are many instances in which illusions and perhaps illusion-maintaining efforts are adaptive (Taylor & Brown, 1988), we are a long way from understanding their long-term consequences for people with high self-regard.

SELF-ESTEEM AND ITS MAINTENANCE THROUGH THE LIFE SPAN

There is now substantial evidence that as people move beyond their 20s, and surely as they reach middle adulthood, they come to realize (if they are fortunate) that some sources of their self-esteem are no longer available. Levinson (1978), for example, found that as men reach their 30s they begin to acknowledge that they will not achieve the goals they set for themselves in their 20s, nor will they achieve their young adult fantasy of what they would be like in maturity. Although people can experience favorable changes in their working models of themselves in adulthood (Vaillant, 1977), Kernberg (1975, 1980) reminds us that many sources of esteem gratification (e.g., physical attractiveness, strength, success, and the admiration of others) are less available in middle age. He provides many clinical examples of older adults who, when confronted with declining vigor, loss of physical attractiveness, and limitations in their career advancement, turn defensively toward adaptive preferences. They devalue what they can no longer attain and derogate others, particularly young competitors whose strength, appearance, and success threaten their self-esteem. These are precisely the strategies deployed by the high self-esteem college students in the studies described in this volume. And although these individuals may transiently maintain self-esteem, that esteem comes at the cost of "a sense of emptiness and loss of meaning in their daily life" (Kernberg, 1980, p. 143; see also Horowitz, 1988).

Another way some middle-aged people protect their self-esteem from lost sources of gratification is by devaluing interests or emotional investments that they had previously held near and dear. This form of adaptive preference is an interesting variation of the strategy employed by high self-esteem students; it is a sort of "downward temporal comparison" (Affleck & Tennen, 1991; Affleck, Tennen, Pfeiffer, Fifield, & Rowe, 1987; Albert, 1977) combined with derogation—in this case, derogation of previous goals and commitments. The cost of this form of self-esteem maintenance is often a misanthropic life philosophy.

We are not trying to suggest that high self-esteem college students inevitably become misanthropic older adults. There is ample evidence that with maturity, many people are able to alter their goals and preferences constructively (Ruble & Frey, 1991) so as to have no need to devalue others or their own earlier aspirations. But our current theories of self-esteem offer few clues as to how these processes unfold, or how representative the esteem-maintaining strategies observed in student samples are to the lives of most adults.

CONCLUSION

The contributors to this volume have presented fascinating theories and provocative findings that begin to solve the puzzle of low self-esteem. They describe the precedents and consequences of low self-esteem and the processes that perpetuate negative self-evaluation. Their findings are valuable to clinical investigators and psychotherapists. Yet we believe that how *high* self-esteem individuals maintain their esteem against threats, and what they construe as constituting a threat, are in their own way puzzling and hold the promise of fresh insights into the intricacies of self-regard across the life span.

REFERENCES

Abramson, L. Y., Seligman, M. E. P., & Teasdale, J. (1978). Learned helplessness in humans: Critique and reformulation. *Journal of Abnormal Psychology, 87,* 49–74.

Affleck, G., & Tennen, H. (1991). Social comparison and coping with major medical problems. In J. Suls & T. A. Wills (Eds.), *Social comparison: Contemporary theory and research* (pp. 369–394). Hillsdale, NJ: Lawrence Erlbaum.

Affleck, G., Tennen, H., Pfeiffer, C., Fifield, J., & Rowe, J. (1987). Downward comparison and coping with serious medical problems. *American Journal of Orthopsychiatry, 57,* 570–578.

Ahrens, A. H., Zeiss, A. M., & Kanfer, R. (1988). Depressive deficits in interpersonal standards, self-efficacy, and social comparison. *Cognitive Therapy and Research, 12,* 53–67.

Albert, S. (1977). Temporal comparison theory. *Psychological Review, 84,* 485–503.

Allgood-Merton, B., Lewinsohn, P. M., & Hops, H. (1990). Sex differences and adolescent depression. *Journal of Abnormal Psychology, 99,* 55–63.

Alloy, L. B., Albright, J. S., & Clements, C. M. (1987). Depression, nondepression, and social comparison biases. In J. E. Maddux, C. D. Stoltenberg, & R. Rosenwein (Eds.), *Social processes in clinical and counseling psychology* (pp. 94–112). New York: Springer-Verlag.

Altman, J. H., & Wittenborn, J. R. (1980). Depression-prone personality in women. *Journal of Abnormal Psychology, 89,* 303–308.

Bakan, D. (1966). *The duality of human existence.* Boston: Beacon.

Baumeister, R. (1989). The optimal margin of illusion. *Journal of Social and Clinical Psychology, 8,* 176–189.

Baumeister, R., & Heatherton, T. F. (1991). *When ego threats lead to self-regulation failure: The negative consequences of high self-esteem.* Unpublished manuscript, Case Western Reserve University.

Becker, J. (1979). Vulnerable self-esteem as a predisposing factor in depressive disorders. In R. Depue (Ed.), *The psychobiology of depressive disorders: Implications for the effects of stress* (pp. 317–334). New York: Academic Press.

Bibring, E. (1953). The mechanism of depression. In P. Greenacre (Ed.), *Affective disorders* (pp. 13–48). New York: International Universities Press.

Brewin, C. R. (1985). Depression and causal attributions: What is their relation? *Psychological Bulletin, 98,* 297–309.

Brickman, P., & Bulman, R. (1977). Pleasure and pain in social comparison. In J. M. Suls & R. L. Miller (Eds.), *Social comparison processes: Theoretical and experimental perspectives* (pp. 148–186). Washington, DC: Hemisphere.

Brockner, J. (1983). Low self-esteem and behavioral plasticity: Some implications. In L. Wheeler & P. Shaver (Eds.), *Review of personality and social psychology, vol. 4* (pp. 237–271). Beverly Hills, CA: Sage.

Brown, G. W. (1984). *Social support and depression.* Unpublished lecture.

Brown, G. W., Andrews, B., Harris, T., Adler, Z., & Bridge, L. (1986). Social support, self-esteem, and depression. *Psychological Medicine, 16,* 813–831.

Brown, G. W., & Harris, T. (1978). *The social origins of depression: A study of psychiatric disorder in women.* London: Tavistock.

Buckner, J. C., & Mandell, W. (1990). Risk factors for depressive symptomatology in a drug using population. *American Journal of Public Health, 80,* 580–585.

Buunk, B. P., Collins, R. L., Taylor, S. E., VanYperen, N. W., & Dakof, G. A. (1990). The affective consequences of social comparison: Either direction has its ups and downs. *Journal of Personality and Social Psychology, 59,* 1238–1249.

Caine, T. M. (1970). Personality and illness. In P. Mitler (Ed.), *The psychological assessment of mental and physical handicap* (pp. 119–145). London: Methuen.

Campbell, J. D. (1986). Similarity and uniqueness: The effects of attribute type, relevance, and individual differences in self-esteem and depression. *Journal of Personality and Social Psychology, 50,* 281–294.

Campbell, J. D., Chew, B., & Scratchley, L. S. (1991). Cognitive and emotional reactions to daily events: The effects of self-esteem and self-complexity. *Journal of Personality, 59,* 473–505.

Chodoff, P. (1973). The depressive personality: A critical review. *International Journal of Psychiatry, 11,* 196–217.

Cofer, D. H., & Wittenborn, J. R. (1980). Personality characteristics of formerly depressed women. *Journal of Abnormal Psychology, 89,* 309–314.

Collins, R. L., & Trobst, K. K. (1992). *Chronic self-esteem and global versus specific reactions to social comparison.* Unpublished manuscript, University of British Columbia.

Coyne, J. C., & Gotlib, I. H. (1983). The role of cognition in depression: A critical appraisal. *Psychological Bulletin, 94,* 472–505.

Crocker, J., & Schwartz, I. (1985). Prejudice and in-group favoritism in a minimal intergroup situation: Effects of self-esteem. *Personality and Social Psychology Bulletin, 11,* 379–386.

Crocker, J., Thompson, L. L., McGraw, K. M., & Ingerman, C. (1987). Downward comparison, prejudice, and evaluation of others: Effects of self-esteem and threat. *Journal of Personality and Social Psychology, 52,* 907–916.

DePaulo, B. M., Brown, P., Ishii, S., & Fisher, J. D. (1981). Help that works: The effects of aid on subsequent task performance. *Journal of Personality and Social Psychology, 41,* 478–487.

Depue, R. A., & Monroe, S. M. (1978). Learned helplessness in the perspective of the depressive disorders: Conceptual and definitional issues. *Journal of Abnormal Psychology, 87,* 3–24.

DeVellis, R. F., Holt, K., Renner, B. R., Blalock, S. J., Blanchard, L. W., Cook, H. L., Klotz, M. L., Mikow, V., & Harring, K. (1990). The relationship of social comparison to rheumatoid arthritis symptoms and affect. *Basic and Applied Social Psychology, 11,* 1–18.

Elster, J. (1983). *Sour grapes.* New York: Cambridge University Press.

Epstein, S. (1983). The unconscious, the preconscious, and the self-concept. In J. Suls & A. Greenwald (Eds.), *Psychological perspectives on the self* (Vol. 2, pp. 219–247). Hillsdale, NJ: Erlbaum.

Fenichel, O. (1945). *The psychoanalytic theory of neurosis.* New York: W. W. Norton.

Fincham, F. D., & Bradbury, T. N. (1988). The impact of attributions in marriage: Empirical and conceptual foundations. *British Journal of Clinical Psychology, 27,* 77–90.

Follette, V. M., & Jacobson, N. S. (1987). Importance of attributions as a predictor of how people cope with failure. *Journal of Personality and Social Psychology, 52,* 1205–1211.

Gibbons, F. X., & Gerrard, M. (1989). Effects of upward and downward social comparison on mood states. *Journal of Social and Clinical Psychology, 8,* 14–31.

Gibbons, F. X., & McCoy, S. B. (1991). Self-esteem, similarity, and reactions to active versus passive downward comparisons. *Journal of Personality and Social Psychology, 60,* 414–424.

Golin, S., & Hartz, M. (1979). A factor analysis of the Beck Depression Inventory in a mildly depressed population. *Journal of Clinical Psychology, 35,* 322–325.

Hamilton, E. W., & Abramson, L. Y. (1983). Cognitive patterns and major depressive disorder: A longitudinal study in a hospital setting. *Journal of Abnormal Psychology, 92,* 173–184.

Hammen, C. L. (1980). Depression in college students: Beyond the Beck Depression Inventory. *Journal of Consulting and Clinical Psychology, 48,* 126–128.

Hesselbrock, M., Hesselbrock, V., Tennen, H., Meyer, R., & Workman-Daniels, K. (1983). Methodological considerations in the assessment of depression in alcoholics. *Journal of Consulting and Clinical Psychology, 51,* 399–405.

Hobfoll, S. E., & Lieberman, J. R. (1987). Personality and social resources in immediate and continued stress resistance among women. *Journal of Personality and Social Psychology, 52,* 18–26.

Horowitz, M. J. (1988). *Introduction to psychodynamics: A new synthesis.* New York: Basic Books.

Ingham, J. G., Kreitman, P., Miller, P. M., Sashidharan, S. P., & Surtees, P. G. (1986). Self-esteem, vulnerability and psychiatric disorder in the community. *British Journal of Psychiatry, 148,* 375–385.

Ingham, J. G., Kreitman, P., Miller, P. M., Sashadharan, S. P., & Surtees, P. G. (1987). Self-appraisal, anxiety and depression in women: A prospective enquiry. *British Journal of Psychiatry, 151,* 643–651.

Jacobson, E. (1975). The regulation of self-esteem. In E. J. Anthony & T. Benedek (Eds.), *Depression and human existence* (pp. 169–182). Boston: Little, Brown.

Janoff-Bulman, R. (1989). The benefits of illusions, the threat of disillusionment, and the limitations of inaccuracy. *Journal of Social and Clinical Psychology, 8,* 158–175.

Kernberg, O. F. (1975). *Borderline conditions and pathological narcissism.* New York: Jason Aronson.

Kernberg, O. F. (1980). *Internal world and external reality: Object relations theory applied.* New York: Jason Aronson.

Kernis, M. H., Grannemann, B. D., & Mathis, L. C. (1991). Stability of self-esteem as a moderator of the relation between level of self-esteem and depression. *Journal of Personality and Social Psychology, 61,* 80–84.

Kiecolt-Glaser, J. K., & Williams, D. A. (1987). Self-blame, compliance and distress among burn patients. *Journal of Personality and Social Psychology, 53,* 187–193.

Klein, M. (1964). *Contributions to psycho-analysis: 1920–1945.* New York: McGraw-Hill.

Klinger, E. (1975). Consequences of commitment to and disengagement from incentives. *Psychological Review, 82,* 1–25.

Lazarus, R. S. (1983). The costs and benefits of denial. In S. Breznitz (Ed.), *The denial of stress* (pp. 1–30). New York: International Universities Press.

Levinson, D. (1978). *The seasons of a man's life.* New York: Ballantine.

Lewinsohn, P., & Teri, L. (1982). Selection of depressed and nondepressed subjects on the basis of self-report data. *Journal of Consulting and Clinical Psychology, 50,* 590–591.

Lewinsohn, P. M., Steinmetz, J. L., Larson, D. W., & Franklin, J. (1981). Depression-related cognitions: Antecedent or consequence? *Journal of Abnormal Psychology, 90,* 213–219.

Linville, P. W. (1987). Self-complexity as a buffer against stress-related illness and depression. *Journal of Personality and Social Psychology, 52,* 663–676.

Mayo, P. R. (1967). Some psychological changes associated with improvement in depression. *British Journal of Social and Clinical Psychology, 6,* 63–68.

Metalsky, G. I., Halberstadt, L. J., & Abramson, L. Y. (1987). Vulnerability to depressive mood reactions: Toward a more powerful test of the diathesis-stress and causal mediation components of the reformulated theory of depression. *Journal of Personality and Social Psychology, 52,* 386–393.

Nadler, A., & Fisher, J. D. (1986). The role of threat to self-esteem and perceived control in recipient reaction to help: Theory development and empirical validation. In L. Berkowitz (Ed.), *Advances in experimental social psychology, vol. 19* (pp. 81–122). New York: Academic Press.

Nadler, A., Fisher, J. D., & Ben-Itzhak, S. (1983). With a little help from my friend: Effect of single or multiple act aid as a function of donor and task characteristics. *Journal of Personality and Social Psychology, 44,* 310–321.

Peterson, C. (1991). The meaning and measurement of explanatory style. *Psychological Inquiry, 2,* 1–10.

Peterson, C., & Seligman, M. E. P. (1984). Causal explanations as a risk factor for depression: Theory and evidence. *Psychological Review, 91,* 347–374.

Peterson, C., Villanova, P., & Raps, C. (1985). Depression and attributions: Factors responsible for inconsistent results in the published literature. *Journal of Abnormal Psychology, 94,* 165–168.

Phillips, L. (1968). *Human adaptation and its failures*. New York: Academic Press.

Pine, F. (1985). *Developmental theory and clinical process*. New Haven, CT: Yale University Press.

Pyszczynski, T., & Greenberg, J. (1987). Self-regulatory preservation and the depressive self-focusing style. *Psychological Bulletin, 102,* 122–138.

Ruble, D. N., & Frey, K. S. (1991). Changing patterns of comparative behavior as skills are acquired: A functional model of self-evaluation. In J. Suls & T. A. Wills (Eds.), *Social comparison: Contemporary theory and research* (pp. 79–116). Hillsdale, NJ: Lawrence Erlbaum.

Ryan, A. (1991). When it's rational to be irrational. *New York Review of Books, 38,* 19–22.

Schafer, R. (1968). *Aspects of internalization*. New York: International Universities Press.

Seligman, M. E. P. (1975). *Helplessness: On depression, development, and death*. San Francisco: W. H. Freeman.

Seligman, M. E. P., & Schulman, P. (1986). Explanatory style as a predictor of productivity and quitting among life insurance sales agents. *Journal of Personality and Social Psychology, 50,* 832–838.

Snyder, C. R. (1989). Reality negotiation: From excuses to hope and beyond. *Journal of Social and Clinical Psychology, 8,* 130–157.

Synder, C. R., & Higgins, R. L. (1988). Excuses: Their effective role in the negotiation of reality. *Psychological Bulletin, 104,* 23–35.

Styron, W. (1990). *Darkness visible: A memoir of madness*. New York: Random House.

Sullivan, H. S. (1956). *Clinical studies in psychiatry*. New York: W. W. Norton.

Swallow, S. R., & Kuiper, N. A. (1988). Social comparison and negative self-evaluations: An application to depression. *Clinical Psychology Review, 8,* 55–76.

Taylor, S. E. (1989). *Positive illusions: Creative self-deception and the healthy mind*. New York: Basic Books.

Taylor, S. E., & Brown, J. D. (1988). Illusion and well-being: A social psychological perspective on mental health. *Psychological Bulletin, 103,* 193–210.

Taylor, S. E., Collins, R. L., Skokan, L. A., & Aspinwall, L. G. (1989). Maintaining positive illusions in the face of negative information: Getting the facts without letting them get to you. *Journal of Social and Clinical Psychology, 8,* 114–129.

Tennen, H., & Affleck, G. (1990). Blaming others for threatening events. *Psychological Bulletin, 108,* 209–232.

Tennen, H., & Affleck, G. (1991a). The meaning and measurement of attributional style: Unresolved issues. *Psychological Inquiry, 2,* 39–43.

Tennen, H., & Affleck, G. (1991b). Paradox-based treatments. In C. R. Snyder & D. R. Forsyth (Eds.), *Handbook of social and clinical psychology: The health perspective* (pp. 624–643). Elmsford, NY: Pergamon.

Tennen, H., Suls, J., & Affleck, G. (1991). Personality and daily experience: The promise and the challenge. *Journal of Personality, 59,* 313–337.

Tennen, H., & Herzberger, S. (1987). Depression, self-esteem, and the absence of self-protective attributional biases. *Journal of Personality and Social Psychology, 52,* 72–80.

Tennen, H., Herzberger, S., & Nelson, H. F. (1987). Depressive attributional style: The role of self-esteem. *Journal of Personality, 55,* 377–393.

Tesser, A. (1980). Self-esteem maintenance in family dynamics. *Journal of Personality and Social Psychology, 39,* 77–91.

Tesser, A. (1991). Emotion in social comparison and reflection processes. In J. Suls & T. A. Wills (Eds.), *Social comparison: Contemporary theory and research* (pp. 117–148). Hillsdale, NJ: Lawrence Erlbaum.

Thompson, S. C., & Janigian, A. S. (1988). Life schemes: A framework for understanding the search for meaning. *Journal of Social and Clinical Psychology, 7,* 260–280.

Vaillant, G. E. (1977). *Adaptation to life*. Boston: Little, Brown.

Watzlawick, P. (1978). *The language of change: Elements of therapeutic communication*. New York: Basic Books.

Weiner, B. (1981). *Human motivation*. New York: Holt, Rinehart & Winston.

Westen, D. (1990). The relations among narcissism, egocentrism, self-concept, and self-esteem: Experimental, clinical, and theoretical considerations. *Psychoanalysis and Contemporary Thought, 13*, 185–241.

White, R. W. (1963). *Ego and reality in psychoanalytic theory: A proposal regarding independent ego energies* (Psychological Issues, Monograph 11). New York: International Universities Press.

Wills, T. A. (1981). Downward comparison principles in social psychology. *Psychological Bulletin, 90*, 245–271.

Wills, T. A. (1987). Downward comparison as a coping mechanism. In C. R. Snyder & C. Ford (Eds.), *Coping with negative life events: Clinical and social psychological perspectives* (pp. 243–267). New York: Plenum.

Wills, T. A. (1991). Similarity and self-esteem in social comparison. In J. Suls & T. A. Wills (Eds.), *Social comparison: Contemporary theory and research* (pp. 51–78). Hillsdale, NJ: Lawrence Erlbaum.

Wood, J. V., & Taylor, K. T. (1991). Serving self-relevant goals through social comparison. In J. Suls & T. A. Wills (Eds.), *Social comparison: Contemporary theory and research* (pp. 23–49). Hillsdale, NJ: Lawrence Erlbaum.

INDEX

ABOUT THE EDITOR

ROY F. BAUMEISTER received his Ph.D in social psychology from Princeton University in 1978 and currently holds the Elsie B. Smith Professorship in Liberal Arts at Case Western Reserve University. Dr. Baumeister has conducted research on self-esteem for two decades, and .he is the author of over 100 professional publications, including his recent books: *Masochism and the Self* (1989), *Meanings of Life* (1991), *Escaping the Self: Alcoholism, Masochism, Spirituality, and Other Flights from the the Burden of Selfhood* (1991), *Breaking Hearts: The Two Sides of Unrequited Love* (1992), and *Your Own Worst Enemy: Understanding the Pardox of Self-Defeating Behavior* (1993). This project was aided by a fellowship grant from the Humbolt Foundation that enabled him to work at the Max Planck Institute in Munich, Germany.